BEYOND AID

To Frédérique
and in memory of Liz

"The world is moving to a new concept of what aid should be about...the new philosophy involves changing the relationship between donor and recipient governments from charity and dependency to interdependence and shared contractual obligation."
Commission on Global Governance, 1995

"To meet new challenges in an interdependent world we must move away from old ideas of 'foreign aid' as a short-term foreign policy tool and towards a cooperative approach where donor and recipient each bring something to the table for the benefit of both... trade, investment and debt relief, much more than aid, are what countries really need in the long run, and these elements must be part of development assistance."
United Nations Development Programme, Publicity Brochure, 1995

"The globalisation process is set to continue and to deepen. And getting off the merry-go-round is simply not an option....[developing countries] must give priority to trade policy reforms, encouraging the private sector to get involved in the process. And they must take better advantage of the market access opportunities available to them in the developed world and, increasingly in the more advanced developing countries."
UNCTAD Secretary-General Rubens Ricupero, 1997

"Investment is the shortest route to development...aid is a life-support system for something that is already dead."
Ugandan President Yoweri Museveni, 1998

Beyond Aid
From Patronage to Partnership

STEPHEN BROWNE

Ashgate
Aldershot • Brookfield USA • Singapore • Sydney

© Stephen Browne 1999

All rights reserved. No part of this publication may be reproduced, stored in a retrieval system, or transmitted in any form or by any means, electronic, mechanical, photocopying, recording or otherwise without the prior permission of the publisher.

Published by
Ashgate Publishing Ltd
Gower House
Croft Road
Aldershot
Hants GU11 3HR
England

Ashgate Publishing Company
Old Post Road
Brookfield
Vermont 05036
USA

Ashgate website: http://www.ashgate.com

British Library Cataloguing in Publication Data
Browne, Stephen
 Beyond aid : from patronage to partnership
 1. Economic assistance - History
 I. Title
 338.9'1

Library of Congress Catalog Card Number: 99-73320

ISBN 0 7546 1133 7

Printed in Great Britain

Contents

List of boxes	*vi*
List of figures	*vii*
List of tables	*viii*
Preface	*ix*
Introduction	1

PART I: THE RISE AND FALL OF AID

1	Origins of aid	7
2	A brief history of aid	19
3	Towards the end of aid?	29
4	Lessons of the aid and development record	39

PART II: FROM PATRONAGE TO PARTNERSHIP

5	Debt forgiveness: waiving not drowning	53
6	Freer trade better than constrictive aid	73
7	Regionalism: expanding lateral partnership	95
8	The information revolution	111
9	Strengthening global development institutions	139
10	Beyond aid	169

Bibliography	183
Index	189

NOTES: The views in this book are the author's own and do not necessarily represent those of the United Nations or its governing bodies.

Unless otherwise specified, the $ sign in this book refers to the United States dollar. The words 'billion' and 'trillion' mean one thousand million (10^9) and one million million (10^{12}) respectively.

List of boxes

Box 1:	The UN development system	8
Box 2:	The chronology of independence	12
Box 3:	Aid defined	15
Box 4:	Guide to debt nomenclature	64
Box 5:	Jubilee 2000 Coalition and debt cancellation	72
Box 6:	Trade - some basic theory	75
Box 7:	Trade glossary	80
Box 8:	ASEAN - an enduring Asian partnership	98
Box 9:	MERCOSUR - the fastest emerging regional cooperation arrangement	102
Box 10:	Origins of the Internet	117
Box 11:	Major global environment agreements of the 1990s	163

List of figures

Figure 1:	Size and growth of the state and economic growth performance, 1980-1995	31
Figure 2:	Long-term aid trend, 1966-1997	33
Figure 3:	Aid as % of GNP of OECD Countries, 1985-1997	33
Figure 4:	Aid volume by major donors, 1974-1997	34
Figure 5:	Share of official concessional finance by major region, 1989-1996	37
Figure 6:	Aid compared with private flows to all developing countries, 1970-1996	43
Figure 7:	Debt outstanding in developing countries, 1970-1995	54
Figure 8:	Net transfer on debt to developing countries, 1970-1995	55
Figure 9:	Net transfer on debt to severely indebted low-income countries, 1970-1995	56

List of tables

Table 1:	Heavily Indebted Poor Countries: Debt and development status, 1995	69
Table 2:	Heavily Indebted Poor Countries: Aid and debt flows, 1995	70
Table 3:	Eight trade rounds	78
Table 4:	Active regional groupings	107
Table 5:	Uneven density of information technology, 1996	119
Table 6:	Applying ICT to development	125
Table 7:	The global UN summits of the 1990s	156

Preface

The decline of aid in its traditional form is a fact of life. We are moving away, rather than towards, the 0.7% target set by the Pearson Commission; at present such traditional aid, as defined by the Development Assistance Committee of the OECD (DAC) reaches barely one-third of this target. This decline has been accompanied by shifts in development thinking away from financial resources to human capital, social capital, policies and institutions. The declining belief in aid as capable of leveraging development in the absence of other essential conditions has been strengthened by the failure of much econometric and empirical research to find a clear correlation between aid flows and economic growth. Nobody would claim that aid, even if its decline could be arrested or reversed, is a necessary and sufficient condition for growth, let alone development. Hence a need to go 'beyond aid'. This book is an important attempt to do so by an author well qualified both by previous research and practical experience.

Stephen Browne accepts the importance and effectiveness of aid as a 'catalyst in friendly circumstances'. But he does argue that at present it is more important to create these friendly circumstances than to increase traditional aid under conditions of 'patronage'. In any case, the transfer of financial resources to poorer countries is usually cancelled out - or more than cancelled out - by the opposite transfer from poor to rich as a result of falling commodity prices, deteriorating terms of trade, debt service, tenaciously lingering obstacles to their exports, transfer of profits from previous foreign investments. It clearly makes sense to look at these negative transfers and remove the paradox of such negative transfers occurring side by side with - and overwhelming - the flow of aid. In particular, one must support the emphasis on the solution of the debt crisis on generous terms, going well beyond the present HIPC (Highly Indebted Poor Countries) initiative in all dimensions (coverage, duration, conditionality etc.). Debt reduction may well be the most effective form of aid, given the vicious circle between debt pressure and deteriorating terms of trade. The same applies perhaps even more strongly to the speedy removal of remaining obstacles to their trade. Although not so easily quantifiable as financial flows, such more direct action 'beyond aid' will certainly have greater leverage on development.

The author also specifically shields emergency aid from any switch into such more effective action. Given a suitably broad definition of 'emergency' to include post-emergency rehabilitation and reconstruction and together with aid effective under 'friendly circumstances' and aid which - through NGOs or otherwise - can be effectively targeted on the poor, this still leaves an ample field for aid, quite possibly more than present flows.

What developing countries can do to advance their development through their own efforts even with diminishing reliance on the direct transfer of aid resources, is well expressed by the sub-title 'From Patronage to Partnership' and developed in Part II of this book. In their pertinence and realism they reflect Stephen Browne's rich relevant experience. As a staff member of the UNDP, and presently serving in Rwanda as the UN development and humanitarian coordinator, he can speak as one at the cutting edge of the attack on poverty and issues of global, regional and national management. His last chapter summarises his proposals better than a brief preface can do. One must hope that they will be widely and carefully studied.

Professor Sir Hans Singer
Institute of Development Studies
University of Sussex

Introduction

The world was very different when aid was born. At 50 years old, aid is in a period of mid-life introspection. It has lived through four phases - this book calls them 'ages' - adjusting to changing perceptions and realities. In the fourth age, beginning in the 1990s, both the perceptions and the realities have altered at an accelerating pace.

The ideological alternatives which dominated interpretations of economics and society are converging rapidly towards a single path of more democracy, openness and markets. The convergence has hastened the arrival of a global economy and coincided with an information revolution of Kuhnian proportions, laying new foundations for development progress. Global inequalities are greater than ever, but there is more evidence of upward mobility. The largest country, accounting for one-fifth of the world's population, is only one of those which, by engaging more fully with the global economy, has demonstrated unprecedented economic growth and recorded rapid human development progress. The graduation of more countries to 'developed' status and the formation of regional blocs to facilitate closer economic and political relations make the North and South divide an artificial one. It is a context in which development assistance no longer fits easily and no longer performs well.

This book is critical of the performance of aid in many of its guises. But it is not a treatise on aid's failure, nor is it a blueprint for its renewal. We should be looking beyond aid because the world has changed too much to need more of the same - bigger and better. It may need less of the same and more of something different. That 'something' is a new and better-managed international order, which accommodates the world as it has become. It will enlarge the opportunities of all countries - rich and poor - to benefit from a less fettered, more open, more inter-connected, more information-rich and more economically dynamic global system which delivers international public goods and tempers the 'bads'.

Development aid has usually been construed as a form of compensation for disadvantage. Yet for as long as there has been aid, the countries which are the major sources of the assistance have also acquiesced in the perpetuation of conditions which handicap the aided. Donors have provided aid partly because many of their actions have made it necessary. And aid is never given freely. To an undiminishing degree, it is bound up in packages which attract the eye, but constrain the hand, of the recipient.

This book maintains that the recipients would do better with less traditional patronage and more opportunities to take control of their own destinies. The opportunities to do so today are greater than they have ever been and the development assistance efforts of the international community should concentrate on enhancing those opportunities.

Within a more constructive global partnership, the exploitation of opportunity is the responsibility of each country, rich and poor. Opening borders to trade and cooperation with neighbouring countries, embracing the information revolution, encouraging foreign investment and engaging fully in the processes of global governance - these are the substitutes for patronage and the complements to the domestic development programmes which a growing number of countries have implemented with such success.

For many countries - and especially those lower in the development ladder - these new commitments will not come easily. They dilute the pre-eminence of national governments, which must increasingly accommodate the activities of non-governmental actors and the private sector; they must also yield sovereignty to the external forces of globalisation. And with more opportunity comes greater uncertainty.

But the alternative is a continuing system of patronage, which gives away a larger measure of control and decision-making to foreign experts in distant bureaucracies. The world must be weaned from the aid mentality that says that development is dependent on aid; that without one there will not be the other. And which has for so long persuaded a large fraternity of aid practitioners that there is no development problem that aid should not try to solve. As the head of an aid agency said recently, donors should no longer "be doing development".

The book is divided into two parts. Part I reviews the origins and evolution of aid, traces the stages in development thinking that have influenced the motivations for aid and the forms in which it has been provided, and traces the decline in aid during the 1990s. This Part concludes with an assessment of the mixed performance of development assistance over half a century.

Underlying Part II is the central idea that in a more equitable and better managed global environment, countries can more readily advance their development status through their own efforts, and with diminishing reliance on the direct transfer of aid resources. This part describes in some detail the five areas in which progress towards a more facilitatory global order has already begun and which deserves more support: a definitive resolution of the external debt problem of the poorest countries; a continuing liberalisation of trade in an equitable manner; an expansion of lateral partnership through different forms of regionalism; acceleration of the information revolution; and reform of the principal global development institutions. This Part concludes with a statement outlining the features of the desirable new era of development partnership.

The book is about the past, present and future of official development assistance (ODA), as it is defined in Chapter 1. There are also references to humanitarian and emergency aid, the necessity of which is not in question and on which the populations of some of the poorest countries continue to depend for their survival. The arguments nevertheless serve as a reminder that all longer-term crises are man-made and can only ultimately be resolved by human will. The roles of aid in facilitation and norm-setting are likely to be at least as effective in helping to bring about sustainable solutions as the provision of traditional forms of development assistance. The rationale for removing the debt burden, building regional cooperation arrangements, opening international markets and pursuing some of the other measures discussed in Part II applies a fortiori to countries in crisis.

Some of the ideas for this book were first presented at a public lecture at the UN University's World Institute for Development Economics Research in Helsinki in April 1997.[1] Since then the themes have been discussed at academic seminars in Cambridge and New York and shared with a number of colleagues inside and outside the UN. Among them are Georges Chapelier, Deirdre Collings, Giovanni Andrea Cornia, Hans D'Orville, Kennedy Graham, Saraswathi Menon, Manuel Montes, Michael Plummer, Rafal Rohozinski, Leelananda de Silva, Cecilia Ugaz and Kanni Wignaraja. They deserve credit for suggesting sources and putting the author right on many points, but they cannot be blamed for any remaining mistakes or misconstruals. Nina Roy, Victoria Zhou and Michele Shortley provided their own inimitable quality of technical assistance on text and tables. Other colleagues in the United Nations Development Programme have been the indirect source of many of the ideas in the book through numerous discussions over the last two years. They may be surprised by the conclusions, but I suspect that few would find themselves seriously at odds with them.

---

1 Published as 'The rise and fall of development aid', WIDER Working Paper No. 143 (1997, Helsinki).

PART I
THE RISE AND FALL OF AID

What is 'aid'? Where did it come from, and why? How has it evolved? How effective has it been? Why is it in decline? What are its prospects? These are some of the questions examined in the first part of the book.

Aid was a product of the immediate post-World War II period which saw the creation of the UN and the beginning of decolonisation, but also the inception of an East-West struggle for ideological influence. The origins of aid determined the motivations which fuelled its steady growth.

A series of aid 'ages' reflected the evolution in development thinking. The concern with economic expansion through capital accumulation was an early influence on aid patterns. As more was learnt about the development process and the special circumstances of the developing countries, however, it became clear that development did not progress along a linear path first travelled by the industrialised countries. There were pressing demographic, technological and other parameters. The global economic environment was also hostile to the efforts of many of the poorer countries to expand trade and break their bonds of debt.

More equitable and effective systems of global governance would have helped developing countries to overcome these constraints. But the record also suggests that developing countries are in a position to help themselves to a considerable degree, independent of aid. In the final age, when aid resources are in sharp decline, there are stronger motivations, but also more opportunities for them to do so.

Part I presents a rather sobering assessment of half a century of development assistance, suggesting that more of the same will be an inappropriate response to contemporary development challenges. The final chapter summarises some of the weaknesses, and anticipates the routes beyond aid proposed in Part II.

1 Origins of aid

No single event determined the start of aid. It grew out of several processes unfolding in the immediate post-war era, and is thus about half a century old. Although becoming a critical ingredient of international relations, aid was an original - and even controversial - notion at the outset. For the first time, resources were to be given away, or lent on generous terms, with none of the rigours of the commercial transaction. Aid required a spirit of altruism, a number of sustaining rationales, and a growing constituency of clients. The story of aid shows how these initial requirements were met. But also, how the world has begun moving away from them after 50 years.

The United Nations system and multilateral aid

Three processes prompted the inception of aid during the 1940s.[1] The first was the launching of the United Nations. The UN concept had been first mooted in 1941 and the name came officially into being at the beginning of 1942. At the end of the war, the human, physical and economic devastation opened a window on the opportunity to safeguard peace through international collaboration among the Allies. A family of new international organisations under the UN umbrella was born, beginning with relief. The United Nations Relief and Rehabilitation Administration (UNRRA), dating from before the end of the war (1943) and set up to address the human ravages of conflict in Europe, has been described as the world's first aid agency.[2] Its existence was relatively short-lived since it quickly fulfilled its mandate, helping to repatriate six million displaced people. Within a few years, UNRRA had been absorbed into the International Refugee Organisation, later to become the UN High Commission for Refugees (UNHCR), while part of its functions were taken on by the new UN International Children's Emergency Fund (UNICEF - now the UN Children's Fund).

The 1940s saw the establishment of several other new UN agencies, designed to address specific areas of developmental - as opposed to

---

1 Browne (1990).
2 The Director of UNRRA was the flamboyant ex-Mayor of New York City, Fiorello La Guardia.

humanitarian - concern. The Food and Agriculture Organisation of the UN (FAO) and the International Civil Aviation Organisation (ICAO) began functioning in 1945, and the UN Educational, Scientific and Cultural Organisation (UNESCO) the following year. Other pre-existing international organisations - including the International Telecommunications Union (ITU) and the Universal Postal Union (UPU), both established in the 19th century - were drawn into the UN family as additional specialised agencies. By 1948, when the International Labour Organisation (a creation of the Treaty of Versailles in 1919) and the World Health Organisation (WHO) had been added, the basis of the UN development system had been laid. But it was by no means complete. Over the ensuing decades, more agencies came into being (see Box 1).

Box 1: The UN development system

Constitutionally, the UN development system is divided into two main parts: funds and programmes whose governing bodies report directly to the UN's Economic and Social Council (ECOSOC) and whose heads are appointed by the General Assembly on the recommendation of the UN Secretary General; and the specialised agencies which are autonomously administered organisations related to the United Nations by special agreements.

1. Among the first group of organisations are the UN's major funding programmes for technical assistance and relief. These are as follows (with headquarters location and starting date of operation):

United Nations Children's Fund (UNICEF, New York, 1946)
United Nations High Commission for Refugees (UNHCR, Geneva, 1951)
UN/FAO World Food Programme (WFP, Rome 1963)
United Nations Development Programme (UNDP, New York, 1965)
United Nations Population Fund (UNFPA, New York, 1967)

This first category also comprises several consultative and research bodies:

United Nations Institute for Training and Research (UNITAR, New York,1965)
United Nations University (UNU, Tokyo, 1973)
International Research and Training Institute for the Advancement of Women (INSTRAW, Santo Domingo, 1976)
United Nations Institute for Disarmament Research (UNIDIR, Geneva, 1980)

In addition, the secretariat of the United Nations comprises various specialised branches in different locations: the United Nations Conference on Trade and Development (UNCTAD, Geneva), the Department of Economic and Social Affairs (DESA, New York), Centre for Social Development and Humanitarian Affairs (UNCSDHA, Geneva), UN Environment Programme (UNEP, Nairobi), UN Centre for Human Settlements (UNCHS or Habitat, Nairobi) and five UN Regional Commissions (ESCAP in Bangkok, ECA in Addis Ababa, ECLAC in Santiago, ECE in Geneva, and ESCWA in Beirut). The International Trade Centre in Geneva is a joint undertaking of UNCTAD and the World Trade Organisation.

II. The second group of organisations comprises fourteen specialised agencies:

International Telecommunication Union (ITU, Geneva, 1865)
Universal Postal Union (UPU, Berne, 1875)
International Labour Organisation (ILO, Geneva, 1919)
International Civil Aviation Organisation (ICAO, Montreal, 1945)
Food and Agriculture Organisation of the United Nations (FAO, Rome, 1945)
World Bank Group
    International Bank for Reconstruction and Development
        (IBRD, Washington, 1946)
    International Finance Corporation (IFC, Washington, 1956)
    International Development Association (IDA, Washington, 1960)
International Monetary Fund (IMF, Washington, 1946)
United Nations Educational, Scientific and Cultural Organisation
    (UNESCO, Paris, 1946)
World Health Organisation (WHO, Geneva, 1948)
World Meteorological Organisation (WMO, Geneva, 1951)
International Maritime Organisation (IMO, London, 1958)
World Intellectual Property Organisation (WIPO, Geneva, 1970)
International Fund for Agricultural Development (IFAD, Rome, 1977)
United Nations Industrial Development Organisation (UNIDO, Vienna, 1985)

The International Atomic Energy Agency (IAEA, Vienna, 1957) is known as an "intergovernmental body under the aegis of the United Nations" but operates in practice very much like a specialised agency.

In parallel with the emergence of the new UN family of organisations, the architecture of a new system of economic and financial governance was being fashioned, also to be loosely included under the UN umbrella. In 1944, the United Nations Monetary and Financial Conference in Bretton Woods, New Hampshire, examined proposals for an international financial clearing system to palliate liquidity imbalances, and for a lending mechanism to facilitate new global investment. The clearing system became the International Monetary Fund (IMF) and the lending mechanism the International Bank for Reconstruction and Development (World Bank). Both began operations in Washington DC in 1946. There was a third set of proposals at Bretton Woods for a commodity-based currency unit, a buffer-stock scheme and a code of trading under the auspices of an International Trade Organisation. Only the code prevailed, but in a modified form, leading to the establishment of the General Agreement on Trade and Tariffs (GATT) in 1948.

The UN family became the core of the multilateral system. The roles of the UN organisations as purveyors of aid developed as their funding bases expanded. The most significant source of such funding was the Expanded Programme of Technical Assistance (EPTA) which began operations in 1950 with initial pledges of $20 million. Proposals for a soft-lending facility under the auspices of the United Nations did not succeed, however. The industrialised powers felt more confident with the non-concessional lending arrangements of the International Bank for Reconstruction and Development. They agreed to back the Bank with 'callable' capital, used to guarantee borrowing on the financial markets at favourable terms. This capital was then on-lent to developing countries at terms which they themselves could not have secured. This arrangement cost the rich countries nothing, and no call has ever been made on their capital.

Aid through the multilateral system was substantially supplemented in 1960, when the donor countries agreed to establish a concessional lending window at the World Bank: the euphemistically-termed International Development Association (IDA). The choice of the World Bank was significant. While the donors overcame their earlier opposition to concessional funding, they wanted it to be administered by an organisation which they effectively controlled (through weighted voting). Thus the prize was denied to the UN, in which the recipients had a much greater influence, providing only for a Special Fund for grant support to pre-investment studies. In 1965, this fund was merged with EPTA to form the UN Development Programme, which has remained the largest of the technical assistance funds of the UN system.

Also in the 1960s, multilateral financing was supplemented by the creation of the three largest regional development banks. The Inter-American Development Bank began operations in 1960, and the African Development Bank and Asian Development Bank followed in 1966. Each of them supplements its lending operations with soft loans and grant funds which qualify as official development assistance (ODA - see Box 3).

Bilateral aid

The second process unfolded as the Allied unity between East and West crumbled. Churchill saw the iron curtain falling in 1946 and in the same year the Soviet Union imposed its first Security Council vetoes. Bilateral aid began to be impelled by growing Cold War rivalry, first manifested by the Marshall Plan.

In his Harvard speech, in June 1947, the US Secretary of State, General George Marshall, determined that Europe "must have substantial additional help, or face economic, social and political deterioration of a very grave character". The speech was vague in its detail, but the intent to extend assistance to the whole of Europe was clear. Within a month, however, the Soviet Union had explicitly rejected participation and ordered the other communist leaders of Eastern Europe to stay away from the Committee of European Economic Cooperation (CEEC), which had been formed in Paris to administer the assistance. Thus the Plan, which from 1948 funnelled $13 billion of assistance from America to Europe over four years (the equivalent of $90 billion today) with rapid and palpable results, inevitably became identified with the fortification of the 'free world' against the encroachment of communism.

With the Marshall Plan under way, President Truman decided in 1949 to build on the experience and widen the geographical horizons of American aid. The US would make "the benefits of our scientific advance and technical progress available for the improvement and growth of under-developed areas...in cooperation with other nations, we should foster capital investment in areas needing development". Truman's resolve was altruistic in expression, but strategic in execution. Although foreshadowing a cooperative effort and recognising the importance of "working through the United Nations and its specialised agencies whenever practical", it was Truman's earlier foreign policy doctrine that was to shape American aid. As a frame of reference, the Act for International Development of 1950, yielded place to the Mutual Security Act of the following year which specified that aid could be given only if it "strengthened the security of the United States".

From behind the ideological curtain, the Soviet Union was rapidly expanding its own programmes of economic assistance. The theatre of rivalry spread to Asia, and the countries encircling the Soviet Union, leading to a new conflagration on the Korean peninsula in 1950. The 38th parallel is now the most tangible memorial of cold war aid, where many soldiers were sacrificed to ideology. The US military effort cost the equivalent of four Marshall Plans, and confirmed the pattern of meshing America's aid with its military security.[3]

Decolonisation

The third process accompanying the birth of aid in the 1940s was the beginning of the independence movement among the former colonies (Box 2). The process began with the Philippines in 1946 (when there were only 74 independent countries) and the constituency of potential recipients quickly grew. There were already 12 new countries when the Afro-Asian Conference was convened in Bandung, Indonesia, in 1955. This was the first manifestation of 'third world' solidarity and it led to the foundation of the 'non-aligned movement' in 1961 (which still exists today). In the light of the Cold War, non-alignment might have meant eschewing foreign assistance from either of the big powers. Sri Lanka was an example. For much of the 1950s, it was concerned to safeguard and strengthen the independence it had won in 1948, and was hesitant about accepting aid from any source.[4]

Box 2: The chronology of independence
Most of the aid-receiving countries became independent or self-governing after 1946, with the independence movement concentrated on Africa, Asia and the Pacific. In Asia, only Iran, Nepal and Thailand, and in Africa, Ethiopia and Egypt were independent by the close of the Second World War. Except for some smaller Caribbean dependencies, the countries of the Americas had gained their independence much earlier. In the Middle-East, most countries became independent during the first half of the century. A few developing countries became independent of others during this period: Bhutan from India in 1949, Namibia from South Africa in 1990 and Eritrea from Ethiopia in 1993

---

3   Strictly speaking, the US aid programme may be said to have begun in the immediate aftermath of the War when technical assistance was provided to the governments of Turkey and Greece to help them to combat emerging pro-communist guerrilla movements. However, it was Truman's 'Point 4' speech which established the global effort.
4   It could afford to do so initially because the Korean War drove up commodity prices from which its export earnings benefited.

(these countries are not included below). Much more recently, the break-up of the Soviet Union led to the renewed independence of the three Baltic states in 1989 and the independence of 11 former republics in 1991.

1946	Philippines *(us)*, Lebanon** *(fr)*
1947	India *(uk)*, Pakistan *(uk)*, French Guiana *(fr)*, Guadeloupe *(fr)*, Martinique *(fr)*, Reunion *(fr)*
1948	Sri Lanka (originally Ceylon) *(uk)*, Burma *(uk)*
1949	Indonesia *(nl)*
1951	Libya *(it)*, Netherlands Antilles *(nl)*, Surinam *(nl)*
1952	Puerto Rico* *(us)*
1956	Gambia *(uk)*, Morocco *(fr)*, Tunisia *(fr)*, Sudan *(uk)*
1957	Malaysia (Malaya) *(uk)*, Ghana (Gold Coast) *(uk)*
1958	Guinea *(fr)*
1960	Benin (Dahomey) *(fr)*, Burkina Faso (Upper Volta) *(fr)*, Cameroon *(fr)*, Central African Republic *(fr)*, Chad *(fr)*, Congo-Brazzaville *(fr)*, Congo-Kinshasa *(be)*, Cyprus *(uk)*, Gabon *(fr)*, Ivory Coast *(fr)*, Madagascar *(fr)*, Mali *(fr)*, Niger *(fr)*, Nigeria *(uk)*, Senegal *(fr)*, Somalia** *(uk/it)*, Togo (Togoland) *(fr)*
1961	Mauritania *(fr)*, Sierra Leone *(uk)*
1962	Algeria *(fr)*, Burundi *(be)*, Jamaica *(uk)*, Rwanda *(be)*, Samoa *(nz)*, Trinidad and Tobago *(uk)*, Uganda *(uk)*
1963	Kenya *(uk)*
1964	Malawi *(uk)*, Zambia *(uk)*
1965	Cook Islands* *(nz)*, Singapore *(uk)*, Maldives *(uk)*
1966	Barbados *(uk)*, Botswana *(uk)*, Guyana *(uk)*, Lesotho *(uk)*
1967	Yemen (South Yemen) *(uk)*
1968	Mauritius *(fr)*, Nauru *(au/nz/uk)*, Swaziland *(uk)*, Equatorial Guinea *(sp)*
1970	Fiji *(uk)*, Tonga *(uk)*
1974	Grenada *(uk)*, Guinea-Bissau *(pt)*, Malta *(uk)*, Niue* *(nz)*
1975	Angola *(pt)*, Cape Verde *(pt)*, Comoros *(fr)*, Mozambique *(pt)*, Papua New Guinea *(au)*, Sao Tome *(pt)*
1976	Seychelles *(uk)*
1977	Djibouti *(fr)*
1978	Solomon Islands *(uk)*, Tuvalu *(uk)*, Dominica *(uk)*
1979	Kiribati *(uk)*, Vanuatu *(fr/uk)*
1980	Zimbabwe (Rhodesia) *(uk)*
1981	Belize *(uk)*, Antigua and Barbuda *(uk)*
1983	Brunei *(uk)*
1986	Micronesia** *(us)*, Marshall Islands** *(us)*
1989	Estonia *(ru)*, Latvia *(ru)*, Lithuania *(ru)*
1991	Armenia *(ru)*, Azerbaijan *(ru)*, Belarus *(ru)*, Georgia *(ru)*, Kazakstan *(ru)*, Kyrgyzstan *(ru)*, Moldova *(ru)*, Tajikistan *(ru)*, Turkmenistan *(ru)*, Ukraine *(ru)*, Uzbekistan *(ru)*
1994	Palau** *(us)*

Key (countries from which independent): USA = us, UK = uk, France = fr, Belgium = be, Netherlands = nl, Italy = it, Portugal = pt, Australia = au, Spain = sp, Russia = ru
*self-governing ** previously under UN mandate

But its example was exceptional. Among the emerging countries, other expediencies soon prevailed. The sacrifice of sovereignty for aid distorted the principles of non-alignment, since many of the developing countries were the targets of aggressive courtship by the two major powers. Khruschev proclaimed in 1956 that the developing countries "need not go begging to their former oppressors" but could obtain aid "free from any political or military obligations". For some countries, such as India, non-alignment was interpreted as allowing aid from both East and West. Other countries, such as Egypt in the 1950s and Somalia in the 1970s, switched their aid allegiances from one bloc to the other.

But aside from vastly expanding the arena of ideological rivalry, the independence movement encouraged other bilateral donors to build aid programmes in the 1950s as a sequel to their colonial obligations. France founded its aid programme on the support of its expatriate population in the ex-colonies. Since it maintained large numbers of public service officials and experts after independence, decolonisation was largely a book-keeping exercise as far as resource transfers were concerned. French aid became more broad-based as the expatriates returned home. Britain leaned more to a policy of graduation, seeking to prepare its colonies for a status at independence which would have enabled them to meet their capital needs from borrowing. The strategy was ill-judged. It would have needed more than a Marshall Plan to achieve this aim, and a series of foreign exchange crises, followed by more borrowing on near-commercial terms, increased rather than diminished a cumulative dependence on foreign aid.

In parallel, several more bilateral donors emerged among the industralised countries which had none of the same military-strategic or post-colonial motivations for providing aid. Although their aid was an obvious adjunct to foreign policy, the programmes of Canada, Netherlands and the Nordic countries (sometimes known as the 'like-minded' donors) fundamentally arose from an altruistic and developmental vocation, linked to the desire to build political bridges to developing countries.

Five aid types

To sum up, two principal forms of development assistance - non-strategic and strategic - emerged from the 1940s. On one hand, non-strategic aid was comprised of multilateral assistance and the more 'altruistic' forms of bilateral aid, intended primarily to respond to the objective development needs of recipient countries. On the other hand, aid was strategic in the military/geopolitical, historical/cultural or commercial senses, serving respectively the political, cultural and market influence of the donors. Part of all bilateral aid has been tied, and the practice has grown of using trade credits in conjunction with aid to stimulate sales of domestic goods and services in the donor country.

Type of aid	*Special characteristics*
Multilateral	Responds to developmental priorities
Bilateral-altruistic	Responds to perceived human needs
Bilateral-political/strategic	Underlines political influence
Bilateral-historical/cultural	Reinforces post-colonial alliances
Bilateral-commercial	Promotes trade, widens markets

These five types were not mutually distinctive. On the non-strategic side, all major donors have subscribed to multilateral aid, through the UN and the development banks, in addition to their bilateral programmes. Over the years, there has been a growth in 'multi-bi' assistance, through which donors have sought to give specific geographic or substantive direction to their multilateral contributions. Also, donor programmes with individual countries have often combined strategic (military) aid with other forms of development assistance. American aid to Israel and Egypt, and French aid to francophone Africa provide examples.

Box 3: Aid defined
In this book, aid is used synonymously with 'official development assistance' (ODA), and broadly follows the definition established by the Organisation for Economic Cooperation and Development (OECD) in the 1960s. 'Official' flows are those of which the sources are the Governments and official agencies of donor countries. They are distinguishable from private flows which include long- or short-term commercial loans (whether or not guaranteed by an official agency), private trade credits, direct investment and investments in bonds and other securities. They include official contributions to private voluntary agencies engaged in development, but they exclude the finances which these same agencies raise from private sources.

Aid comprises resources that are channelled to 'developing' countries, either directly or through the intermediary of a multilateral institution or private voluntary organisation. Aid is not confined to resources allocated to independent countries, however. In the case of France, for example, aid statistics include the substantial transfers to its remaining colonies and dependent territories ('*départements et territoires d'outre-mer*', the so-called DOM/TOMs) although the figures are listed separately.

Aid is 'developmental', but that term is rather imprecise. Normally, ODA excludes resources provided to developing countries for relief, emergency and humanitarian (including refugee) purposes. In practice, the distinctions between development and relief aid are often not clear. However, using their own definitions, donors appropriate resources for development and for relief separately, in the latter case usually setting aside a reserve to be drawn down as needs demand. When there are major emergencies, special pledging conferences may be called to raise supplementary relief resources. These are not ODA.

Formally speaking, ODA excludes all assistance of a military nature, but here also there are margins of ambiguity. For example, donors use ODA to support paramilitary and police forces, for which the rationale is presumably that the training can be turned to useful civilian applications. For the most part, however, assistance directed to military recipients is excluded from classification as aid, even though development assistance appropriations are sometimes tied closely to the provision of military assistance.

The terms of aid are concessional, meaning that aid is provided either as grants in funds or in kind, or as loans at costs low enough to be discounted to values that are small in comparison with the total original disbursement. Loans are determined by the OECD to be concessional, and therefore eligible as ODA, if they have a 'grant equivalent' value equal to a minimum of 25 per cent.

To facilitate measurement, aid is usually defined to include only those forms of assistance that involve identifiable financial transfers: either capital, goods (food and commodities) or services (technical cooperation) purchased with aid funds. Reckoning aid in these terms leaves out of account other implicit transfers which may be significant but which do not lend themselves easily to measurement. One important example is price subsidisation: essential goods sold by developed countries to developing countries at prices below world market levels, or purchases of exports from developing countries at higher than prevailing levels.

Not all of the resources reported as aid are available for delivery to developing country recipients. A proportion is absorbed by the general administrative budgets of aid agencies, while intrinsic to every aid project there are costs of management and execution. There is a wide variation in the proportion of project budgets taken up by administrative costs. In the case of IDA credits, there is an annual 'commitment' fee on the undisbursed portion and a 'service' charge of 0.75 per cent on disbursements. At the other end of the scale, complex projects may absorb high proportions of their overall values *in costs of execution.*

In financial terms, the actual transfer of technical assistance resources is limited. Some 75% of the value of bilateral projects is spent in the donor countries or on the products, services and expertise of the donors. The aid transfer has to be reckoned in terms of the value of the training, expertise and equipment provided.

2 A brief history of aid

Aid, and the rationale for providing it, has evolved through several phases, which are presented here as 'aid ages'. The three ages, while not wholly distinctive, illustrate the prevailing fashions of development theory, helping to explain the assumptions under which development assistance has been given.

The first age: development through capital and growth (1950-1965)[1]

The post-War world was Keynesian. The British economist, a leading architect of the Bretton Woods institutions, was closely identified with theories that linked economic growth to capital investment. Growth theory, little used in economic analysis before the war, became the essence of development studies. Indeed the terms were essentially synonymous. Reconstruction under Marshall, a process which focused heavily on restoring dynamism to the economies in Europe, clearly perceived capital as the ingredient of progress. Development theory built on that experience.

At the heart of the theory was the 'incremental capital-output ratio (ICOR)', considered to be a stable function over time, which assumed that increases in capital investment led directly to output growth.[2] Several economists in the 1950s[3] considered that the capital-orientated development experience of the industrial countries could be directly transplanted to the developing world. With the neo-classical theorists, the argument ran, the returns on capital would be higher in the developing world where capital was scarcer relative to other factors of production, particularly labour.

The influence of these western theories - built around the so-called Harrod-Domar model - could also be seen in the first national plans of the developing countries[4] and 'public investment plans' still form the centre-pieces of some World Bank Consultative Group (aid mobilisation) meetings. The role of aid was to bridge the domestic resource gaps of the developing countries by raising the rates of productive investment. A seminal work from this era was one of the fullest expositions to that date of

1   The notion of 'ages' has been partly inspired by Hyden (1994).
2   See, for example, Harrod (1939).
3   Kuznets (1954); Rostow (1956).
4   de Silva (1984).

a development model.[5] In the stages of economic growth, the first condition for 'take-off' was a rise in the investment rate, which could be achieved through an exogenous injection of capital.

A further refinement of Rostow was developed in 1966 by Chenery and Strout, outlining the role for aid more comprehensively.[6] It was another stages-of-development approach, also known as the two-gap model: during the first two stages of economic development, aid was required to bridge the difference between capital investment needs and domestic savings (the internal gap), and to finance the necessary increase in imports (the external gap).

Much of the essence of these theories is lost in paraphrase. There were other critical aspects of these and other theories, but they were given insufficient attention by the development school during this first age of aid. Rostow's third condition had been the emergence of a political, social and institutional framework that facilitated ongoing expansion - a fundamental concept of sustainability that underlies today's fashionable governance debate. Chenery and Strout also laid stress on the importance of technical assistance and the development of skills as an essential accompaniment to capital and as fundamental to absorptive capacity.

Almost since its inception, the United Nations had also been drawing attention to the importance of directing aid to supporting 'social productivity' in the interests of global welfare. During the first age, however, donor attention was mainly fixed on the safer alternative: capital investment. It stemmed from a basic misgiving - which is now returning - about the practice of giving away, rather than lending, funds to the developing world. Technical assistance was a gift with uncertain returns, unless it came embodied in the exportable goods and services of bilateral donors. Multilateral technical assistance was the least dirigible of all, especially through the UN, where the industrial countries soon lost their voting majority as the world body gained new members.

Aid from the Soviet bloc carried many of the same proclivities and it came in similar wrappers. Socialist principles, handed down from the commanding heights of heavy industry, had served Soviet economic advance well. They also emphasized capital investment, as manifested in the vast Soviet industrial and infrastructure projects that began to appear in the developing countries.

The first age of aid was thus dominated by development models which perceived development paths as unilinear, exalting capital investment as the

---

5   Rostow (1960).
6   Chenery and Strout (1966).

engine of economic growth. It was a paradigm of modernisation, of aping the North. It was also a model in which the State - within the new sovereign countries - was expected to play a leading role as planner and investor. Thinking during this age encouraged the growth of capital transfers through concessional loans and grants to the governments and public sectors of developing countries.

The second age: interdependence and basic needs (1965-1980)

During the second age - from the mid-1960s to the mid-1970s - misgivings were already arising over the supposedly beneficial connection between aid and savings,[7] and even the pro-aid Pearson Report[8] described as "very weak" the correlation between aid and growth.[9] The development debate also became more complex, and more ideological. It was conducted on at least two planes: the plane of international economics, but now also at the micro-level of the individual.

International economic arguments turned on the concept of dependency, and anticipated today's debate on the pros and cons of globalisation. In its benign version, the argument contended that developing countries stood to benefit from the increasing interdependence of the North and South, particularly with respect to trade. The benefits of openness in the economies of some East Asian countries could already be seen to result in rapidly growing exports, as well as inflows of direct investment. Such evidence provided fertile ground for the 'trade-rather-than-aid' school, according to which developing countries could arguably earn more than they could be provided through concessional transfers.

But there was another, quite different, view which saw the benefits of interdependence flowing mainly in one direction, towards the rich countries. This view looked more closely at the quality of trade and investment, and saw other disadvantages of interdependence.[10] Many developing countries

---

7   For example, Griffin (1970).
8   Pearson (1969).
9   A more rigorous study from the 1980s concludes: "The main empirical result of this chapter ['Aid as Instrument of Development'] is a negative one, namely that there appears to be no statistically significant correlation in any post-war period, either positive or negative, between inflows of development aid and the growth rate of GNP in developing countries when other causal influences on growth are taken into account." Mosely (1987), p.139.
10 From the ideological left, integrated global markets were a mirror of the exploitative patterns within capitalist economies. One of the foremost exponents of this view was Amin (1970) who spoke of the developing countries as the economic periphery around a centre of metropolitan powers.

have traditionally depended on the export of primary products, and the terms of trade have moved against them for most of the post-War period. While the expansion of industrial markets could lead to growth in demand for developing country exports, increasing protectionism in those markets - especially during these years, before the benefits of successive global trade negotiations began to bear fruit - succeeded in limiting market access.[11] The benefits of foreign investment could be mitigated by lop-sided terms in the initial negotiations, and by multinational corporations extracting additional advantages through devices such as transfer pricing.

Underlying the arguments of the trade pessimists was the continuing belief in the importance of industrialisation as the central engine of growth, and the need to protect infant domestic industries in order to facilitate their expansion.[12] Trade policy was dominated by strong preferences for import substitution, whereby investments were channelled into domestic industries to produce goods previously imported. Virtually all developing countries - and developed countries before them - raised import barriers to protect new industry. The more dynamic economies, however, moved quickly from policies of import substitution to export promotion, exposing their domestic firms to competitive conditions on the global market and successfully jumping the protectionist hurdles in the western markets.

In hindsight, the most serious weakness of the system of international governance that came out of the post-War period was the absence of a regulatory trade organisation which would have more aggressively enforced the mutual reduction of trade barriers in the developing and developed economies. It was not until the 1980s, and the Uruguay Round of trade negotiations, that conditions became more propitious for free trade. In the absence of a strong trade regime, reliance was placed on the financial mechanisms of the Bretton Woods institutions. But neither the export production promoting loans of the World Bank, nor the temporary borrowing mechanisms of the IMF (extended by the compensatory financing facility in 1963 and the compensatory and contingency financing facility in 1988), could possibly have compensated for the chronic payments crises of the countries which were pursuing a protective and inward-looking development path, and which were suffering from long-

---

11 UNDP estimated in its 1994 Human Development Report that the cost to developing countries of protectionism in the textile and clothing markets was $50 billion, and in agrarian commodities, $22 billion. An earlier study by the OECD estimated that a 30% reduction of OECD border measures would result in $90 billion of benefits for developing countries. (1992, OECD Development Cooperation Report, Paris). These figures are higher than the OECD's estimates of annual aid flows.
12 See, for example, Krueger (1995).

term declines in real commodity prices. Developing countries quickly accumulated debts to the Bretton Woods institutions which could neither be forgiven nor rescheduled. And since both bodies were governed through a weighted voting system, their major clients could do little to change the operating principles.

During the early 1970s, the Organisation of Petroleum Exporting Countries (mainly the Arab States and Iran) staged its own spectacular demonstration of trading dis-order when it used its power as a cartel to raise oil prices substantially. OPEC's success gave impetus to the demands of developing countries in the UN for a 'new international economic order', unpopular with the industrialised countries at the time, but incorporating several goals which are even more urgent two decades later. However, OPEC also highlighted the ambiguity of southern solidarity since the major costs of the oil price increases were borne by the developing countries (and the major gains by the commercial banks of the North).

Another consequence of OPEC for development assistance was the sudden emergence of new donors in the Middle-East. For the decade of the 1970s as a whole, OPEC aid was equivalent to one quarter of the total from the OECD countries, although it has diminished drastically since.

At one level, the second age was characterised both by the laissez-faire school of economic openness, and the radical detractors arguing for the de-linking of developing countries from the international economy. Both schools were sceptical about aid. The marketeers contended that aid was superfluous in a global economy increasingly dominated by private capital. The de-linkers argued for more collective self-sufficiency among developing countries, among which the OPEC countries were still counted.

Politically, however, aid retained its respectability, gaining wider official acceptance as a legitimate form of compensation for disadvantage. Aid came to be associated with quantitative targets,[13] somewhat analogous to a global tax scheme. For two principal reasons, however, targeting has not served aid well. First, these targets have remained out of range of nearly all the major donors, and thus seemingly irrelevant. Second, targets have implied that aid had become an automatic requirement based on arbitrarily determined supply levels, rather than a response to carefully defined needs. (Development problems would not have been solved if the targets had been consistently met). By helping to substitute declamation for debate, targeting may have even hastened the eventual demise of non-strategic aid.

---

13 The Pearson Commission had advocated that each developed country should raise its expenditure on official development assistance to 0.7% of GNP, a target subsequently endorsed by the UN and adopted by the OECD DAC.

Nonetheless, the nature of development processes themselves were receiving much greater attention during this phase, and this analysis was eventually to have an important influence on aid programmes and on future global cooperation. Two issues first became more prominent during the 1970s: the environment and population.

In 1972, the UN sponsored a conference in Stockholm on the 'human environment', which examined the quality of human life and the natural resources that support it. There was growing concern about the sustainability of economic growth and the 'carrying capacity' of the natural world. The concerns emanated mainly from the developed countries. Many developing countries were even sceptical about participating because they construed conservation as anti-growth. After the conference, notwithstanding the establishment of the UN Environment Programme, interest in environmental concerns diminished within the international community - North and South. Many in the developing countries continued to see a trade-off between environment and economics. And environmental dangers were perceived to be mainly local: if it was 'not in my back-yard' (NIMBY), it wasn't a global concern. But when in the 1980s, more reliable scientific evidence linked 'local' environmental degradation to global meteorological changes, and as the signs of global warming began to appear, environmental management concerns rose to the top of the development agenda.

In the 1970s, the focus on human indicators - as opposed to merely economic ones - became stronger as the fundamental differences in southern development parameters were more clearly recognised. There were significant demographic differences. Because industrialisation had preceded the major advances in epidemiology in western countries, they had not experienced rapid population increases. In many developing countries, however, populations were large and growing rapidly and the poverty which accompanied this growth made western modernisation models based on technology seem unsuited. Small was suddenly beautiful and more basic ('intermediate technology') production methods more appealing.[14] This was also the era in which the basic needs of people rather than economies began to receive more attention.[15]

The orthodox economic reaction was to advocate 'redistribution with growth',[16] and begin to recognise that even in the more macro-economically dynamic developing countries, but especially in the more slothful ones,

---

14   Schumacher (1974).
15   International Labour Office (1977).
16   Chenery (1974).

intractable poverty prevailed. As with the environment, donor interest stemmed not just from altruistic concern, but also from more selfish preoccupations arising from what was perceived as the demographic explosion in the South. Aid for most population control methods in developing countries - in spite of their highly disputable connection with development progress - began to flow generously, leading to the establishment of a separate multilateral agency (the UN Population Fund, UNFPA).

The third age: structural adjustment and the rise of the NGO (the 1980s)

In the third age, the dependency chickens were returning to roost. The surplus global savings balance of the 1970s - accumulated in part by the huge increase in unspendable export earnings by OPEC - had stimulated substantial lending to developing countries. By the turn of the new decade, the unfamiliar phenomenon of 'stagflation' was assailing the developed countries and the costs of borrowing had mounted rapidly. The South was heavily in debt and in 1982, Mexico came close to defaulting. After two decades of aid, most of the developing countries were much further away than ever from closing the two gaps of the Chenery-Strout model. The banking system accommodated partially. The most exposed commercial banks absorbed some of the losses through bad-debt provisions, and limited grant aid was diverted to provide for official debt restructuring. With these measures, and with a bout of enforced fiscal repression in the South, the crisis eased for the major borrowers.

The Bretton Woods financial mechanisms, originally established to regulate global imbalances, took none of the hits, but responded with more short-term lending. By mid-decade the flow of funds had turned around so that the developing countries as a whole became the net creditors of the World Bank and IMF. These costs of financial dependence were attributed by World Bank economists at the time, not only to the disadvantages of interdependence, but also to policy failure on the part of the borrowers.[17] To the uncertainties of trade, and the burden of debt in the developing world, had been added the necessity for comprehensive structural adjustment, essentially a set of policy measures designed to close the internal and

---

17   For example, Please (1984): "..unpropitious external circumstances were intensified further by the widespread failure of developing countries to take effective steps to assure their ability to meet the debt-service obligations on the large flows of funds obtained from commercial banks during the second half of the 1970s."

external resource gaps.

With the World Bank's first structural adjustment loan in 1980, a new aid phase of macro-economic governance had begun, in which the choices for the developing countries - and hence a large measure of their economic sovereignty - were further circumscribed. From here on, there would be a much greater degree of consensus among the donors about the conditions for lending as well as aid provision. Donors were more determined to elicit conditions for the type of assistance provided, in addition to the conditions imposed by the tying of aid to home exports.[18] This age, therefore, added a new strategic spin to aid motivation.

The beginning of the decade was also the time when consensus about aid within donor countries broke apart. In 1980, Willy Brandt published the first report of his Commission. The 'programme of survival' urged for a new compact between North and South, and Marshall-style 'massive transfers' which would reap their own dividends in global economic stimulus. Pearson had made the same case a decade earlier, but less convincingly. The public was mobilised to press governments for action on what would have been a revisited new world economic order. Momentum developed amongst pro-aid lobbies in western countries in the months before the much-heralded development summit of 22 world leaders meeting in Cancun, Mexico, in 1981.

But the summit was a disappointment for the new aid lobbyists. Its timing during the sharp economic down-turn in the world economy was scarcely propitious. What helped to doom it, however, were the conservative positions of the new administrations in the USA and UK, which displayed a new zeal for market mechanisms, an unwavering belief in the power of private capital, and hostility to the notion of government-sponsored economic stimuli. In some western policy-makers' books, neo-Keynesianism was a failed concept and the notion of new massive transfers was still-born.

While there was no substantial increase in aid flows, official development assistance nonetheless remained quite buoyant during the 1980s. One stimulant was the channelling of more resources through non-governmental organisations (NGOs) in both donor and recipient countries. The Brandt momentum had not been wholly dissipated. More importantly, the drama of the famines that recurred in 1983 in eastern Africa was now

---

18   It has been estimated that, on an average, 75% of the value of bilateral technical assistance projects returns to donor countries: 21% to the originating donor as administration costs, and the remaining 54% to the originating donor, or other donor countries for the purchase of goods and services. The more tied is the aid, the larger the proportion returning to the originating donor. Browne (1990).

being disseminated through the global media. The western public responded generously through the charitable organisations which seemed better able and more inclined than government and multilateral agencies to meet the succession of emergencies. The growing importance of NGOs as agents of development and relief assistance - which predated the 1980s but grew visibly during that decade - signified the rise of popular interest and engagement. NGOs supplemented, and in some cases supplanted, the roles of governments and official agencies. In recipient countries, NGOs helped to give louder expression to, and meet more directly, the needs of the underserved populations. In donor countries, they demonstrated greater speed and responsiveness in mobilising and delivering aid.[19]

Notwithstanding these efforts, however, evidence was accumulating that more aid on any scale - while it helped to temporarily alleviate the plight of the victims of crisis - was not likely to engender significant and sustainable advantages for the neediest in the developing world. The African famines, real and potential, were occurring or threatening to occur in some of the most generously aided countries and were in all cases attributable to subtle factors of human origin which aid was seemingly unable to influence. A proportion of aid was being diverted to other purposes; even when it reached its legitimate targets, it did not appear to facilitate beneficial change.

The 1980s have been described as a defining decade: serious economic setbacks (and negative growth) in Latin America; stagnation, famine and continuing human misery in Africa. There were also harsh, if belated, reappraisals of aid programmes. "Does aid work?" asked one exhaustive study in 1986. Yes - but only partially, was the response.[20] As the decade wore on, the cherished adjustment process was in serious doubt. Macro-economic stabilisation, where it was not blown off course by emergencies, was unrealistic in its prescription and politically clumsy. As a result of dismal evaluations, donor governments began to lose confidence in aid, and in its use by their client governments.

---

19 Among many other sources on the role of NGOs are Korten (1990) and Clark (1991).
20 Cassen (1986).

3 Towards the end of aid?

The 1990s have witnessed a number of important development watersheds. The limitations of central planning have been exposed and there has been a marked convergence in development policy prescriptions in favour of market-oriented economics. The graduation of several developing countries to middle and upper income status has provided important lessons about the benefits of openness to the global economy. And recent experience has also underlined the importance of sound and stable governance and cohesive policy environments. The value of institutional factors, long ago foreshadowed by development theorists, can now be seen more clearly than ever.

These momentous changes have altered the rationales for aid in a fundamental way. International relations are now based less on ideological considerations, and more on the economic. Aid is not only differently motivated, its role in relation to the now widely accepted prescriptions for development progress also needs to be reappraised. For a number of reasons - some of which could have been anticipated, and some not - these changes in global relationships have been accompanied by a sharp reduction in traditional forms of aid from the traditional sources.

The global age?

The end of the Cold War and the disintegration of the last modern empire heralded the fourth - and last? - aid age. The fall of the Berlin Wall, the reunification of Germany and the democracy movements in Eastern Europe, exposed the vulnerabilities of communism, politically and economically. Within two years, economic hardship brought on by misguided and half-hearted Soviet reforms, had also broken the union apart.[1] Central planning

---

1 While change in Eastern Europe had been spurred by the yearnings for democracy and more open markets, the break-up of the Soviet Union had been mainly precipitated by a failure of leadership in Moscow. This failure stoked the separatist fires in some (but by no means all) of the Soviet Republics and the resulting revolutions were initially of state-hood, rather than of democracy or economic reform. In the aftershocks of the revolutions in Europe and the former Soviet Union, the ideological debate has not yet been cleanly resolved, and will not be as long as there are ex-communists in positions of influence. Outside the region, Cuba and North Korea have proved so far impervious to ideological change, while in China, political change is occurring only slowly.

had been grievously exposed as untenable. Although not a simple triumph of capitalism over communism, the trend underlying these momentous changes has been unmistakable.

The failures of central planning in Europe and Central Asia have only served to crown a growing consensus about the most appropriate development path. Virtually all programmes of reform - whether among developing countries or post-communist transitional economies - centre on common objectives facilitating greater openness and economic integration, and the application of market principles: trade and financial liberalisation, encouragement of foreign investment, and the fostering of conditions favourable to free enterprise. In conjunction with this trend, two key pillars of global economic governance - the International Monetary Fund and the World Trade Organisation - are moving towards near-universal membership. We are in a global age of converging development paradigms.

These more uniform patterns of progress are the basis of the much vaunted globalisation process, of which the principal pillars are the liberalisation of trade and investment, and the spreading information revolution, discussed in detail in later chapters. Because globalisation is an inexorable process, it makes little sense to debate in favour or against it. The concern is over impact on individual countries, whose performance and prospects will be increasingly determined by the degree to which they have successfully adjusted to globalisation.

The countries of East Asia are usually held up as examples of highly successful long-term development performance. Typical among them is South Korea. In the 1950s, it was one of the world's most impoverished and poorly endowed countries. Yet from 1965 until 1990, the Korean economy yielded annual average real growth per person of over 7 per cent. By 1996, Korea had a per capita level of income of over $10,000 dollars and had joined the OECD. For the four East Asian 'tigers' taken together (Hong Kong, Korea, Singapore, Taiwan) high and steady growth raised income per person from less than one-sixth of the US level in 1965 to well over half today.

The progress of these countries could be ascribed to development strategies consistent with increasing openness and liberalisation. The fact that among them, Korea has experienced a sharp economic retrenchment in 1997-98 only serves to highlight the fact that the country was relatively less successful in developing a transparent and well-regulated financial sector adequate to the task of managing huge private inflows of capital. For globalisation also insures a measure of regulation by revelation. In Indonesia and Thailand - both countries which have also derived considerable dynamism from the export of goods and services and the import of private capital - financial governance systems were found to be seriously wanting and they have paid a high price through a sharp economic down-turn.

The decade of the 1990s can also be dubbed the era of 'good governance', a term which encompasses a wide range of institutional connotations.[2] There is now a much clearer understanding of the conditions in which the state could play a beneficial role in the contemporary development process. Contrary to the prevailing wisdom of the post-war period when large state apparatus was considered essential for reconstruction and industrialisation, an effective state today is not one which necessarily commands substantial resources. Although the economic role of the state has grown almost everywhere, a comparison between the western industrialised countries and the countries of East Asia, including China, shows a negative correlation between the size of government spending and growth performance. An economically large state in the developed countries reflects a more elaborate social welfare system. Economically smaller states are more conducive to growth, but less protective (see Figure 1 below).

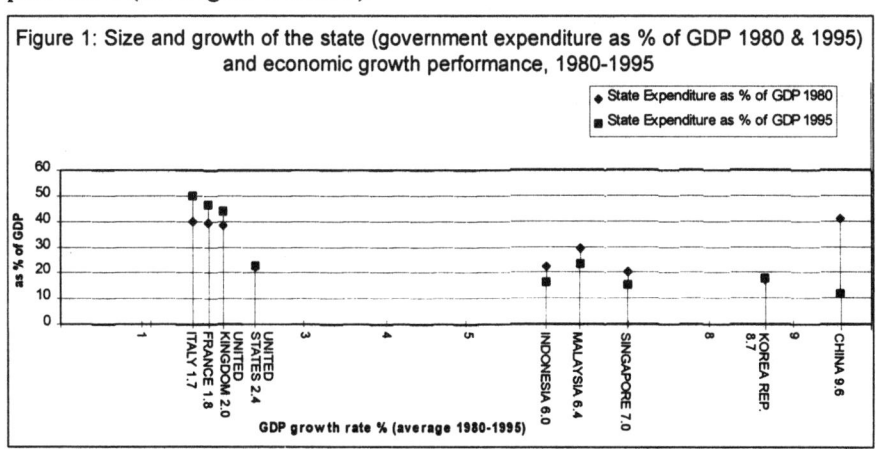

Figure 1: Size and growth of the state (government expenditure as % of GDP 1980 & 1995) and economic growth performance, 1980-1995

Sources: UNDP and World Bank

An important lesson of the East and Southeast Asian experience has been that an effective state must be a strong state, able to provide political stability, set down - and help ensure the observance of - a clear set of laws and regulations, allow for a creative and entrepreneurial environment and maintain transparent and consistent policies, while being accountable to the

---

2 The expression would seem to have been a Franco-British invention dating from 1990. It was first cited in a speech by President Mitterand and subsequently taken up by British Government officials.

population at large. The crisis of 1997-98 has only served to underline the importance of sound domestic governance, as well as the retention of the confidence of the private sector, particularly where a country is widely exposed to the international economy.

The importance of sound governance is also highlighted by the examples of countries where governance has broken down or has not been sustainably established. In the 1990s, more countries than ever have been seriously impacted by internal conflict and humanitarian crisis: Burundi, Rwanda, Congo (Brazzaville) and Congo (Kinshasa), Sierra Leone, Liberia, Sudan, Comoros. Somalia has fallen apart politically and territorially and has virtually ceased to exist as a country. The breakdown of Moscow-centred control systems at the end of the Soviet empire has also precipitated crises within the newly independent states, particularly in the Caucasus and the Balkans. Within Russia itself, there are strong centrifugal forces straining the federation.

Falling development assistance

The last age has seen a marked decline in aid (Figure 2). According to the data of the OECD Development Assistance Committee (DAC),[3] levels of development assistance from 21 donor countries in 1997 were the equivalent of almost $48 billion. In real terms, this figure is no higher than thirty years earlier following a 30% fall since 1992. In 1997, the proportion of DAC country GNP given as aid fell to 0.22%, the lowest it has ever been, making the original target of 0.7% even remoter (Figure 3). The signs are of continuing decline in 1998. The fall in aid is mainly accounted for by the G-7 countries. Aid from the US[4] and Italy peaked in 1992, Japan and France in 1995 (Figure 4). The further heavy fall in US aid in 1997 was due to the reclassification by OECD of Israel - the largest recipient, receiving $2.2 billion in 1996 - out of developing country status. Some of the smaller donors have increased their aid levels, but they provide little compensation for the decline in aid in the 1990s.

Taking a longer-term view of the performance of the previous largest donor shows even more graphically how weak has become the official support for aid in the USA. In 1997, the US Government's appropriation for

---

3 Http://www.oecd.org.
4 It could be argued that the USA is even beginning to put aid into reverse. More and more frequently, countries are being subjected to economic sanctions, intended to hinder them economically. Since 1993 sanctions have either been imposed or threatened by legislation no fewer than 60 times, targeting 35 countries.

Towards the end of aid? 33

Figure 2: Long-term aid trend ($ millions at 1994 values), 1966-1997

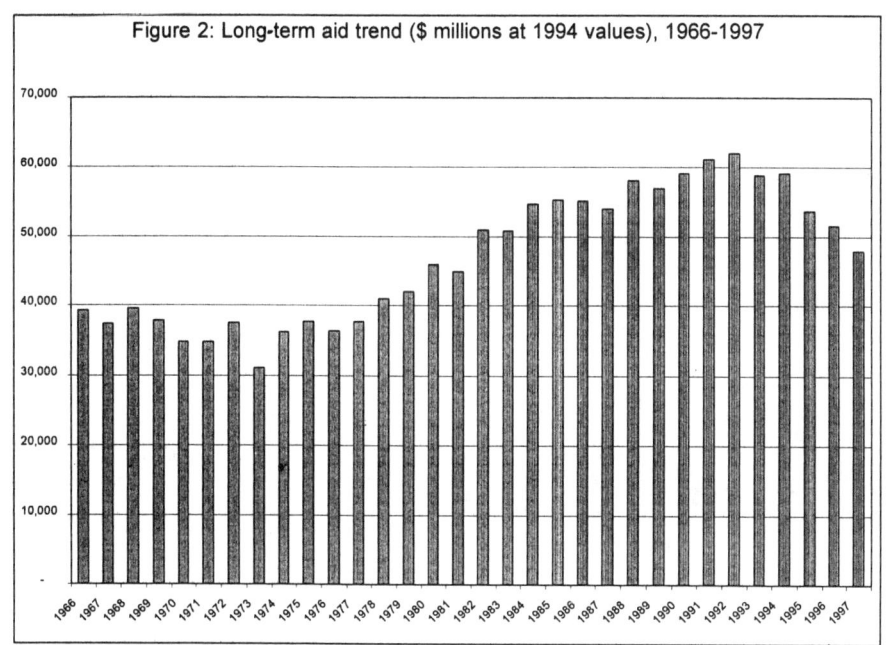

Source: OECD/DAC

Figure 3: Aid as % of GNP of OECD Countries, 1985-1997

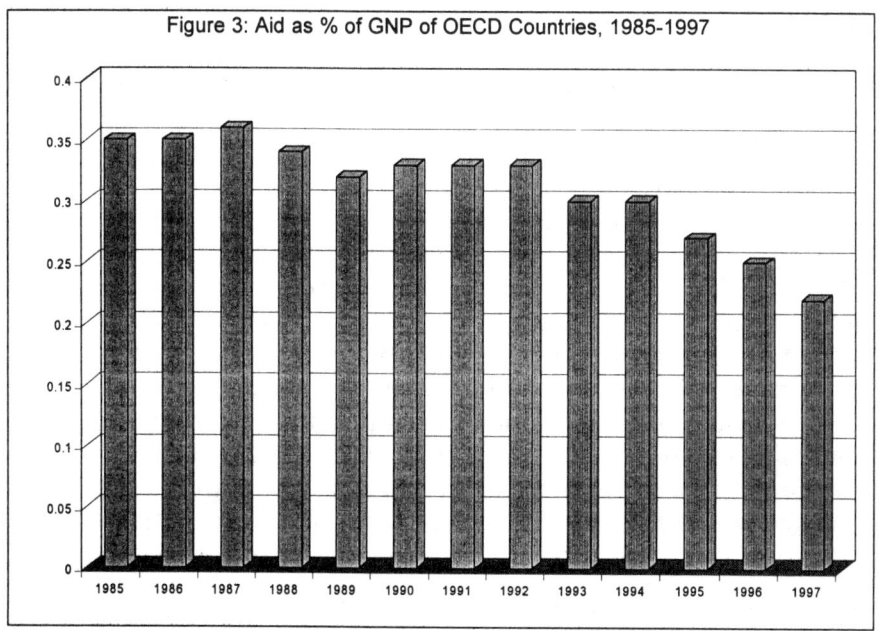

Source: OECD/DAC

Figure 4: Aid volume by major donors ($ millions), 1974-1997

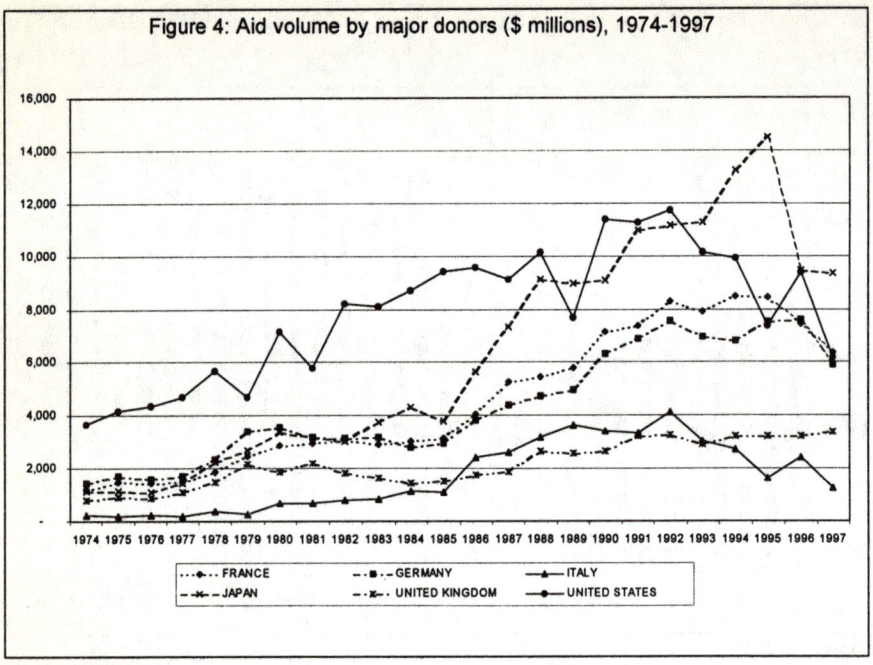

Source: OECD/DAC

'foreign aid' (which includes military and humanitarian assistance), was less than 1% of total federal outlays. This amount compares with the equivalent of $51 billion in 1947 (in 1997 values), more than 17% of federal spending.[5]

The overall decline in development assistance to traditional recipient countries is, moreover, understated by the OECD data, in at least two important senses. First, since 1990, the Soviet bloc countries almost ceased their own aid programmes and became recipients of aid and other less-concessional forms of assistance. The traditional recipients have thus suffered a double 'loss'. Figure 5 shows that between 1989 and 1996, the proportion of aid going to Europe and Central Asia rose (from 0%) to 20%. In the same period the share of Sub-Saharan Africa fell from 40% to 34%.[6] The fears expressed by the African countries in the early part of the decade about aid 'diversion' to their detriment have been wholly borne out.

Secondly, the amounts of development assistance are overstated by the data because of a growth in the importance of emergency aid. Between

---

5 US Congressional Budget Office (1997), The Role of Foreign Aid in Development, CBO, Washington.

1990 and 1995, emergency and refugee assistance grew from $1 billion to $3 billion and the costs of peace-keeping activities through the UN, from $500,000 to almost $3.5 billion. Together these figures are equal to well over one tenth of the aid total.

What have been the causes of the decline? To some extent, it might have been predicted. The end of bipolarity in international relations and the steady ascendancy of democratic market economies in the 1990s has undermined the geo-political rationale for bilateral assistance. Some traditional aid recipients have lost their strategic attraction. The western donors have reduced their interest in several African countries once considered ideologically pivotal - Angola, Congo (Kinshasa), Sudan - while Russia has had neither the means nor the motivation to provide Vietnam, North Korea, Cuba and other former client states with aid on the same scale as before.

However, it would be an oversimplification to ascribe a decline in aid to the ending of the Cold War. As discussed earlier, aid has been motivated by many considerations besides the geo-political. In fact, the rising importance of political and commercial factors in the provision of aid has arguably made it more - rather than less - strategic and less developmental.[7] For example, the USA has maintained its politically-motivated assistance to Israel and Egypt, while there are several new recipients of politically and commercially-oriented western aid: in particular, South Africa and the newly-independent countries in Eastern Europe. In fact the decline in geo-politically motivated aid has been at least matched by the increase in aid to the new states formerly in the Soviet Union.

It was also predicted that, as military spending by the major powers fell following the end of East-West rivalry, development assistance might benefit from a growing 'peace dividend'. The fall in global military spending after 1987 was substantial, from nearly $1 trillion in that year to

---

6 In the aftermath of the break-up of the Soviet Union, the OECD revised its definitions of recipient countries, creating two categories (Parts I and II) in 1993. The former includes the traditional developing country recipients, augmented by 8 of the successor states of the Soviet Union, plus Albania and the former Yugoslavia. The latter category - which receives 'official aid' as opposed to official development assistance - includes the remaining successor states plus some central and eastern European countries. (Israel was added in 1997). OECD's aid data normally refer to the Part I recipients only. The data in Figure 5 refer to Parts I and II countries. The 'diversion' in ODA has been in favour of the new Part I recipients only, but the diversion in aid using the augmented definition (ODA plus official aid) - which is mostly taken from the same sources in donor countries - has benefited more than a dozen other middle income countries of Europe.
7 See, for example, Riddell (1996).

less than $800 billion in 1994. In that seven year period, the potential cumulative dividend amounted to over $900 billion, about three times the spending on aid in the same period.[8] For various reasons, however, the reductions in military spending did not result in a switching of national budgets in favour of aid. In the major western countries - not all of which significantly reduced their military spending - the dividend was used to repay national debts and reduce the budget deficit. The cuts in military spending by the western powers have also drawn attention to spending levels in the developing countries. Many major recipients of aid spend substantial proportions of their budgets on arms and armies and in Sub-Saharan Africa as a whole, military spending increased five times in real terms between 1960 and 1990. The peace dividend is thus potentially even larger within the major aid recipient countries themselves.

One of the major reasons for declining aid budgets by many of the donors has been related to a general move towards fiscal restraint. In the case of the USA - now enjoying a budget surplus, almost alone among OECD countries - balanced budgeting was a strong political issue. In the case of the countries of the European Union, budgetary stringency was related to the need to conform to the terms of the Maastricht treaty (which has given a target maximum budget deficit of 3% of GNP) prior to unifying their currencies in 1999.

But the budget strait-jacket is obviously not the full explanation. Aid is a rather small component of national budgets, which could be protected even when spending is being constrained. The fact is that the political constituency for aid is weakening, based on a growing disillusionment with the relevance and effectiveness of aid. The next chapter, by drawing conclusions about the effectiveness of aid based on a half-century of experience, examines in more depth the basis for these growing concerns.

---

8 ul Haq (1995).

Figure 5: Share of official concessional finance by major region, 1989 - 1996

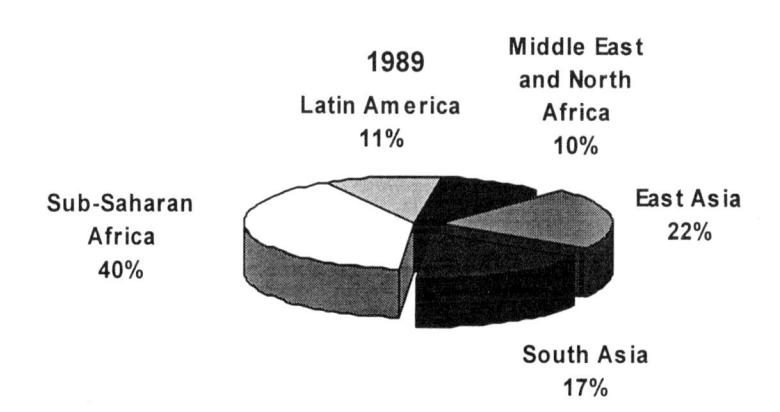

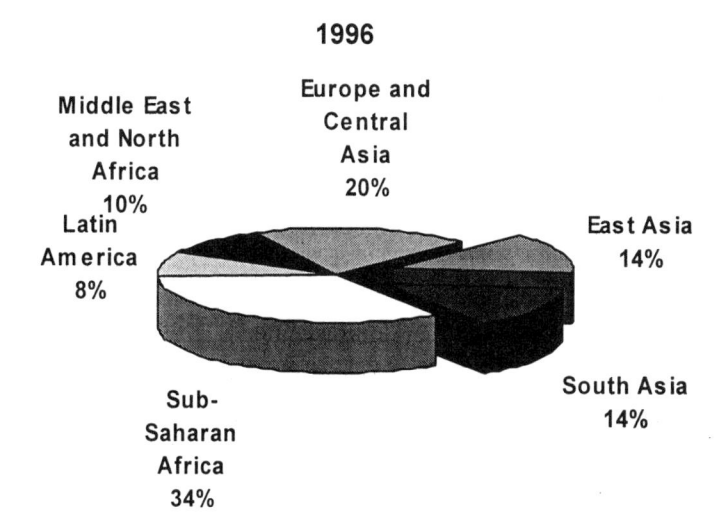

1989
- Latin America 11%
- Middle East and North Africa 10%
- East Asia 22%
- South Asia 17%
- Sub-Saharan Africa 40%

1996
- Middle East and North Africa 10%
- Europe and Central Asia 20%
- Latin America 8%
- East Asia 14%
- South Asia 14%
- Sub-Saharan Africa 34%

Note: Official concessional finance includes official development assistance and official aid to middle- and low-middle income countries, and excludes official development finance to high-income countries.

Sources: OECD/DAC and World Bank

4 Lessons of the aid and development record

The theoretical rationale for aid developed in the 1950s and 1960s was appealing, but it has proved to be unrealistic. It implicitly assumed a predominant role of the state in the financing and management of the development process. As we saw, it envisaged a role for aid in the temporary filling of three gaps: the domestic resources gap, the external payments gap, and the skills gap.

Perceptions about the appropriate role of the state have since evolved to a considerable degree. Many governments are moving away from ownership and control of the economic levers. The autonomy of all governments is being increasingly circumvented by the freer flows of trade, capital and information. While there are concerns voiced about the rampant instincts of neo-liberalism, the record of public management has scarcely been reassuring: statism has been correlated with stagnation and the persistence of penury.

Aid has been valuable in bridging resource gaps, but has often not provided a sustainable solution. In the case of the external gap, the long-term deterioration in trading conditions for commodities - and the burden of debt - have proved a hindrance. The skills gap was not a matter only of lacking technical expertise, nor even of organisational and management capacities. Additional institutional and policy capacities were also required, which technical assistance has not adequately provided. Yet it is unclear how or whether aid could have made the important difference.

These are some of the lessons drawn in this chapter. They provide reasons why aid may be in its final age, and why we should be looking for a different basis for development cooperation, explored in Part II.

The changing role of the state

The twentieth century will have seen the rise and fall of big governments in powerful states. From the prevailing *laissez-faire* doctrine of economic management and commerce at the beginning of the century, two major wars were to underscore political and territorial rivalry and deliver fatal blows to business confidence, severely disrupting international trade and investment. The conduct of, and recovery from, warfare greatly enhanced the economic role of the state in the present century. Three other sets of events also contributed to the rise of statism, occurring respectively in the 'second', 'first' and 'third' worlds.

The first of these was the Russian Revolution in 1917, which led to the abolition of private property and the spread of state control into all economic activity throughout the country. With the expansion of the Soviet Union's sphere of influence into its neighbouring satellites, central economic planning became prevalent in many parts of Europe. A second cause was the Great Depression of the late 1920s and early 1930s, which obliged Governments of the non-communist world to suddenly take a much greater hand in economic stabilisation. The hardship which resulted also helped to pave the way for an expanded role of the state in managing welfare programmes. The third series of events took place within the aid era. The decolonisation process discussed above brought into being more than 100 newly independent nation-states. The reach of those governments grew with the nation-building process, reinforced by the prevalent development paradigm of public investment in key areas of the productive economy.

The growing economic role of the state was an important institutional backdrop to aid. Although the notion of development assistance was initially controversial, it soon came to be accepted as a means of international resource transfer somewhat analogous to a welfare system. It was also a public welfare system, from richer government to poorer government. Towards the end of our period, however, the role of the state is undergoing what may be termed a 'triple transition', resulting in a diminution in the power and influence of central governments, on both domestic and international planes.

In the first place, there is a return to more widespread neo-liberal thinking about economic management and a renewed belief in the power of free markets. At the level of the state, governments are withdrawing from planning and yielding the ownership and management of large parts of the economy to private interests. These interests are increasingly global. Economies are interlocked through transnational ownership and management, through the almost instantaneous transfers of capital across borders, and the rapid migration of information and knowledge. Secondly, therefore, governments are increasingly beholden to actions and circumstances taking place outside their borders. The third transition is to tribalism: the retreat by individuals and communities into groups that transcend or ignore political or territorial boundaries, and which are bound by similarities of religion, ethnicity or culture. Groups within and between nation-states are challenging the legitimacy and authority of central governments.

There are both positive and negative ramifications of each of these transitions, but all are inexorable. Accompanying these developments, aid has also evolved. It is no longer largely confined to transfers between governments. Private charities and aid organisations have hugely expanded their roles in both development and relief activities, and governments are channelling more resources through these non-governmental organisations. More than a quarter of the aid of Sweden, Switzerland and Norway is channelled through northern or southern NGOs.

Internationally, aid efforts are beginning to facilitate global processes by making markets work better. New systems of global governance are helping to compensate in those areas - such as environmental externalities - unseen by markets, or where individual states are relatively powerless - such as drug trading. Individual states and their governments will have a diminishing role as active participants in development processes, but a growing role as regulators and as governors of regional and global management systems. These issues are explored in more depth in Chapter 9.

Capital as aid

Official capital. As discussed earlier, the neo-Keynesian and neo-classical theories of development were predicated on the assumption that capital would reap the highest returns when applied to countries where it was relatively scarce. More capital would yield more growth, and assist the developing countries to catch up the richer ones. The role of aid was primarily of gap-filling: to prime the capital accumulation process, and to help pay for necessary imported inputs.

The role of aid in productive investment has been exhaustively investigated through project evaluations. For the most part, these project evaluations have shown positive outcomes. For example, the World Bank reported average rates of return of over ten percent on its capital projects during the 1960s and 1970s in every major region and almost every sector. A more recent assessment found a higher average rate of return of 17% on projects completed between 1990 and 1994.[1] The results from other development banks have been similar.

These positive results would be sufficient evidence of the effectiveness of aid if they were accompanied by proof that such capital aid had also had

---

1 World Bank: Annual reviews of project performance audit results, Operations Evaluation Department, Wasington DC.

beneficial consequences for macro-economic growth. However, empirical studies arrive at the opposite conclusion. Already in the 1970s, studies showed a negative correlation between aid and domestic savings.[2] More recently, research has shown that there has been no significant correlation between aid and growth.[3] This apparent conflict between good project performance and the poor overall performance of aid as a stimulant to growth has been called the 'macro-micro paradox'.[4] But the paradox can be readily resolved. In some countries, capital aid replaces, rather than supplements, the domestic savings or the private foreign capital that might have funded the investments. Continuing aid can discourage savings. Thus, the overall (macro-economic) effects of incoming flows are increased consumption, not increased investment.

This conclusion cannot be generalised because the circumstances of each developing country have been very different. The amounts of investible funds within aid programmes have varied enormously from recipient country to recipient country. In some, the inflows have been large relative to GNP, in others quite small. High inflows have gone to countries with consistently high savings rates and higher investment rates (Malaysia, Korea). These countries - showing a high correlation of aid to investment - have needed capital aid least, but have put it to the most productive use. High investible inflows of aid funds have also gone to countries with low domestic savings rates, in which investment and savings have remained at chronically depressed levels. These were the countries - showing a low correlation of aid to investment - which needed capital aid most, but have used it least well.

Although there are many variants of these relationships, it is tempting to concur with some critics that capital aid either goes to countries that do not need it or those that cannot use it. The 'displacement theorists' conclude that in the neediest countries aid has been diverted to other than productive uses and has removed the incentive for recipient governments to improve fiscal and monetary discipline and raise public and private savings performance.

Private capital. As the following diagram shows (Figure 6), private capital flows to developing countries, in different forms, have increased substantially since 1970, the major part of the increase occurring in the 1990s. Private capital flows to developing countries now exceed by between 4 and 5 times the flows of aid. There have been several distinct phases in this evolution. During the 1970s, there was a steady rise in private

---

2 Griffin and (1970) Weisskopf (1972).
3 Mosely (1987). Other studies include Boone (1996).
4 Mosely, ibid.

lending, followed by a decline; from 1980, foreign direct investment (FDI) has grown steadily, and these flows were augmented by portfolio finance and bond lending from the late 1980s.

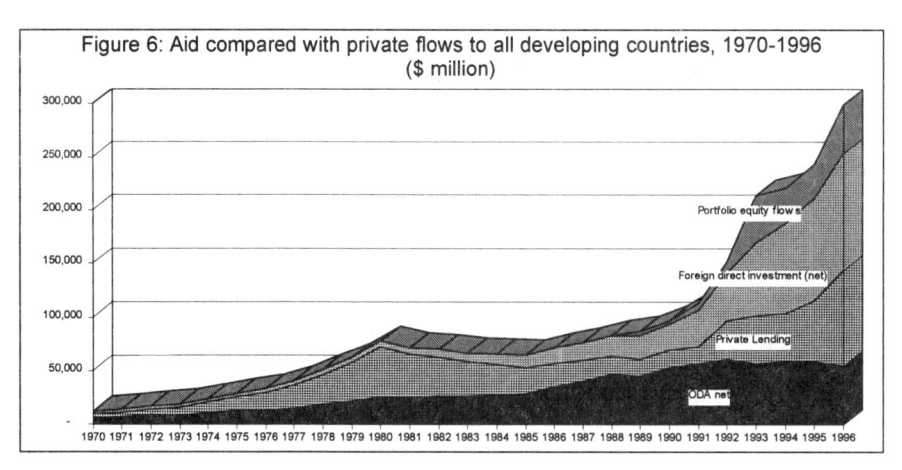

Figure 6: Aid compared with private flows to all developing countries, 1970-1996 ($ million)

Source: OECD/DAC and World Bank

The rise in private lending to developing countries during the 1970s can be explained in large part as a balance of payments need. In 1973 and again in 1979, the substantial rises in the price of OPEC oil left the oil-importing countries with substantial new requirements for capital which, in the absence of adequate official capital, could only be met from the large surpluses of the high-income, oil-exporting countries. The monetary recycling occurred in one of two ways. In the first place, the Organisation of Petroleum Exporting Countries (OPEC) - mainly the Arab states and Iran - became important sources of augmented official aid, as mentioned earlier. But recycling also occurred through the intermediary of Western commercial banks where a major portion of the 'petrodollars' were deposited. These deposits augmented the rapidly rising liquidity of the euromarkets, and banks responded to the capital needs of developing countries with large new lending operations. Between 1972 and 1976, the total value of private bank lending to developing countries more than doubled in real terms. The substitution of aid by private capital is nothing new.

The oil shocks were followed by a global liquidity crisis, with higher interest rates and stagnation in the developed countries at the end of the 1970s. Those countries which had adjusted their economies during the decade and retained an export earning capacity were able to surmount their indebtedness. But the serious debt problems from which many developing countries are suffering originated during this period. For the poorest among them - mainly in Sub-Saharan Africa - the responsibilities of creditor have shifted steadily from private to official (bilateral and multilateral) lenders, placing the onus for alleviating the debt burden mainly on the governments of the OECD DAC countries, and on the Bretton Woods institutions.

During the 1980s, the inflows of FDI and of portfolio capital were mainly to the more economically dynamic and politically stable developing countries in which foreign investors have shown growing confidence. Among the developing countries, the ten largest hosts received two thirds of foreign direct investment and the smallest 100 recipients received only 1%. (The ten largest hosts, however, account for over 35% of the population of the developing countries). However, FDI is proportionately significant in many smaller economies; for 11 Sub-Saharan African, 18 Latin American, and 3 Asian countries, FDI represented more than 10% of gross investment.[5] Also, the number and importance of recipient countries is growing and much more could be done to accelerate the process.[6] In India - the country with the largest numbers of those in absolute poverty - a programme of domestic economic reform encouraged a tripling of foreign direct investment inflows in 1995 alone.

Apart from FDI, the more dynamic economies have also seen a revival of private lending during the 1990s, partly a reflection of the successful floating of bonds and other instruments on the international capital markets. These inflows, in addition to helping to plug the trade gaps, went largely into the private sector and have helped to replace the need for aid. The experience of 1997-98 in East and Southeast Asia, however, illustrates the importance of sound policies and well managed financial sectors in economies which have become heavily reliant on private capital. Maintaining an overvalued exchange rate, allowing the banking sector to maintain too many bad loans, and to channel funds increasingly to unproductive and untradeable sectors such as property, are weaknesses that are eventually found out by foreign holders of capital. Inflows of private capital are a measure of the confidence of investors in the soundness of the economic management of a host country. When that management is perceived to be strong and backed by solid financial and other regulatory institutions, then private capital marks its confidence. But when policies

---

5 United Nations (1998).
6 "While a heartening range of countries have been successful in putting in place the prerequisites and then in generating and attracting private flows, many others have only just begun to take the first steps on this path. Against the background of scarce global aid resources, what is required is a combination of policies and efforts to help countries progress steadily from heavy aid-reliance to a strong capacity to raise and attract adequate private financing." OECD, op.cit.

and institutions are perceived to be unsound, capital withdraws.

This section is a paraphrase of a considerable body of research, to which it does not do justice, but from which the conclusions are clear. External capital - whether from official or private sources - has been an essential component for development but not a sufficient one. In open, well-managed economies which have given priority to export expansion, external capital has been productively used, and private capital and foreign investment have come to replace aid (in the form of capital from official sources). Flows of external private capital, however, are potentially volatile. Sound macroeconomic management and a well regulated financial sector are necessary to promote confidence in the host economies and minimise the risk of capital flight.

In more stagnant and closed economies, capital aid has been a poor primer of investment. It has been less productively used and has tended to dampen domestic savings and investment efforts. The difficulties of such economies in meeting their balance of payments requirements have been compounded by poor export performance and by an adverse global economic environment in which terms of trade deteriorated sharply (especially for oil-importers), global growth declined and the costs of capital rose. The gap-filling needs of many of these economies have been met by both private and official capital, but borrowing has led directly to an intractable debt burden, from which an early release is necessary.

In sum, there has been a poor correlation between the provision of capital aid and development progress. The uneven performance of developing countries in the use of official and private finance can be explained by strengths and weaknesses of domestic policies and institutions, the degree of openness of the economies and the varying impact of adverse global economic conditions.[7]

Aid and trade

Trade augments the domestic markets of developing countries, most of which are small, and is a dynamic stimulus to demand, having consistently grown faster than world output in the post-War period. The record of development has amply illustrated its importance. Most of the developing countries which have achieved high and sustained economic growth have followed open and outward-orientated development paths supported by rapid export expansion.

One of the principal justifications for aid was as a temporary expedient

---

7   Burnside and Dollar (1997) and World Bank (1998b).

for developing countries to fill an external payments gap and sustain imports. Aid has indeed been essential to countries subject to sudden external shocks - such as a collapse of export prices - or crisis needs, for example food shortages following poor harvests. But over the longer term, development assistance would have served developing countries best by stimulating trade expansion and facilitating their capacity to export. In this respect, aid in its different forms, and the policies followed by the donors have been unhelpful at best, and at worst have proved an impediment to trade expansion. Commodity and food aid has been used as a long-term substitute for trade; the tying of aid has distorted trading conditions and terms; and the protectionist policies of the donor countries have annulled some of the potential benefits of aid by putting up barriers to exports from the developing countries.

Commodity and food aid. The Marshall Plan established the pattern of commodity aid and was the inspiration for the US Food for Peace programme enacted by Public Law 480. Food aid from the major grain exporters - which is channelled either bilaterally or multilaterally (e.g. through the UN's World Food Programme) - has become a widespread form of external gap-filling, constituting some ten percent of total aid value overall, and much more in the instance of some individual donors. A major reason for the popularity of long-term food aid with some donors is that it allows the major food producing donors to dispose of substantial quantities of surplus produce (which in the case of the European Union have been accumulated as a result of overproduction stimulated by farm subsidies). In times of humanitarian crisis, food aid has been of critical importance, for example during the East African emergencies of the 1970s and 1980s. But as a developmental resource, the utility of food aid has been questionable.[8]

Where food aid directly replaces commercial imports and where it reaches those who are too poor to buy food, it can free domestic resources for other purposes. Food aid is often monetised from local sales and the proceeds used to finance development projects. 'Micro' gains from the provision of food aid can usually be demonstrated, although there are also documented misuses of food aid due to the difficulty of effective targeting of needy recipients. But, as with capital assistance, food aid - particularly where it has been provided over a long and continuing period - has tended to have deleterious 'macro' consequences. Food aid dependence has depressed domestic food prices and inhibited efforts to stimulate domestic food production in some countries.

---

8 Raffer and Singer (1996).

Protectionism. The post-War period has been one of un-free trade. Developing countries have had to face a hostile protectionist environment, particularly for certain commodities in whose production they have the greatest comparative advantage: agricultural commodities in raw and processed form, and garments and other non-technological consumer goods. Under multilateral auspices, there have been many initiatives to achieve freer and more equitable trading conditions, but the results have been mixed. Attempts by the UN (notably UNCTAD) and the European Union to try to compensate for market forces and build commodity protection agreements, or provide compensatory funds, have been expensive and unsustainable, since they only address one side of the transaction (supply) in the face of declining or weak demand. To the extent that these kinds of safety net have been effective, at least in the short term, they have discouraged diversification of exports away from the protected commodities.

Eight rounds of global trade negotiations under the General Agreement on Trade and Tariffs (GATT), leading to the creation of the World Trade Organisation (WTO), have encouraged much freer trade, although a high degree of protectionism by the richer countries still persists in agricultural and textiles trade. UNDP and the World Bank have calculated that the costs to the developing countries of unequal access to markets are several times larger than the value of net aid transfers,[9] prompting the conclusion that the need for aid would diminish if the richer countries concentrated harder on making the rules of the game fairer.

This lesson was not heeded by bilateral donors supporting the Eastern European countries and the newly-independent states of the former Soviet Union. Donors have extended long-delayed and selective financial and technical assistance closely tied to home expertise. But much of this assistance has been negated by the raising of trade barriers against the same countries to protect donors' domestic markets.

Aid as donor export support. The commercial motivation for bilateral aid has always been strong and an important proportion - about one-third for donors overall, substantially higher for some of them individually - is tied to the purchase of goods and services in the respective donor countries. It can be applied as a more general support mechanism, or as a specific subsidy, when it can take the form of a 'mixed credit' (in which aid is associated with a trade loan).

---

9 United Nations Development Programme, Human Development Report 1992 (1992, New York, Oxford University Press); also Finger (1994).

Aid tying is motivated by a belief that aid can act as an economic stimulant in the home country and circumvent export competition, but there is no solid basis for believing that either objective is actually achieved. For recipient countries, tied aid of course constitutes a net gain in terms of resource transfers, but it distorts trade. Analysis shows that tying reduces the value of the aid by up to 15%, through rent-related cost increases of the goods and services procured.[10] There are also various indirect costs of tied aid for recipients. Goods and services provided may be of low priority, excessively capital-intensive and otherwise technologically incompatible. Aid tying also creates dependency on continuing imports from the donor country.

In sum, a combination of aid and the protectionist stances of the donor countries has inhibited and distorted trade for developing countries, rather than assisting in the creation of export capacity. Again, the fundamental question is whether the recipient countries would have been better off without long-term food and commodity assistance and tied aid. While the transfers of resources would have been substantially less, developing countries would have been subject to fewer commercial pressures and distortions.

The hostile trading environment would still have been a hindrance, but developing countries could have done more to help themselves. The examples are provided by those (for example in East Asia) which did break through very successfully into global markets. Initially, they raised tariff walls to protect their own emerging industries, but pursued policies of greater openness by encouraging a vibrant private sector and liberalising trade and capital flows. An analysis of development performance since 1970 found a significant correlation between more economic openness and higher growth among developing countries.[11] With the conclusion of the Uruguay Round, the establishment of the WTO and the prospects of a continuing liberalisation of the trade environment, the opportunities for trade expansion have increased further. Not all countries will benefit in the short term, particularly the smaller ones dependent on one or a few commodities facing global oversupply. For these countries, aid may still be needed for a transitional period. But aid will only serve a useful purpose if it does more to facilitate trade, and less to underwrite the commercial interests of donors.

---

10 Catrinus Jepma, 'The case for aid untying in OECD countries' in Stokke (1996) and Morrisey (1993).
11 Sachs and Warner (1995).

The role of technical assistance

As we saw earlier, the importance of a 'third gap' in development needs was anticipated during the first aid age. While a major role of aid was to serve the ends of economic growth through support to investment, it was recognised that the capacity to absorb capital was constrained by low skill levels, as well as weak management and organisational capacities. The emergence of a political, social and institutional framework that facilitated ongoing expansion was also a condition for 'take-off'.

Technical assistance programmes have focused on training and human resource development as a means to close the third gap. There have also been many tangible results. Thousands of wells have been dug, schools, hospitals and roads built, slums cleared, and myriad other benefits provided to improve people's lives. But technical assistance has been much less successful in fostering the processes and the institutions needed to underpin and, more importantly, sustain beneficial change. As a UNDP analysis of African aid concluded a few years ago, "almost everybody acknowledges the ineffectiveness of technical cooperation in what is or should be its major objective: achievement of greater self-reliance in the recipient countries by building institutions and strengthening local capacities...".[12]

There are numerous examples of this shortcoming. Donors have very often established autonomous project management offices to run 'their' projects, without careful consideration of how these offices are to be integrated into the existing administrative structures, once the projects end. Also, donors have provided considerable assistance to organisations while not questioning whether those organisations are still relevant or effective. Aid has supported agricultural marketing boards which have introduced persistent price distortions, often contrary to the longer-term interests of the farmers they are intended to serve; or state trading organisations which have inhibited the development of more private sector led trade enterprises. For many years also, technical cooperation has funded government-run tourism and hotel training schools for government-run hotels, when the wholesale privatisation of tourist facilities would have resulted in much better and economically self-sufficient services, for which private managements would have found their own training solutions.

Technical assistance has tended to ignore the larger picture, analagously with the 'macro-micro paradox' of capital project aid. It leaves out of account the strengthening of institutions (as opposed to just organisations), including the subtle norms and rules of conduct which guide individual and

---

12 UNDP (1993).

collective behaviour. Equitable and sustainable progress will remain elusive if there are not adequate standards of honesty and transparency in bureaucracy, if the rule of law does not prevail, if there are no clear legal frameworks that safeguard property rights, or if people are barred from influencing the decisions of leaders.

The now fashionable emphasis on 'good governance' in aid programmes may raise awareness of the importance of the institutional context of development. But there are dangers that the term will be interpreted subjectively by donors through a prism of western democratic ideals. The current enthusiasm for supporting western-style elections in a growing number of countries, for example, should not obfuscate the need to create other conditions necessary to sustain more participation and openness.

Fundamental questions remain, however: how much influence can external assistance be expected to have on the enormously subtle and society-specific institutional factors required for sustainable change? The development record would seem to indicate that the important institutional changes in developing countries have occurred largely un-aided: as a result of enlightened leadership, the expressions of popular discontent and many other sources of domestic pressure. Should the role of aid be confined to more passive forms of technical assistance such as the establishment of norms?

PART II
FROM PATRONAGE
TO PARTNERSHIP

Whatever the motivations for aid, it has traditionally been seen as compensation for disadvantage. As a means of compensation, however, it has been rather ineffective. Some developing countries have progressed well with limited amounts of aid. Others have received generous amounts but have remained poor and aid-dependent. Experience shows that strong domestic institutions and consistent and appropriate policies are the key to development progress. A positive domestic environment for development appears to be much more important than the size of aid allocations, which exert a very uncertain influence on policies and institutions.

In the context of the global development environment, the concept of compensation becomes ambiguous. The same donor countries which provide aid to the poorest countries are also their largest external creditors, reluctant to alleviate the crippling burdens of debt which actually inhibit spending in poor countries on their human development. The same donor countries have also raised trade barriers against the commodities, textiles and processed goods exported by the aid recipients. These debt and trade aberrations lead to transfers of resources in a reverse direction to aid.

But the global environment is changing. It provides new opportunities for poorer countries which they must grasp, and which the rich must not hinder but help to encourage. Trade is becoming freer and more open. Markets are also expanding regionally, where neighbouring countries want to take advantage of complementarities. There is an information revolution under way which could bring substantial benefits. And to continue to improve the management of the global development system, for the benefit of all countries, reforms must be pursued.

All countries, however we designate them, can forge closer partnerships in these areas for mutual benefit. A new and fairer world order offers greater promise for continuing development than systems of compensation that have accompanied traditional forms of patronage.

5 Debt forgiveness: waiving not drowning

A fundamental thesis of this book is that any discussion on the objectives and effectiveness of aid is inadequate if the broader conditions of the global economic environment are not taken fully into account. Capital has been a critical ingredient of the development process but the growing debts incurred as a result of private and official borrowing from abroad have turned sour for some middle-income countries and many of the poorest countries with a diminishing capacity to repay them. We have seen that the crisis is not a new one. But, as this chapter shows, it has been addressed through incremental financial measures which have done little to diminish the impact and may have exacerbated the crisis in some instances.

The cost of this external debt is a critical component of the wider debate on aid, because it represents a huge financial imposition, translating into real deprivation for many of the world's poorest people. Set against this massive impediment, aid becomes a means of compensation. Debt makes aid more necessary. But alleviating debt would remove part of the need for aid, and equally important, removes the often humbling conditions imposed by creditors on the borrowing countries.

The debt crisis perpetrates other iniquities. Even more than aid, it underlines the seemingly indefinite dependence of the poorest countries on the richest and on the financial institutions which they dominate. Debt drives a wedge of incognisance between the practices of financial management and the brutish realities of human development. The debt negotiations conducted in the boardrooms of creditor banks examine rows of numbers in abstraction from their real meaning in terms of sustaining livelihoods in the borrowing countries.

Perhaps the most singular iniquity of all is that those who ultimately pay the real costs of debt in the poorer countries are not those who authorised the loans, nor those in the borrowing countries who gained the principal benefits from them, but those who are already the most destitute. The debt crisis is a manifestation of some of the worst aspects of the global political economy. It has serious implications for the role of aid and for global economic governance.

The amount of the debt

At the end of 1996, the total outstanding debt of the developing countries stood at almost $2.2 trillion ($10^{12}$), equivalent to nearly 40% of their total GNP. It has grown steadily in both absolute and relative terms. In 1970, the outstanding debt was a little less than $60 billion,[1] or barely 7 % of GNP. By 1980, it was over $600 billion and by 1990, nearly $1.5 trillion (see Figure 7).

The numbers are more dramatic for the category of severely indebted low income countries (see Box 4 for definitions). At the end of 1995, their unpaid debt stood at $226 billion, exceeding by nearly 30% their combined GNP. In crude terms this means that the total economic value of the most indebted economies would not be sufficient to honour their debt obligations. The outstanding debt has exceeded their total economic value since the late 1980s.

Outstanding debt is a stock. More meaningful in a developmental context are the financial flows and transfers associated with lending. For the developing countries as a whole, the pattern is shown in Figure 8. Net transfers on debt are determined by subtracting from inflows of new lending the repayments of loan principal and interest. From the late 1980s

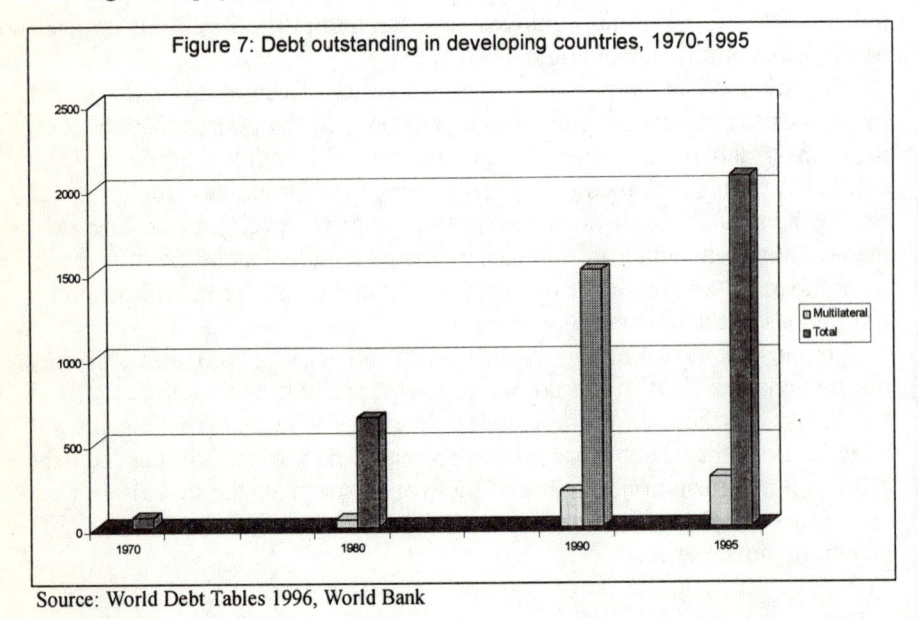

Figure 7: Debt outstanding in developing countries, 1970-1995

Source: World Debt Tables 1996, World Bank

---

1 This figure excludes the relatively small amounts of short-term debt, for which accurate data are not available for that year.

until 1991, the net transfer to developing countries as a whole was negative. During the present decade, there has been a modest positive balance. But the picture is again worse for the severely indebted countries (Figure 9). Rather than increasing, disbursements have shown a downward trend, while service payments have remained stubbornly high. Consequently, in the 1990s the net transfer has been barely balanced or negative.

The figures for debt service reflect payments actually made, not what is owed, the latter being larger. From the mid-1980s, there has been a steady build-up of arrears by the developing countries, which are cumulatively added to the total debt stock. In 1980, the arrears on long-term debt amounted to less than $2 billion, but by 1990, they had reached $60 billion and are over $100 billion today.

Origins of the debt crisis

We saw in an earlier chapter how private bank lending to developing countries rose rapidly during the 1970s. The origins of the huge liquidity volume which facilitated these increases derived from the development of

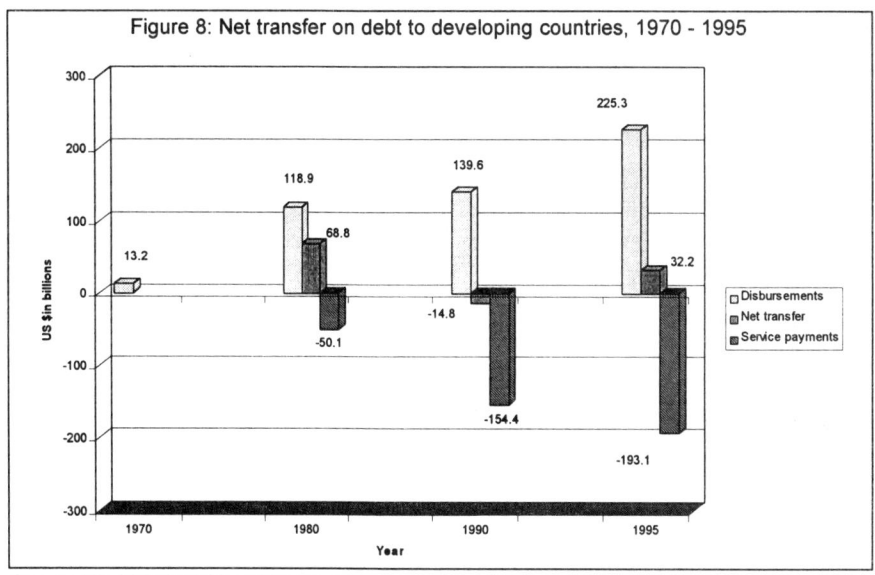

Figure 8: Net transfer on debt to developing countries, 1970 - 1995

Source: World Debt Tables 1996, World Bank

56 *Beyond Aid: From Patronage to Partnership*

Figure 9: Net transfer on debt to severely indebted low-income countries, 1970-1995

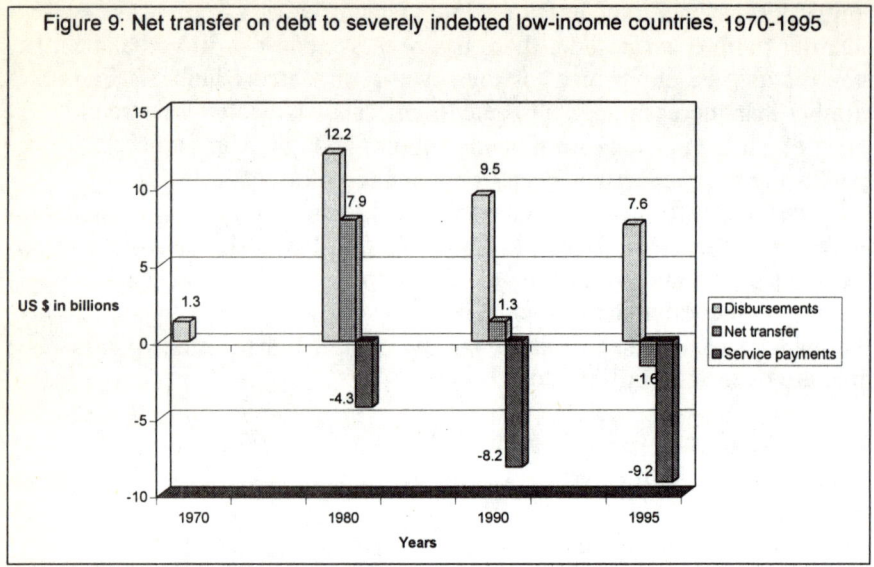

[Chart showing US $ in billions for Disbursements, Net transfer, and Service payments across years 1970, 1980, 1990, 1995:
- 1970: Disbursements 1.3
- 1980: Disbursements 12.2, Service payments 7.9, Net transfer -4.3
- 1990: Disbursements 9.5, Service payments 1.3, Net transfer -8.2
- 1995: Disbursements 7.6, Service payments -1.6, Net transfer -9.2]

Source: World Debt Tables 1996, World Bank

the first major transnational capital market - the 'euromarket' - in the preceding decade. Initially, the euromarket consisted mainly of US dollars accumulating offshore (in London banks). These were augmented by a huge speculative outflow of dollars from the US in 1972 accompanying the weakening dollar exchange rate. More dollars stayed abroad because of domestic US policy, which placed restrictions on interest-rates on deposits and limited bank credit. Deposits in the euromarket were unfettered by reserve restrictions and transactions were virtually unregulated. From a few billion US dollars in the early 1960s, the euromarket was worth more than $100 billion a decade later, rising to $1,500 by 1980.[2] The market became progressively more diversified by currency and financial centre.

When the oil-exporting countries raised the oil price four-fold in 1973-74, a substantial volume of petrodollars was added to this international market, while a huge demand developed in the oil-importing countries for finance to bridge their yawning balance of payments gaps. Private bank lending was attractive to both sides. The banks had default-free sovereign countries as their guarantors.[3] The borrowing countries were getting access to cheap money at short notice and with no macro-economic conditionality. The accumulation of debt was premised on the assumption of relative

---

2 Loxley (1986).
3 Strictly speaking there had been two cases of default in the post-war period: Korea in 1947 and (partially) Ghana in 1966.

stability in real interest rates and buoyant export earnings.

By the late 1970s, of course, these judgements were being seriously undermined by developments in the global economy. In 1979-80, oil prices were hiked further, putting additional pressure on the balance of payments of the oil importing countries. Their trade woes were further exacerbated by increases in the price of imported manufactures and a fall of about 30% in the prices of primary commodities, on which many countries depended for their exports. In the industrialised countries, the advent of monetarist policies in response to high inflation encouraged sharp rises in interest rates which, coming on top of the deflationary impact of the oil price rises, predictably succeeded in dampening prices, but also precipitating the worst economic slump since the 1930s. Nearly all the private bank lending had been contracted at variable interest rates. As a result of the monetary squeeze, the key London Inter-Bank Offered Rate (LIBOR), which governs the cost of most private loans, rose from 8.7% in 1978 to 16.5% in 1981. Meanwhile, the large amounts of private finance which had been flowing in to the developing countries during the 1970s had been utilised for a variety of purposes including investment in shares and property. For the most part, there were no mechanisms in place in the borrowing countries to ensure that private loans were used productively to generate a foreign exchange surplus.

A landmark of financial history was the near-default of Mexico in the summer of 1982. Within a few months of each other, Mexico and Brazil, two of the largest private borrowers abroad, told their creditors that they would declare themselves insolvent if their debts were not rescheduled. Their stance sowed panic in financial markets, because the western banks now felt hostage to their debtors.[4] The banks came face to face with insolvency. But this was only the end of the beginning of the debt crisis.

Addressing the crises

Out of the 1980s, two rather different types of debt crisis have emerged. On one hand, there have been the problems of the more dynamic and open economies of Latin America and Asia. As globalisation has proceeded, these economies have gained considerable benefit from a widening array of sources of private external finance. But, as foreshadowed by earlier experience, this growing dependence on finance from private sources, has brought other problems. While the role of the state in the management of

---

4 Miller (1986).

these economies has been loosened, governments have failed to put in place adequate mechanisms of supervision to ensure the sustainability of these new financial arrangements.

On the other hand, there has been the less visible but more intransigent crisis of the poorer countries. For the most part, they have had to depend more heavily on external financing from official bilateral and multilateral sources. This dependence has continued to increase, imposing a growing burden on the economies and their people.

Middle-income countries. In 1985, three years after the Mexican crisis broke, the US launched the 'Baker Plan' (named after the Secretary of the Treasury of the time), which was at least an acknowledgement that the crisis existed and that coordinated action might be needed to address it. The plan first took shape at the Plaza meeting in New York in September 1985 among the five largest industrial countries and was outlined at the World Bank/IMF annual meeting in Seoul the following month. The plan prescribed new financing of $29 billion for the borrowing countries over three years, two-thirds of it from the commercial banking sector and the rest from the World Bank and Inter-American Development Bank. There was to be an additional earmarking of funds from the IMF.

In addition to signalling official concern, the Baker initiative had three important features. First, it made a virtue of liquidity by proposing to solve the crisis with more lending. The solution to the private borrowing crisis was (mostly) more private borrowing. Secondly, however, the multilateral institutions were to be brought into the picture, adding their own conditions to their lending. Thirdly, the plan was voluntary and, partly for that reason, it went unheeded.

The next attempt at a concerted effort to reduce commercial debt was the Brady Plan of 1989, which also bore the name of the US Treasury Secretary. Brady, like Baker, was aiming mainly at the middle-income countries of Latin and Central America. Unlike Baker, this plan was complex in conception and brought the World Bank and IMF more centrally into debt rescheduling. Somewhat belatedly, it was recognised that the outstanding debt was unpayable but could be reduced in return for guarantees from the World Bank and IMF. The Brady plan embodied the controversial principle that the multilateral institutions should cover the ill-judged costs of commercial lending.

Under the plan, part of the outstanding debt was replaced with 'Brady bonds' with a lower face value and longer repayment terms. Twelve countries have benefited from debt rescheduling under this scheme which has covered nearly $200 billion of outstanding debt. With lower interest rates, more buoyant trade and a restoration of confidence in the borrowing countries, the debt crisis for these countries seemed to abate in the 1990s. Some evidence can be adduced from the debt figures for the Latin and Central American countries. During the first half of the 1990s, the outstanding debt stock has risen more slowly than before, while the arrears actually fell between 1990 and 1995.

Now the major commercial borrowers in Latin America and Asia - the emerging economies - face a different challenge. Their liquidity needs can be readily met from private markets, but the continuing dependence on short-term capital still has its perils. Poor macro-economic management of a borrowing country can disguise a debt crisis and once revealed, the problems are compounded by a rapid withdrawal of capital (particularly portfolio investments which can disappear overnight).

Mexico provided a new landmark with its crisis of liquidity at the end of 1994. But it was largely self-inflicted. Instead of addressing the fundamental problems of its trade imbalance by, among other things, devaluing its currency, the government had had growing recourse to borrowing through the sale of bonds. Following some of the principles hallowed by Brady, the IMF led the rescue and helped enforce the corrective measures. Confidence was quickly restored. In 1997, however, the governments of Thailand, Malaysia, Indonesia and South Korea ran into similar trouble. In large measure, the problems were precipitated by overvalued exchange rates, but they went much deeper. The stubborn reluctance to devalue, until forced to do so by a collapse of confidence in international financial markets, was related to the fragile state of their financial sectors and the unproductive utilisation of external loans. Much of the foreign borrowing had been used to finance short-term speculative activities and unproductive investments. The loans could not be collateralised by assets.

For these emerging countries, which have developed a heavy reliance on private capital - foreign direct investment and portfolio investments, in addition to banking loans - the debt crisis was no longer merely a matter of misjudging global economic developments. The series of crises in the late 1990s has been symptomatic of a failure by the state to put mechanisms in place to ensure against financial insolvency in the public and private sectors. In all the stricken countries, new stock-markets and a plethora of new finance and banking institutions had grown up without adequate supervision or control, and often with privileged connections to those in power. The financial sector had in turn supported many enterprises and transactions with doubtful returns, for which no adequate financial monitoring procedures existed, and in the absence of strict bankruptcy provisions.

In all crises, there is a tendency to seek out scapegoats. As some of the emerging economies succumbed to internationally transmitted financial turbulence, their governments first failed to admit to the problems and then sought to blame the globalisation of finance for the activities of private banks, portfolio managers and currency speculators. This is like leaving the door open and being surprised by the draught. Openness to international markets, from which the dynamic economies of Latin America and Asia have benefited, needs to be mirrored by transparency in domestic financial and corporate markets. The crises of 1997 were provoked by imperfect governance as well as poor judgement. The picture of a head of government playing Canute to the waves of speculative finance until overwhelmed by the necessity to shore up a shaky domestic banking sector will for long be remembered as a turning point.

The crisis for the middle-income countries can be addressed if the governments of those countries take adequate measure of the dependence of their economies on the range of sources of private finance, and put in place the mechanisms necessary to ensure transparency and sustainability. In developmental terms, these mechanisms should be there to ensure that the state can fulfill at least two key functions: sustainability of finance and sustainability of employment. First, it must guarantee adequate continuing financing for infrastructure and other public goods. While financing for these purposes can be met increasingly from private foreign sources, governments should ensure that the longer-term needs of development projects are not put at risk by the shorter-term instincts of private investors. Many of the problems inherited from the 1970s reflected a failure to resolve this incompatibility. The desire for private banks to see a fast turn-around of their capital prompted many of the borrowers to channel funds into speculative ends.

A second area of responsibility is related to the first. While a growing proportion of the labour force of these countries is being absorbed by the private sector, which depends increasingly on foreign sources of finance, the government retains the responsibility to ensure that a measure of social protection is guaranteed to the most vulnerable. In a transparently managed economy with strong financial control mechanisms, the first people to lose their jobs when companies become insolvent are those who had primary responsibility for the financial arrangements. The last victims should be the lowliest employees. Unfortunately, in many of today's emerging economies, the exact opposite occurs, as recent experience in Southeast Asia has shown. The protests of the early victims of the crisis in Indonesia contributed to the ouster of the president, but his removal could not have brought their jobs back.

Low-income countries. The debts of the low-income countries are substantially derived from official lending from bilateral and multilateral sources. These debts are largely the responsibility of creditor governments, which have full capacity to diminish them. But despite the enormous human costs of the crisis, it has not been given adequate priority.

In the 1970s, many of the poorest countries were buffeted by the same adverse economic conditions as those in the middle-income category: a sharp increase in the cost of imports of oil and manufactured goods, falling commodity prices, shrinking export markets and rising costs of borrowing. These adverse circumstances led directly to a huge increase in external debt which, as we saw above, was proportionately much worse for the low-income countries. By 1995, the debt-to-export ratio of the severely indebted low income countries was more than twice as high as for other regional categories of countries. More than 60% of the outstanding debt of the severely-indebted low-income countries is owed to official bilateral sources, a further 20% to multilateral sources, the balance to private sources. Of the official debt, some two-thirds is owed to the Paris Club governments (essentially OECD/DAC countries), most of the remainder to Russia[5] and some Latin American countries.

A few of the severely indebted countries have successfully renegotiated their commercial debt through the London Club (see Box 4). In 1997, Côte d'Ivoire restructured $7.2 billion and Senegal $118 million. Senegal and Mauritania also concluded recent buyback agreements[6] with assistance from the World Bank's Debt Reduction Facility.[7] However, the debt crisis of the low-income countries can only be resolved by agreement with official bilateral and multilateral creditors.

A concerted attempt to address the problem of official bilateral debt began at the summit of the G-7 countries in Toronto in June 1988. The meeting decided on a set of conditions for debt rescheduling for the severely indebted countries in Paris Club negotiations. In 1991, these conditions became refined as the Enhanced Toronto Terms, under which debt

---

5 Russia is to join the Paris Club and, as part of its agreement, it will write off a substantial proportion of the debt owed to it by the poorest countries.
6 See United Nations Conference on Trade and Development (1997).
7 The Debt Reduction Facility was established in 1989 under the auspices of the International Development Association of the World Bank. It makes funds available in the form of discounted obligations to commercial banks, and is conditional on medium-term adjustment policies.

repayments falling due within a 12-18 month period may be rescheduled. Official concessional loans (on ODA terms) may be rescheduled on a very long-term basis, while for export credits there is a choice of options, including partial write-off and rescheduling at concessional rates.

Under the Naples Terms agreed in December 1994, countries with per capita income less than $500 or a net present value (discounted) debt-to-export ratio of over 350%, which have remained in compliance with IMF and Paris Club conditions for three years, will be eligible for a 67% reduction in 'pre-cut-off' date loans. Other countries are eligible for a 50% reduction. These terms are intended to be definitive and granted on the understanding that the debtor country will not return to the Paris Club for subsequent rescheduling.

This succession of agreements recognised the urgency of official debt rescheduling. But in terms of alleviating the burden, the impact has been very limited. In fact, since the first Toronto agreement, the scheduled repayments for the poorest countries have steadily increased, not decreased. But because the additional debt service is largely unpayable, the arrears have been added to the outstanding debt stock, further increasing repayment obligation in the future.

Perhaps ironically, however, the most problematical part of the debt portfolios of the low income countries is the multilateral, owed to the World bank, the IMF and the regional development banks, all institutions created mainly for the benefit of the poorer countries. These institutions and the major creditor countries have been very slow in addressing the multilateral debt problem.

As already discussed above, the international financial institutions have been increasingly drawn into the debt rescheduling picture since the 1980s and have been assuming a growing portion of the outstanding debt of the severely-indebted low-income countries - over 20%. More important, the multilateral institutions account for about half of the debt service payments of this group of countries. The privileged position of the World Bank and the IMF is due to their status as preferred creditors, which is in turn derived from their statutory need to retain the top credit rating in financial markets and enable them to benefit from borrowing on the most favourable market terms.

But this status can lead to awkward financial manoeuvering in order to honour the terms of multilateral debts. For example in 1990, Guyana had to arrange a short-term commercial loan to pay its arrears to the IMF, to clear the way for that institution to advance a new credit to pay off the bank. Similarly, Peru used funds in 1993 from the US Treasury and the EximBank of Japan to pay its IMF arrears, and have its bilateral creditors paid back with new IMF finance. Similar accommodations have been made for World Bank loans, again with bilateral funds.[8] Gradually, the severely indebted countries have been weaned away from IBRD (non-concessional) lending from the World Bank and onto easier IDA loans. The World Bank has created a 'Fifth Dimension' programme which uses repayments on past IDA loans, supplemented by new grants from creditor countries, to provide funds to the severely indebted countries to enable them to pay off interest on remaining IBRD loans.

These circular Peter-to-Paul transactions raise serious questions about the contemporary role of the World Bank and IMF which have traditionally been seen respectively as a major source of development finance and a lender of last resort, but which in most years since 1990 have been withdrawing more from the developing countries than they have been paying out. The IDA in Sub-Saharan Africa - traditionally the most important source of development finance in the continent - transferred less than $1 billion in net terms in 1997, and made net withdrawals from Côte D'Ivoire and Kenya, two of its largest borrowers.[9]

The need to do more for the poorest

During the 1990s, the urgency has been mounting for more action on multilateral debt, with the focus on the 41 countries defined by the World Bank as Heavily Indebted Poor Countries (HIPC).

To illustrate the current plight of the 41 Heavily Indebted Poor Countries, some basic data have been provided in Tables 1 and 2. All but eight of the HIPCs are in sub-Saharan Africa. All but seven are in the category of countries classified by the United Nations Development Programme as having low human development levels (measured by income, health, education and literacy variables). Debt stress is substantially an African affliction and coincides with levels of least development. It also affects some of the most generously aided countries.

In about one third of the countries, public debt (for which governments are responsible) is larger in value than the total GNP; in Nicaragua, Sao Tome, Guinea-Bissau, Guyana, Mozambique and Congo (Brazzaville) the debt is twice or even several times higher. In Sao Tome, where the average income is less than $1 per day, each inhabitant currently owes nearly $2,000 in debt. In Nicaragua, the ratio is even higher.

---

8   See Raffer and Singer (1996).
9   World Bank, Annual Report 1997 (Washington DC).

Box 4: Guide to debt nomenclature

External debt consists of   long-term debt + short-term debt + use of IMF credits.

Long-term debt consists of   public debt (incurred by a government) and
publicly-guaranteed debt and
private non-guaranteed debt

Public and publicly-guaranteed debt consists of unpaid loans from
official creditors (individual governments or multilateral finance institutions) and
private creditors (commercial banks or bonds)

Flows and transfers

Loan disbursements *minus* repayments of principal *equal* **net resource flows** on debt

Loan disbursements *minus* repayments of principal *minus* interest payments *equal* **net transfers** on debt

Heavily Indebted Poor Countries (HIPC): *a category of 41 countries defined by the World Bank and IMF in 1996 as having serious debt problems. The countries are:*

Angola	Guinea	Nigeria
Benin	Guinea Bissau	Rwanda
Bolivia	Guyana	Sao Tome
Burkina Faso	Honduras	Senegal
Burundi	Kenya	Sierra Leone
Cameroon	Laos	Somalia
Central African Republic	Liberia	Sudan
Chad	Madagascar	Tanzania
Congo (Brazzaville)	Mali	Togo
Congo (Kinshasa)	Mauritania	Uganda
Cote d'Ivoire	Mozambique	Vietnam
Equatorial Guinea	Myanmar	Yemen
Ethiopia	Nicaragua	Zambia
Ghana	Niger	

Severely Indebted Low Income Countries (SILIC): *an earlier defined category of debt-stressed countries. The SILICs excluded Angola, Benin, Bolivia, Burkina Faso, Chad Laos and Senegal from the HIPC category, but included Afghanistan and Cambodia. In almost all SILICs and HIPCs, the major portion of the outstanding debt is to governments and multilateral institutions.*

Paris Club: *a forum serviced by the French Trésorie which brings together debtor countries with their official creditors, mainly from the OECD countries. The Paris Club was formed in order to avoid defaults on officially guaranteed export credits and ODA loans through short-term rescheduling. The first time a debtor country visits the Paris Club is known as the 'cut-off' date. Since 1988, the Paris Club has developed new criteria (under so-called 'Toronto Terms' and 'Naples Terms') for reducing the debt burdens of the SILICs.*

London Club: *a forum for debtor countries to renegotiate external commercial debt with commercial banks.*

The human plight of these indebted countries can be illustrated with reference to those in the most precarious situations. Mozambique has a per capita income of $80 - the lowest in the world according to World Bank calculations. In 1992, the country emerged from a debilitating 16-year civil war which killed one million of its people (6% of the total population), destroyed two-thirds of its primary schools and one third of its rural health units. Half of the country's children have stunted growth and 200,000 under fives die each year from preventable diseases.[10] Life expectancy is 46 years, only 39% of the population have access to health services. The adult literacy rate is 40%.

Yet in spite of frequent rescheduling, Mozambique's outstanding debt still stands at $5.6 billion (in present value terms), or more than 10 times the value of annual exports. In 1997 alone, the country owed its creditors $196 million, or $13 for every inhabitant - the equivalent of two months of average income. In 1997, debt servicing absorbed one third of government spending and the proportion is rising. The country already spends twice as much on debt servicing as it does on education and health combined. Mozambique is a recipient of substantial amounts of aid, but overwhelmingly the major proportion goes on relief and rehabilitation; development assistance is more modest. With debt relief, the country could immediately enjoy a dividend enabling it to substantially increase public spending on health and education.

Ethiopia is the second poorest country of the world in terms of income per head. Life expectancy is 48 years, only 46% of the population have access to health services, and 25% to safe water sources. The enrolment ratio at primary and secondary school level is only 20%. Ethiopia's public health spending is modest in per capita terms, but it spends four times as much on debt servicing.

In Tanzania, the third poorest country, life expectancy is 50 years. Only 42% of the population have access to health services, 38% to clean water. The adult literacy rate is 67%, but primary and secondary enrolment is only 44%. By all accounts, the health and education sectors are in a state of rapid deterioration, precipitated by falling public expenditures. In local currency terms, total education spending in the first half of the decade was only one third of the level ten years earlier; health spending fell by 50%. Today, the country spends four times as much on debt servicing as on health and education combined.

These three countries may be among the most precarious, but their plight well demonstrates the close connection between the burden of debt

---

10 Oxfam International (1997).

and human survival in all the HIPCs. "A child born in a HIPC is 30% less likely to reach their first birthday than the average for all developing countries...a mother is three times more likely to die in childbirth."[11] Truly, for these countries, the crisis is a matter of life or debt.

In fact, there is nothing inevitable about the persistence of debt and the handicap of debt servicing imposed on the poorest countries. In September 1996, the World Bank and IMF launched the HIPC initiative, the most far-reaching debt relief mechanism to date. The initiative belatedly takes a broader view of the debt crisis. Rather than examining the terms of individual loans and determining methods of rescheduling them, the initiative addresses the problems of the 41 countries in a comprehensive way. It is their overall indebtedness with respect to all sources, and their ability to repay which determines their eligibility for relief.

There are two phases of debt relief. An initial phase of three years, leading to debt reduction under the Naples terms (see above), must first be completed. At this point, a country is subject to a debt-sustainability analysis. If this analysis determines that the country will have an unsustainable burden of debt in three years time, then in a second phase, it undertakes another 3-year IMF programme, on completion of which it is eligible for further debt reduction. This further reduction is made from a trust fund comprising $500 million from World Bank profits on its lending programme, $600 million from the African Development Bank and Inter-American Development Bank, and other funds contributed by bilateral donors.

By 1998, it was unfortunately still too early to determine the extent to which the HIPC initiative might provide a more definitive solution to the debt crisis of the poorest countries, but the signs were not promising. The first countries which would seem to have qualified for relief were Uganda and Bolivia with 10 years or more of compliance in IMF programmes behind them but with a continuing prospect of unsustainable debt in spite of positive growth and moderate inflation levels. The HIPC terms could have been interpreted to provide both Uganda and Bolivia with significant further debt relief from 1997, but some of the major donor countries enforced a delay until 1998. In the case of Uganda, Oxfam estimates the delay 'cost' the country $193 million, equivalent to six times the annual health budget.[12] Of the three countries described above, Ethiopia will not qualify for HIPC initiative relief until the end of the year 2000; Mozambique and Tanzania until at least 2002.

---

11 Oxfam International, ibid.
12 Oxfam International, ibid.

From all initial indications, the HIPC initiative is too little too late for countries with desperate economic conditions that impinge directly on the lives of their poorest people. The debt reduction conditions are seriously insufficient even by the most generous interpretations. The fundamental weakness of the initiative is that - like most debt reduction schemes that have preceded it - it appears to treat the problem as one of liquidity, rather than one of basic solvency.

Most of the HIPC countries have been accommodated by increments in liquidity over many years, but their economies are not merely illiquid, they are fundamentally insolvent. And they are insolvent for reasons which usually cannot be influenced in the short-term even by the most well-meaning of governments. These fragile economies are still chronically dependent on one or a very few commodities for their export earnings. The fortunes of their primary production sectors are at the mercy of unfavourable weather conditions and natural disasters. Like Mozambique, some are recovering from widespread civil conflict. A few are still embroiled in it. Their terms of trade have declined in the long term and their export prospects remain dim. They lack the domestic resources to make the necessary investments in human capacity, precisely because in many cases, their budgets are being drained by long-standing debt obligations. Those obligations may themselves be related to the profligacy of irresponsible preceding administrations.

Most of the present governments cannot be blamed for these adverse circumstances. Yet the multilateral creditors are holding them to account for sustained better economic performance, before considering them eligible for debt relief. The indicators which attract detailed scrutiny - and which determine debt 'sustainability' - are two ratios: the ratio of the present value of the outstanding debt to exports,[13] and the ratio of debt service payments to exports. Debt 'sustainability' is achieved when the first ratio lies within a range of 200-250% or below and the second within a range of 20-25% or below. As can be seen from the table, nearly all the HIPCs lie outside - often far outside - these ranges. But even these measures of disadvantage are clearly inadequate. The capacity to repay should also take into account the fiscal burden of debt repayment which, as illustrated above, can be of a crippling nature. Other measures of disadvantage, such as export concentration, should also be included in the determination of solvency.

---

13 The present value of debt is obtained by calculating all future debt servicing obligations until full repayment of the debt, and dividing them by a discount rate. If the discount rate is equal to the original interest rates of the loans the present value will be equal to the face value of the debt.

Aid and debt

The world has become divided into the indebted and the chronically indebted. In the 1970s, there were huge increases in transnational borrowing world-wide, some retrenchment in the 1980s and further huge increases in the 1990s. But while the rising tide has lifted some vessels it has almost drowned others.

Most countries are afloat, even if they are not all perfectly seaworthy. The middle and higher income borrowers have increased their dependence on foreign capital in a growing variety of forms: private bank loans, bonds, foreign direct investment, portfolio holdings. Some have not put in place the regulatory mechanisms to withstand a sudden withdrawal of capital in a crisis of confidence. But they can be bailed out with more liquidity and they can usually reverse the leakages with a return of confidence. For those countries which have gained the most from external exposure, these ebbs and flows are some of the caprices of financial globalisation, and they can be accommodated.

Many other countries are floundering badly, however. Today's most heavily indebted countries have been obliged to restructure and reschedule their external obligations repeatedly, not diminishing the outstanding debt but seeing it increase, while its composition hardens around a growing multilateral core. As a press release put it recently, some of the poorest countries are 'drowning not waiving'. But even the waivers are insufficient to set countries right and shake off the millstone of debt.

Yet while the international community can mobilise some $100 billion to bail out the middle and higher income countries of Asia - equivalent to about half of the total outstanding debt of the 41 Heavily Indebted Poor Countries - no HIPC has been cured of its debt problem in the present decade and there is no prospect of cure under the most recent debt alleviation scheme.[14]

These chronically debt-bound countries are not in a liquidity crisis, but a solvency crisis. If they were firms, many would have been declared bankrupt. The managers would have been fired and some of the assets saved. Countries cannot disappear economically. But in practice the managers are invariably saved and many of the assets - including the vulnerable poor - allowed to suffer. Under the present bail-out regime, salvation cannot even be guaranteed by responsible economic management,

---

14 The $100 billion is in non-concessional loans, which will be repaid to the creditors, while the HIPC debt problems will only be resolved through grants of ODA. However, the developmental impact of solving the HIPC debt problem will be immeasurably greater.

Table 1: Heavily Indebted Poor Countries: Debt and development status, 1995

	Human Dev. Rank (out of 175)	GNP $ US Per Head	Public Debt as % of GDP
Angola	157	410	—
Benin	146	370	57
Bolivia	113	800	46
Burkina Faso	172	230	39
Burundi	169	160	—
Cameroon	133	650	106
Central African Rep	151	340	—
Chad	164	180	36
Congo (Brazzaville)	130	680	282
Congo (Kinshasa)	142	120	184
Cote D'ivoire	145	660	144
Equatorial Guinea	135	380	—
Ethiopia	170	100	—
Ghana	132	390	55
Guinea	167	550	74
Guinea-Bissau	163	250	270
Guyana	104	590	347
Honduras	116	600	75
Kenya	134	280	48
Laos	136	350	47
Liberia	—	—	—
Madagascar	152	230	114
Mali	171	250	32
Mauritania	150	460	125
Mozambique	166	80	205
Myanmar	131	—	—
Nicaragua	127	380	460
Niger	173	220	52
Rwanda	174	180	40
Sao Tome	125	350	381
Senegal	160	600	45
Sierra Leone	175	180	72
Somalia	—	—	—
Sudan	158	—	—
Tanzania	149	120	138
Togo	147	310	67
Uganda	159	240	33
Vietnam	121	240	29
Yemen	148	260	—
Zambia	143	400	101

— data not available
Sources: United Nations Development Programme, World Bank

Table 2: Heavily Indebted Poor Countries: Aid and debt flows, 1995

	Aid as % of GNP	Debt servicing as % of GNP (a)	Debt service as % of govt expenditure (b)	Debt as % of exports (c)	Debt service as % of exports
Angola	11	—	—	278 (a)	13
Benin	17	3	11	221	8
Bolivia	11	6	12	223	29
Burkina Faso	24	2	10	294	11
Burundi	32	5	—	388 (a)	28
Cameroon	10	6	70	410	20
Central African Rep	19	4	—	243 (a)	7
Chad	24	2	10	140	6
Congo (Brazzaville)	25	48	87	423	14
Congo (Kinshasa)	—	—	81	702	55
Cote D'ivoire	25	47	38	340	23
Equatorial Guinea	—	1	—	308 (a)	14 (a)
Ethiopia	23	2	18	383 (a)	14
Ghana	9	6	—	219	23
Guinea	11	3	14	340	25
Guinea-Bissau	74	3	61	1,882	67
Guyana	—	21	58	367	27
Honduras	—	15	55	208	31
Kenya	10	15	26	148	26
Laos	14	1	5	184	6
Liberia	—	—	—	339 (a)	8 (a)
Madagascar	—	4	73	485	9
Mali	25	8	13	145	13
Mauritania	28	11	11	270	22
Mozambique	101	7	19	989	35
(Myanmar)	—	—	—	442 (a)	32 (a)
Nicaragua	46	10	114	1,358	39
Niger	25	5	36	346	20
Nigeria	neg			274	12
Rwanda	96	7	17	656	—
Sao Tome	—	35	—	1,846	24
Senegal	17	7	20	141	19
Sierra Leone	36	21	17	499	60
Somalia	—	—	—	3,745 (a)	150 (a)
Sudan	—	—	—	3,057 (a)	87 (a)
Tanzania	30	—	54	525	17
Togo	14	3	16	212	6
Uganda	19	4	16	271	21
Vietnam	6	3	18	82	5
Yemen	5	4	27	189 (a)	3
Zambia	21	11	32	318	174

— data not available
Source: IMF, World Bank (a) 1994 (b) public service debt (c) present value

fiscal rectitude and trade openness. For many, there are literally no prospects at all of escape from debt if the conditions do not change, barring an economic miracle.[15]

Debt burdens like these make development aid more meaningless. Donors which provide the extra dollar for technical experts, training or imported goods would do better to put the equivalent into debt cancellation. As the main creditors - indirectly through the multilateral institutions, or directly through bilateral loans - they bear the main responsibility for the future solvency of the poorest countries. But under present practice the donor countries are locking themselves into indefinite limited debt alleviation and indefinite limited aid. If they contributed sufficiently to reduce the debt burden, they could begin to dispense with both obligations. Then, for even the poorest countries, sound economic management would bring its own rewards, instead of having them cancelled out by debt servicing obligations.

The mechanisms are already in place to make the definitive transformation, but they are not being used with adequate generosity. The eligibility terms of the HIPC initiative should be interpreted much more generously and the time frame for application shortened. To finance debt cancellation, the World Bank's Trust Fund should be substantially augmented by the major creditors, but also by the World Bank which holds reserves currently in excess of $17 billion. The IMF's liquidity could be boosted if it sold a portion of its own gold reserves. A proposal to make an additional $2 billion available by this means has already been tabled, but it is being opposed by a few of the largest donors.[16]

Donors have begun to write off some of the outstanding official debts owed to them by the poorest countries. In 1997, for example, the British government announced its own $220 million debt initiative for the poorest countries of the Commonwealth. Other donors have forgiven all or part of outstanding official loans to individual borrowers in recent years, but the overall impact on the total debt stock has been limited. In the late 1990's the Jubilee 2000 coalition was formed to put pressure on creditor countries to cancel debt by the end of 1999 (see box).

---

15 One of the 41 HIPCs may soon be saved by just such a miracle. Equatorial Guinea - a small country of 400,000 people - has recently discovered oil. Helped by export revenues in 1996 and 1997 of over $300 million, its GDP grew by 40-50% in those two years. Not many HIPCs will be so fortunate.

16 Both multilateral institutions are reluctant to cash in a part of their reserves because they claim that doing so would affect their credit ratings, and thus their capacity to continue borrowing funds on the money markets. The argument, however, is untested. It also sounds somewhat disingenuous coming from institutions owned by both the creditors and the debtors and when considered against the true debt plight of the poorest countries.

> **Box 5: Jubilee 2000 Coalition and debt cancellation**
> Jubilee is formed of Church groups and development organisations in the UK and elsewhere, campaigning for a cancellation of the 'unpayable' debt owed by the world's poorest countries. One of the aims of the coalition is to gather over 20 million signatures on a petition to influence the G-7 countries. This petition will be presented to the G-7 leaders at their meeting in Germany in June 1999.
>
> The campaign has already had some probable influence. The British Government has been pressing for faster debt relief since the September 1997 meeting of Commonwealth Finance Ministers in Mauritius, and has expressed sympathy with the aims of the movement. During 1999, there has also been a more lenient attitude by the Governments of the US - which is ready to examine the possibility of selling IMF gold stocks to alleviate debt - and of Germany, since the change of leadership. Although not a G-7 member, Canada is also entertaining a total cancellation of the debt of African countries.

Debt forgiveness needs to be undertaken with minimal additional conditionality, while the process should provide certain assurances to the creditor countries that a clean break can be made with chronic indebtedness. Sustainable solutions will require comprehensive agreements which take into account the specific status and prospects of each of the crisis-stricken countries. Hitherto, agreements have been inadequate because the problems of each country have been examined in different forums - Paris Club meetings, IMF/World Bank consultations, donor meetings and consortia - addressing different aspects.

It is therefore proposed that comprehensive agreements for each country be negotiated through a single forum which brings representatives of the government together with the main bilateral, multilateral and commercial creditors, other donors (including non-governmental agencies) and the UN system. Preparations for the forum would include a complete survey of the economic, social and humanitarian status of the country, and a presentation of alternative projections of progress. These scenarios should lead to alternative financial solutions for debt forgiveness in the short-term, and outright cancellation in the longer-term, leading to eventual independence from development aid. The solutions could include the explicit agreement by debtor governments to channel converted debts and savings of debt service into health, education and other social development funds.

Ultimately, the purpose of debt cancellation is self-sustaining development in the crisis countries. In announcing its recent write-off of debt to the poorest countries, the British government stated that "the long-term objective is to do away with the need for aid".

6 Freer trade better than constrictive aid

From the time of the classical economists, trade has been justified on the grounds of 'comparative advantage', by which the global economy benefits from commercial exchange (see Box 6).

In the post-War period trade has always expanded, pulling the global economy up with it. Since 1950, the world's total output has grown five and a half times. In the same period, the volume of goods traded internationally has increased 16-fold, accounting for 7% of world output in 1950 and 15% in 1995. Trade in services is now growing even faster than trade in goods: 12% versus 9% per year since 1985. The global economy is becoming steadily more integrated, with trade - as well as international financial flows - providing the engine of expansion.

For developing countries, maximising the benefits from trade growth means maximising external revenues. The real economic advantages of trade derive from an expansion in import purchasing power, more exports leading to more imports. This is where the comparison with aid comes in. Aid - as the 'gap-filler' - also expands the foreign purchasing power of developing countries, but with aid come limitations which induce new borrowing, or which are attached to conditions of purchase, or both. Aid distorts trade in a way intended to bring benefits. However, it has been estimated that if aid ceased, but instead the providers of aid lifted all restraints on imports from developing countries, the revenue benefits would be at least twice as large as the value of aid.[1] Free trade without aid may thus be seen as doubly superior to a combination of donor aid and donor protectionism: more value and fewer conditions.

If trade expansion is controversial in the context of increasing globalisation, it is because the benefits will be unevenly distributed and because the process of short-term adjustment to freer trade may be painful for some countries. The wave of trade liberalisation unleashed by the Uruguay Round will bring benefits to the world economy as a whole, accelerating trade expansion. But the poorer countries which have benefited hitherto from various forms of privileged trading conditions may be set back in the short-term. The important questions are whether those trade privileges were desirable in the longer-term; whether they constituted a

---

1 Commission on Global Governance (1995).

form of aid that is ultimately unsustainable. Also, expanding trade is stimulated by, while helping to catalyse, changes in domestic economies and not all of those are comfortable. Thus, the arguments are not against trade itself. Only about how to maximise the benefits from its expansion, while minimising the adjustment costs.

This chapter is about trade as an alternative to aid. It is a subject as old as aid itself. However, since aid began, trade has never been freer or potentially fairer as now and the advantages of trade can be newly appraised. The chapter traces the process of trade liberalisation, and in particular the Uruguay Round and its aftermath; assesses the potential benefits from freer trade for development prospects; and reviews the need for developing countries to promote more openness in their economies to take full advantage of trade liberalisation.

Freeing world trade

Trade liberalisation is returning and history can be a guide to the future. Much more than a century ago, in the 1840s, when the world was dominated - as now - by a limited number of global economic powers, Britain began a process of reducing export and import duties. The most significant and initially controversial measure was the repeal of the Corn Laws which levied tariffs on imported grain. Britain's 'Manchester creed' was taken up in continental Europe and, with rather less enthusiasm, in the United States. The 'unequal treaties' imposed by the western powers on Japan kept that country's markets open.

Free trade was the basis for rapid industrialisation in the latter part of the 19th century and until 1914. During this period, global economic output expanded steadily, bringing growing prosperity to the people of the more advanced countries. It has been estimated that the share of exports in world output rose from 5% in 1870 to nearly 9% in 1913.[2] This period of expansion was strongly supported by an almost universal currency standard. In the early part of the 20th century, some nine-tenths of the world's population lived in countries with currencies convertible into gold or silver. The development of transport and communications links also facilitated economic globalisation. This was the golden age of the railway and the steamship. The Suez Canal opened in 1869, the Panama Canal in 1914. Telecommunications were steadily improved.

These developments have been replicated by similar kinds of advance,

---

2 Maddison (1995). As we saw above, the proportion was lower in 1950 than in 1913.

> **Box 6: Trade - some basic theory**
> Economists since Adam Smith and David Ricardo in the 19th century have used arguments about comparative advantage based on costs in order to explain the rationale for trade. Trade theory has evolved to encompass the realities of the global economy, but the principle of comparative advantage is still sound.
>
> The original version of the theory was based on a comparison of costs of production determined by labour. Trade occurs because these comparative costs differ. Imagine two countries (A and B) producing the same two goods. Even if country A has an absolute advantage over country B in the production of both goods - i.e. it uses less labour per unit of output for each - it has an interest in trading. Country A will specialise in the production and export of the good in which it has a comparatively greater cost advantage and import from B the good in which it has a comparatively smaller cost advantage. In other words, as long as relative production costs differ among countries there are gains to be made from trade.
>
> Actual patterns of trade are determined by wages. In a comparison of the US and Britain in the 1950s, it has been shown that in a wide range of industries, American productivity was higher, but because UK wages were lower, Britain had a comparative trading advantage in those industries in which its productivity was comparatively less inferior.[3]
>
> International comparisons of labour productivity and wage-rates still help to explain trade patterns today. However, a more sophisticated version of the theory needs to take into account other factors of production besides labour: land, capital, technology, information and entrepreneurial skills. Neo-classical theory predicts that a country will export goods produced with factors of production which it has in relative abundance, and import those made with factors in which it is relatively scarce.
>
> The implications of neo-classical theory are that trade is based on differences of factor endowments: the greater the differences, the more the opportunities for trade. Natural endowments are the basis for much trade in primary commodities, of course: Australian wool, Brazilian coffee, Canadian wheat, Saudi oil. But in manufactures, there is extensive trade among countries with somewhat similar endowments, for example within Europe. This suggests that, over and above factor endowments, there are what are called 'external economies' helping to create comparative advantages. The emergence of computer-based industries in Silicon Valley in the US, watch-making in Switzerland, financial services in London and other such clusters, indicate that international specialisation - reinforced by trade - can grow up in the modern technological and service sectors as a result of historical or other reasons, such as government support.
>
> The implications for developing countries are that they can benefit from trade through the development and promotion of exports on the basis of a variety of different factors which can be turned into a comparative advantage: low labour-cost activities; endowments of natural resources; special locational and touristic benefits; information technology and communications applications, among others.

3 Krugman (1996).

at much higher technological levels, in recent years. However, the second contemporary phase of liberalisation is occurring after a prolonged period during which the global economy was more fragmented and protectionist.

The First World War did not only take a serious toll in human lives, it severely disrupted international economic exchange. The Great Depression overtook the western economies from 1929, as countries deflated, finally abandoning the Gold standard when they could no longer maintain fixed parities. A decade later, governments were again attempting to exert greater control over economies, as they had done in the mercantilist days, before free trade.

Thus, as noted earlier, the aid era began in a much more constrained international economic climate and the efforts to liberalise trade have occurred against a backdrop of renewed mistrust of openness. In addition to retaining their protectionist barriers, the advanced economies were slow to return to currency convertibility. The newly independent countries were also shy of convertibility and even today, many of their currencies are protected by strict exchange controls. Openness was not on the economic agenda, which was dominated by a paradigm which might be described as statism-in-one-country. In any case, countries were concerned about the short-term inflationary consequences of liberalisation. In India, for example, convertibility was quickly followed by rapid price increases and the policy was abandoned.

There was sufficient concern to begin opening markets again, however, for the 50 members of the United Nations to draw up proposals for an International Trade Organisation (ITO). The ITO was to have been the permanent watchdog of protectionist practices, under the auspices of the UN system, which would have ensured near-universal membership. Its charter, approved at a conference in Havana in 1948 also included rules on employment, commodity agreements, restrictive business practices, international investment and services.[4] Looking back, it is ironic to reflect that that such a charter should have been approved in Cuba, and effectively quashed by the United States, when the Congress declared itself unwilling to ratify it in 1950. The world had to wait 45 more years before agreement could be reached on the establishment of the World Trade Organisation - outside the UN system but with a much expanded membership - designed to establish and implement the legal ground rules for international commerce. In the meantime, only one element of the ITO was agreed to: a framework for trade negotiations called the General Agreement on Tariffs

---

4 World Trade Organisation, www.wto.org.

and Trade (GATT), signed by 23 founder members, known as 'contracting parties'.

The real costs of the failure of the ITO are a matter of speculation. GATT was an imperfect and partial substitute which, significantly for the developing countries, excluded all commodity trade. It was left to the UN Conference on Trade and Development (UNCTAD), some 20 years later, to re-start negotiations on international commodity agreements. Even though confined to manufactures, the post-War experience of negotiating for more trade openness has been slow and it has proceeded in a piecemeal fashion, advancing through a series of GATT 'trade Rounds' instigated by the dominant powers. This one-sidedness is evident from the limited membership of the GATT. The table below, summarising the eight trade Rounds, shows that participation was limited until the Tokyo Round in the 1970s (see Table 3).

The first five trade Rounds were exclusively concerned with cuts in tariffs. The scope of the Kennedy and Tokyo Rounds was broadened slightly, but some of the resulting agreements (or 'codes') were signed by only part of the membership - mostly industrialised countries - making them 'plurilateral' rather than multilateral. These Rounds nevertheless succeeded in reducing the average tariff rates on industrial goods traded among the contracting parties from 40% to 6% by the end of the Tokyo Round in 1979. But many obstacles remained for the developing countries. Key export items remained outside the negotiations and even attracted new barriers. The Multi-Fibre Arrangement (MFA), first drawn up in 1962 and still in force, placed quotas on individual exporters of textiles and clothing. The MFA actually penalises export success by the developing countries since quotas are applied to additional countries and additional products as significant shares or growth rates in the world market were reached.

The MFA was a manifestation of the serious shortcomings of GATT. It was one means by which, after seven Rounds of trade negotiations, the limited success in reducing tariffs was also stimulating other forms of protectionism. By the 1980s, it was also becoming evident that the GATT was much less relevant to contemporary trade realities. The agricultural sector, the object of massive subsidisation by the major trading powers - the USA, European Union and Japan - continued to lie entirely outside the agreement. In addition to commodities, GATT did not address trade in either services or intellectual property, which were also of special interest to developed countries.

Table 3: Eight trade rounds

Years	Name/Place	No. of Countries	Coverage
1947	Geneva	23	Tariffs
1949	Annecy	13	Tariffs
1951	Torquay	38	Tariffs
1956	Geneva	26	Tariffs
1960-61	Dillon Round, Geneva	26	Tariffs
1964-67	Kennedy Round, Geneva	62	Tariffs, anti-dumping
1973-79	Tokyo Round	102	Tariffs, non-tariff measures, 'framework agreements'
1986-94	Uruguay Round	123	Tariffs, non-tariff rules, services, intellectual property textiles, agriculture, WTO and institutions

Source: WTO

The Uruguay Round

The most recent Round has been by far the longest and most comprehensive of all, finally establishing a basis for universal and equitable trade liberalisation under the supervision of a new international agency, the World Trade Organisation. It is useful to describe these negotiations, and their outcome, in some detail. The process helped to establish a comprehensive new framework for trade relations and saw a considerable evolution in the policy stances of all trading countries.

The Uruguay Round, which ran from 1986 until 1994, represented an important threshold in a number of senses. At the outset of the negotiations, the developing countries were chary. They had not taken a full part in past Rounds, and the outcomes had been of limited benefit. The developed countries acknowledged this caution. The Ministerial Declaration at the opening conference in Punta del Este stated that "the developed countries do not expect the developing countries, in the course of trade negotiations, to make contributions which are inconsistent with their individual development, financial and trade needs."

But the climate changed during the Round, and a less political and more business-like approach began to be taken by all participants. In fact, as they proceeded, the negotiations were increasingly perceived as being among a heterogeneity of trade partners and not purely between developed and developing countries, North and South. Many of the negotiations remained two-sided. But in the agriculture negotiations, for example, the 'Cairns

Group' of countries pitted Australia, Argentina, Canada, Thailand and other major grain exporters against the strongly protectionist countries such as the US, EU, Japan and Korea. In this sense, the Uruguay Round achieved a certain maturity. Trade interests cut across some of the aid donor-recipient boundaries that had so often characterised - and stymied - global negotiations in the past.

Another important change that occurred during the Round was the recognition by a growing number of countries of the merits of openness. Many countries shed their inhibitions about protectionism and made unilateral offers of tariff reduction. There is no doubt that these gestures helped to ensure progress in other areas in which protectionism had become enshrined, such as agriculture.

The issues on which progress was recorded may be grouped into four areas: market access, trade rules, new areas and institutions.

Market access covered tariffs and non-tariff barriers on manufactures, natural resource and tropical products, textiles and clothing and agriculture.

There was substantial progress in the Uruguay Round on the reduction of tariffs. The overall objective had been to achieve a general tariff cut of one-third on all industrial products and this target was actually surpassed (38%). The cuts made by the developing countries, whose tariffs had further to fall, were greater than those made by the developed. By the end of the Round, the developed countries were imposing average tariffs on imports from developing countries of 4.5%, but this was higher than the average tariff rate on imports from all sources (3.9%). Moreover, the tariff cuts were less on many products of particular importance to developing countries, including textiles and clothing, leather, rubber footwear and travel goods. On tropical and resource-based products, the tariff reductions by developed countries ranged up to 45%.[5]

The Round also resulted in a marked increase in the proportion of 'bound' tariffs (see Box 7) offered by all countries. By the end of the Round, the developed countries had bound virtually all their tariffs, and the developing countries raised the proportion from 13 to 61%.[6] Binding has two important positive consequences: first, it provides a ratchet to ensure that the gains from tariff-cutting are consolidated. Secondly, it gives greater certainty to trade. While not eliminating entirely the threat of sudden increases in tariffs (since binding limits are sometimes set above prevailing tariff rates), binding ensures much greater tariff stability. There was also progress in the de-escalation of tariffs and the reduction in tariff peaks.

---

5   Safadi and Laird (1996).
6   Overseas Development Institute (1995).

> **Box 7: Trade glossary**
>
> **Generalized System of Preferences (GSP):** negotiated under the auspices of the United Nations Conference on Trade and Development (UNCTAD), the GSP provides preferential tariff treatment for selected imports of manufactured goods from developing countries into developed countries.
>
> **Most Favoured Nation (MFN) principle:** MFN lies at the heart of multilateral trade and is in Article I of the original GATT. It is an ambiguous title which means in practice that countries cannot discriminate among their different trade partners: under WTO rules, if a country grants a trade preference to one country, it must grant it to all. (The GSP - above - abrogates this principle).
>
> **National treatment:** this is another of the basic principles of the new trading system. It specifies that, once a product, service or intellectual property has entered a country, they must be treated in an identical manner to products of national source, in all respects.
>
> **Non-Tariff Barriers (NTBs):** these have grown in number and complexity, partly in response to lower tariffs. NTBs include quotas, licensing systems, special levies, VERs (see below) and various rules stipulating the exact configuration, content, health standards and packaging of imported products to conform with domestic market requirements.
>
> **Tariff binding:** the agreement not to raise tariffs on particular imports above established upper limits.
>
> **Tariff escalation:** designed to protect domestic production of processed products, importers apply lower tariffs on the import of raw materials and semi-finished goods, and higher tariffs on the finished products.
>
> **Tariff peaks:** application of higher tariffs on goods which importing countries judge to be sensitive, and for which they wish to provide protection for their domestic producers.
>
> **"Tariffication":** the substitution of non-tariff barriers to trade by tariffs. One of the important outcomes of the Uruguay Round has been to convert many trade barriers into tariff regimes which are easier to monitor and to which liberalisation measures can be more easily applied.
>
> **Voluntary Export Restraints (VERs):** also known as 'orderly marketing arrangements', VERs are imposed by importing countries on selected products making rapid inroads on their domestic markets. VERs are 'grey area measures' because their conformity with GATT/WTO regulations is doubtful.

Non-tariff market access measures also advanced during the Round, providing more potential benefits to developing countries. One was the gradual elimination of 'voluntary export restraints' on the exports of footwear, electronics and travel goods. Another was the agreement to phase out the Multi-Fibre Arrangement (MFA) whose quotas on the export of textiles and clothing has been a hindrance to many developing countries. The MFA and its successor agreements, which have prevailed for more than 40 years, were in direct contravention of the 'Most Favoured Nation' (MFN) principles of the GATT. Now the MFA is due to end in 2005, and in several phases, more and more categories of products will be brought within the normal ambit of WTO's rules, while quotas will be steadily raised.

With textiles and garments, the other very important production sector for developing country trade is agriculture. For the first time, the Uruguay Round also brought agriculture within the GATT/WTO framework. The importance of agriculture - including tropical products - cannot be overstated. While only 13% of developing country exports overall are agricultural, according to GATT/WTO sources, the proportion is above 20% for more than half of them.

Sugar, which is of critical importance to several tropical developing countries (and which can also be produced by natural and synthetic means in temperate northern climates), is one of the products which has been the most affected by intervention.[7] Both the US and the European Union impose heavy restrictions, allowing imports by strict quota and value, while subsidizing their own domestic producers and exporting their surpluses. The result is heavy distortions of the world market and lower prices overall. Grains have also been subjected to similar strict controls by the developed countries. Japan and Korea have traditionally banned the import of rice entirely, for example.

The Uruguay Round prescribed three sets of changes. First, non-tariff barriers (NTBs) - consisting, among other things, of quantitative import restrictions, variable import levies, minimum import prices, discretionary licensing and VERs - will be 'tariffied'. Secondly, there will be reductions in levels of support given to domestic farmers. Thirdly, export subsidies will be gradually diminished.

Trade rules. This is the second general area in which the Uruguay Round achieved significant results. They will largely redound to the benefit of the developing countries, since a stronger rule-based trading system will help to prevent the imposition of ad hoc and subjectively determined impediments

---

7 See Krueger (1995).

to their exports into the larger markets of the developed countries.

Under the old GATT, developed countries allowed themselves to resort to certain 'safeguards' - temporary import restrictions - to protect their domestic industries. The Agreement on Safeguards provides for their more flexible use, but in a more disciplined manner. All existing safeguard measures are to be phased out and countries will have to demonstrate serious harm to their domestic industries if any new measures are to be approved. The phase out will be over a longer period for the developing countries.

Stricter rules are also going to be applied to so-called anti-dumping practices which, since the 1980s, have been used as a principal bilateral trade weapon by the US, EU and Australia against Asian countries (including Japan). Anti-dumping measures, which contend that exporters are charging prices below costs of production, have hitherto been able to take advantage of rather vague GATT rules. The Uruguay Round agreement provides for clearer rules on the application of such measures, and requires that they be phased out within five years. However, it is by no means clear how effective the WTO can be in challenging national anti-dumping laws through the new disputes mechanisms. Somewhat ominously, anti-dumping protection has been taken up by more countries in recent years.

New areas. One of the most important features of the Uruguay Round has been the inclusion in the negotiations of new areas relevant to modern patterns of trade. In addition to agriculture, these areas have included trade-related intellectual property rights (TRIPs), trade-related aspects of investment measures (TRIMs), and services. From the outset, negotiations in these areas were controversial. They tended to split countries along North-South lines, even though the potential benefits from resulting agreements will be highly differentiated.

Although intellectual property is already regulated by multilateral regimes under the auspices of the World Intellectual Property Organisation (WIPO), the intent of TRIPs was to strengthen the rules against counterfeiting and ensure that license fees were paid for the production of goods incorporating patents. The agreement essentially reinforces existing conventions and brings their supervision within the WTO enforcement mechanisms (which inevitably brings into question the continuing need for an independent WIPO).

TRIPs is the Round's one major example of legislating for an increase in protectionism. In the early stage of the negotiations it was opposed by countries like Brazil and India which were (and are) major importers of technology, directly or through foreign investment. The positions of those two countries - and the middle-income East Asian countries - has been mollified as they have further developed their own patentable technologies (for example, the rapidly growing software sector in India). But the limitations which TRIPs impose on the dissemination of technologies and, just as importantly, patented products like pharmaceuticals, present impediments to development. Private corporations can legitimately claim that intellectual property protection is necessary to foster innovation, but when such innovations are of widespread developmental interest - for example vaccines and agricultural research - it is important to seek ways in which they may be kept in the public domain.

The discussions on TRIMs recognised that certain measures governing foreign investments had impacts on trade patterns. There are several types of such measures. One is the 'local content' stipulation which requires that a minimum proportion of production inputs be purchased locally. A second is the "trade balancing" requirement which limits the volume or value of imports by an enterprise to the equivalent volume or value of exports. Under the TRIMs agreement, these practices are to be phased out over a period of from 2 years for developed countries, to between 5 and 7 years for developing.

Liberalising investment along these lines is likely to be beneficial to all host countries. The above restrictions distort trade and act as a disincentive to foreign investors, for whom host countries draw up incentive schemes as compensation. The aim should be a gradual elimination of investment conditions as well as incentives.

At the closure of the Uruguay Round, some of the major investing countries wanted to pursue negotiations on investment on a more comprehensive basis, with the intention of drawing up a Multilateral Agreement on Investment (MAI). This agreement was intended to be all-encompassing, replacing the need for the many prevailing bilateral agreements, and leading to a lowering of all remaining barriers to foreign investment. Starting in 1995, the discussions have been conducted, not by the WTO, but among the 29 members of the Organisation for Economic Cooperation and Development (OECD).

The ultimate purpose of further investment liberalisation is sound. But the OECD, often perceived as the 'rich man's club' by developing countries, is not a true multilateral forum. Although the OECD has claimed that the countries participating in the MAI negotiations represent over 90% of the current foreign direct investments sources, and 75% of its current destinations, many significant investing countries - including Malaysia, Singapore and Brazil - are not taking part. More important, a large number of the world's potential investment hosts - for which an agreement to facilitate tomorrow's investment expansion should be intended - are not represented at all. Partial negotiations such as these are contrary to the spirit of multilateralism which the new WTO has come to epitomise, now that its membership has become closer to universal. Countries should not be asked to sign any agreement which they did not have a hand in negotiating.

In the area of new issues, another important feature of the Uruguay Round was the inclusion of negotiations in the vast services sector. The exclusion of services would have been an aberration, since taken as a whole the sector accounts for more than half the GDP of most countries and a rapidly rising proportion of their exports. Its inclusion means that WTO now covers all key aspects of trade. Yet, the proposal to add services to the agenda was initially controversial, some developing countries seeing it as a means to force them to open their doors to foreign banking, media and other areas in which they wanted to retain national control. Again, however, as the talks progressed, the negotiating climate became more positive, with developing countries recognising the advantages to their own economies of liberalisation in tourism, shipping, construction and other areas in which they had comparative advantages.

The Round led to GATS, the General Agreement on Trade in Services. It is founded on the same general premises as the GATT, and is the basis for a process of steady liberalisation in all services sectors. No tariff or other generalised protection mechanism is to be applied in services. Countries opt in gradually, choosing which of their service activities to offer for liberalisation, and then applying MFN and 'national treatment' principles (see Box 7). Countries can choose initially to limit their obligations to liberalise and phase out these limitations. In practice, the developed countries have made the most commitments under the GATS, and the poorer countries the least.

To ensure continuity in the trade liberalisation process, the WTO has a 'built in agenda' setting out a programme of negotiations on products and services which were not addressed or on which discussions were not completed during the Uruguay Round. The first of the post-Round negotiations to be completed was on Basic Telecommunications Services, an agreement involving 69 countries, 40 of them are developing. The agreement is significant because of the rapidly growing importance of telecommunication services. They are currently valued at over $600 billion, of which $50 billion are traded[8] (a major part consisting of international telephone calls). Both output and trade are growing much faster than global

---

8   World Bank, Global Economic Prospects and the Developing Countries, (1997, Washington).

averages. Rapid technological advances and increased competition have lowered costs and raised access to telecommunications services, from which more countries can benefit as trade is liberalised. Developing countries participating in the agreement have mostly only agreed to limited market access, but have a lot to gain from liberalisation.

Another area of post-Round liberalisation is in the trade of information technology products (computers, telecommunications equipment, semiconductors, semiconductor manufacturing equipment, software, and scientific instruments). An outcome of the December 1996 Ministerial Conference in Singapore was an agreement to eliminate customs and other duties on these products, as soon as countries accounting for 90 percent of world trade in information technology products had agreed to participate. This threshold was reached by September 1997.

The continuing agenda also includes financial services and maritime transport, which have not progressed as well. The liberalisation of other services will soon be brought into negotiations, and agricultural protection and subsidy is due to be further scrutinised.

Labour standards and the environment. There are two areas of controversy which have also been considered for inclusion in trade negotiations, because they are thought to give unfair trade advantages to certain countries. The first concerns labour standards. Some of the developing countries are accused of employing child workers and paying them wages that are considered artificially low - or not paying them at all - and subjecting them to poor health and safety conditions. There is no doubt that the accusations have substance, and that child labour is used in the manufacture of traded goods. There is also little argument about the sometimes cruel and exploitative conditions under which children are employed, and child labour is outlawed by conventions drawn up by the International Labour Organisation (ILO).

But while it is entirely legitimate for the world community to continue to press for action to alleviate the worst miseries associated with child labour, the issue does not belong in trade negotiations. Individual countries may show their indignation with the practice, but trade laws are neither fair nor effective as the means to improve conditions. Child labour is used unevenly between and within countries (including in industrialised countries and by the corporations of industrialised countries). Children are employed seasonally, sometimes on a part-time basis. There are circumstances in which children are utilised for their special dexterity and employed humanely. Bilateral sanctions are unacceptable in trade, which is now mostly governed by multilateral rules. To try to impose trade-related norms under WTO auspices would, as often as not, unfairly discriminate against some countries, while not successfully targeting the worst examples of exploitation. Child labour concerns belong in an ILO forum.

Poor environmental standards have also been invoked as an excuse for brandishing the threat of trade sanctions, and bringing the issue within the WTO. There is probably truth in the assertion that growing global competitiveness may lead to laxer environmental practices in the production of traded goods. But lax standards are found in all countries - developed and developing - and it would be invidious to single out certain countries, and specific products and sectors within them. There is certainly a case to be made for a multilateral approach to improving environmental standards world-wide - and it is made elsewhere in this book - but the desire to link environment to trade is another form of back-door protectionism which does not belong in the WTO.

Institutions. The Uruguay Round rewrote the GATT - governing trade in goods - created the GATS (services) and TRIMs (investment measures). It then needed a body to supervise the implementation of these and other agreements, with powers and scope much broader than the GATT secretariat. This was the WTO, which officially opened its doors for business in January 1995.

The WTO is much closer than the GATT secretariat to being a universal organisation. During the Uruguay Round, 31 countries joined, and by 1990 WTO had 132 members, with a waiting list that includes China and Russia. The WTO has a status independent of the United Nations system, and is seen as one of the major components of the international policy system, along with the Bretton Woods organisations. Because the negotiating process has been institutionalised, there should no longer be a need for more Rounds. Every two years, its highest governing body - the Ministerial meeting - reviews progress and provides the opportunity to examine the scope of the ongoing agenda.

A key mechanism of the WTO is the disputes procedure, which greatly tightens GATT practices. Under the GATT, a complaint from one of the contracting parties about the trade practices of another prompted the formation of a disputes panel, a process of deliberation, then a report. At any stage, the process could be delayed almost indefinitely by the defending party. Under the WTO, the whole process must be completed within a year, unless voted out by the WTO Council, consisting of all the members. Because decisions are binding, and backed by sanctions, the mechanism has begun to prove its worth. By the end of 1997, over 100 complaints had been filed (as against 300 in GATT's 47 year history), and one third of them had been brought by developing countries.

Beyond the Uruguay Round

In sum, the Uruguay Round has led to a widespread liberalisation of trade in products and services, and laid down a definitive framework for a continuation of the process. The trading rules are now more transparent and more inclusive and liberalisation is expected to facilitate even faster trade expansion. Measured in terms of income growth, the estimates of the overall gains for global welfare range from $212 billion to over $500 billion. For the developing countries, the estimates are from $86 billion to $122 billion.[9] The exact numbers are not important, and the gains may take several years to work through. However, the expected benefits are expected to be very large.

In the short-term, however, the Round will bring a lot of winners, but also some losers. The gains will be differentiated by region and product group. For developing countries as a whole, the first ten years (1995-2005) are expected to yield additional annual export growth of over 1%. The main beneficiaries will be the Asian economies followed by Latin America. But Africa may see negative growth.[10]

There are three reasons for the potential difficulties of Africa, which also apply to some Caribbean and Pacific countries. First, the terms of trade of several countries may deteriorate because of higher prices of imported food, as producer and export subsidies are phased out in exporting countries, following liberalisation in agriculture. Second, many of these countries currently have a limited range of exports and will not be able to take more than marginal advantage of increased market access for manufactures and services, at least in the short-term.

The third reason is the most important of all, however. In those markets in which they trade, many exporters of primary commodities in Sub-Saharan Africa (SSA) and the Caribbean will either have gained little from the WTO agreements, or will have seen any special advantages they had undermined. A majority of the SSA countries depend on two or three agricultural commodities for more than three-quarters of their export earnings. Approximately two-thirds of Africa's exports are sold in the European Union. The perils of this chronically narrow dependency are

---

9   Safadi and Laird, op.cit.
10 Overseas Development Institute, op.cit.

compounded by the decline in real prices of commodities exported by SSA countries. In the 1980s, average prices declined by 45%, with limited recovery since then. Several Caribbean countries depend on a single commodity - bananas - for over 50% of their export earnings.

Hitherto, preferential access for African-Caribbean-Pacific (ACP) country exports into the European Union has been governed by the Lomé Conventions, under which virtually all SSA countries (except South Africa) benefit from some trade preferences. There will be no impact on petroleum and other fuels, which enter Europe duty-free. Also, industrial products will benefit from tariff reductions - to less than 3% for most of their manufactured exports. But, while Lomé allows free access for certain unprocessed commodities, the EU's Common Agricultural Policy applies escalating tariffs to processed commodities. The Uruguay Round went some way to de-escalating these tariffs,[11] but they continue to present obstacles to the export of higher value-added goods.

The ACP countries will also see their relative advantages in their traditional markets undermined, since the generalized improvements in market access resulting from the Uruguay Round will be extended to other countries not previously enjoying privileged access. For example, some of the banana exporters of the Caribbean face special problems. Several exporting countries in Central American exporters (with the strong backing of the US multinational corporations concerned) have challenged the Lomé privileges under the disputes mechanism and they are due to be phased out under WTO rules.

Since the 1970s, selected exports from developing countries have benefited from the Generalized System of Preferences (GSP) accorded by some developed countries. The GSP is a derogation of the multilateral system in several respects. It goes against the MFN principles, it is negotiated bilaterally and applied selectively. GSP has nevertheless been of some incremental benefit, but the major gainers have included the strongest trading countries such as South Korea and Hong Kong.

There are financial support schemes designed to shelter commodity exporters from income declines. Under the European Union's Lomé agreements, the 'STABEX' system helps to stabilize export incomes by providing compensatory payments when prices of exports fall. The IMF also introduced conditional lending under its Compensatory Financing

---

11 For example, raw tobacco attracts a 17.5% tariff (down from 21.8%) but manufactured tobacco attracts 26.5% (52.6%); rough wood attracts a zero tariff, wood-base panels 6.8% (down from 10.0%); hides, skins and leather exports in raw form attract zero tariffs, as finished products they attract 4.4% (7.2%).

Facility (CFF) to countries experiencing balance of payments difficulties. For many years, the United Nations Conference on Trade and Development (UNCTAD) attempted to get agreement on a Common Fund, intended to stabilize prices by creating buffer stocks of certain commodities.

However, none of these schemes is in the long-term interests of the developing countries. When commodity prices decline over the long run, as has been the case for many developing country exports, no scheme can indefinitely support export incomes. Under STABEX, payments are determined by moving averages of incomes over several years. Thus, transfers fall if there is a downward trend in export prices. The CFF induces higher indebtedness. Buffer stocks become unaffordable. Even when the falls in export prices are short-term, stabilization schemes discourage diversification of products and markets, which is ultimately the best insurance against fluctuations.

Maximizing the benefits of trade liberalisation

In the world as a whole, the gaps in income between the richest and the poorest countries have tended to widen over time. The richer and middle-income countries have grown generally faster than the poorer. There is nevertheless considerable evidence that, particularly during the last two decades, there has been an unmistakable process of convergence among the economies that have been relatively open. The more open economies among the poorer countries have grown faster than the open economies of the richer countries, among other reasons because the former have reaped the advantages of importing capital, and the most recent technologies, from the latter.[12] The countries that continue to lag in growth, therefore, are mainly the poorer ones which have remained relatively closed. The obvious implication is that, as more of the poorer countries open their economies, they can expect to grow faster and catch up. And as trade is bolstered by growing liberalisation, the opportunities for gain are commensurately greater.

This returns us to the question posed at the beginning of the chapter: how then can all developing countries hitch themselves to this moving trade vehicle, and maximize the benefits from it?

The previous section helped to illustrate that openness will not be an automatic prescription for growth, particularly for many of the poorer

---

12 Edwards (1998) and Sachs and Warner (1995) also present considerable evidence from many sources in support of convergence.

countries with relatively narrow trade bases. For them, openness, combined with more competitive global trading arrangements under the WTO, could bring short-term disadvantages, among other reasons, through an exacerbation of their terms of trade and a loss of special market access privileges. This at least is the static view, and assumes that many of the poorer countries remain over-dependent on a very few export commodities, propped up by compensation schemes and special privileges. But all developing countries can gain from openness, if they can begin to take the necessary measures in their own economies. The measures needed are both short and long-term and they reach outside the trade sector into a wider range of domestic economic reforms. Many of the measures will be difficult to implement and will imply quite fundamental changes of policy emphasis. However, they will help to turn openness to sustainable advantage and allow more countries to move further away from aid dependence.

Trade policy reform starts with the changing role of governments. In many countries, the state continues to play a preponderant role in economic management and places a heavy bureaucratic hand on foreign trade. In the future, governments need to play a more facilitatory, and less directive role. And this role needs to be consistent with outward-looking economic strategies.

As we saw in an earlier discussion of the aid ages, state-sponsored trade policy has favoured import substitution, as the basis for fostering infant industries behind import barriers. Trade regimes became more 'inner-oriented' and the state placed little priority on supporting and promoting exports. When countries ran into balance of payments difficulties, their instincts were to further restrict imports (those which did not serve the immediate needs of protected domestic industries), rather than to seek to increase foreign exchange through exports. Behind protective walls, the producers of import-competing goods had little incentive to expand production faster than the domestic market. Producers made the easy choice between the sheltered domestic market, in which they often enjoyed a monopoly and where they could derive rent-boosted profits, and the more competitive international market. The over-protectiveness of governments in these countries meant that domestic producers were ill-prepared for openness.[13]

A number of fundamental domestic policy changes are implied by a more outward-oriented approach. They will entail a reduction in the protection of those domestic industries which have been favoured by import-substitution policies, and the pursuit of measures in support of

---

13 Krueger, op. cit.

industries which can benefit from international market opportunities. There will be social costs as a result of the transition, mainly in the short term. But a process of liberalisation is a necessary alternative to protective policies that have led to economic stagnation in many poorer countries. The uncomfortable changes will be a better guarantee of future prosperity.

The new policies aimed at the protected industries will include de-monopolization in order to promote greater efficiency and competitiveness. These monopolies may be in the public or private sectors, and are likely to have been harbouring over-staffing, guaranteed employment and unrealistically high wages. The process is therefore likely to lead to a fall in employment and wages. Domestic economic liberalisation thus has to be complemented by the aggressive encouragement of new activities in which the country can build on international comparative advantage in addition to traditional commodity production. Part of the necessary diversification process will be the move into higher value-added processing of these traditional commodities which, while still confronted by tariff escalation in developed country markets, can begin to take advantage of better market access conditions: hides to leather goods, coffee and tea to beverage products, for example. Processed products can take advantage of the fact that their share in total agricultural trade grew from 33% to 46% between 1983 and 1993.[14] Diversification will also mean building up other industries to produce new products and services, including tourism.

Building up an export sector will require private capital, including foreign direct investment. Investment will only flow, however, in a favourable climate of stability and policy consistency. Fiscal schedules and foreign exchange regimes should be transparent and predictable. Legal and regulatory frameworks, including company laws and investment codes, should be conducive to a vibrant private sector.

Improvements in infrastructure will also be necessary in many countries to support the shift to an outward-oriented strategy. The upgrading of physical infrastructure will in most cases require considerable new resources and is not realizable in the short-term. In the area of information and communications technology, however, rapid improvements are possible if governments are ready to de-monopolize and privatize their post and telecommunications authorities and encourage foreign investment and technology imports. The enormous short-term benefits that could flow from liberalisation in this area are discussed in a separate chapter.

There are also many initiatives for countries to take in the area of trade promotion and the interface with the world economy. Governments and the

---

14 UNCTAD (1996).

private sector should work together to ensure that the fullest means of support are provided to the export sector. Three of the most important resources are information, finance and promotional activities. First, exporters need the information about markets and their corresponding tariff and other entry conditions; transportation facilities and costs; and so on. Such information is particularly important in the wake of the Uruguay Round which has helped to change so many of the conditions and parameters of trading. Second, exporters, particularly those of a small or medium scale, need trade finance of both a pre- and post-shipment nature. Third, exporters can gain from trade fairs, chamber of commerce tours, and networks of trade attaches in order to learn about markets.

A major priority for trade promotion is the diversification of markets. Hitherto, trade for many countries has been locked into traditional patterns determined by post-colonial ties, and these have been reinforced by the self-serving trade-aid programmes of donors. There are obvious impediments to geographical diversification, such as the absence of convenient transport links, and language barriers. While these obstacles have not prevented some of the more dynamic developing country exporters from penetrating new markets, there is still considerable scope for lateral trade, particularly among contiguous developing countries. The forging of stronger regional linkages can help to foster such trade by expanding market spaces, also the subject of a separate chapter.

Aid and trade: the do's and don'ts

If history ended with the collapse of communism and central planning, it is tempting to believe that globalisation is hastening the demise of economics. At the end of the 20th century, the world is returning to a liberalised global economy. But, unlike in the previous century, it is a world of many more independent countries linked by a web of institutional and economic integration. In the 1990s, the degree of harmonization has deepened further: a single global economic system is emerging, in which openness to trade and finance is a principal common feature. Its new custodian is the WTO.[15] It was not always so in the post-War period. As we have seen in this chapter, the process of prising open the world economy has been agonizingly slow, but it culminated in a Uruguay Round whose success was dictated by an increasingly strong economic logic. Looking back, aid can be viewed as a form of foreign exchange compensation for the deficiencies of a highly

---

15 Sachs and Warner, op. cit.

imperfect trade environment, unable to guarantee stability - let alone growth - of export earnings for a large number of developing countries. There was a temptation to blame that system and try to correct for it. However, even in the dark days of growing protectionism, there were countries which, by adopting aggressive outward-looking economic policies, could break into and profit spectacularly from the world trading system. Examples are South Korea, Singapore, Hong Kong, Taiwan, Malaysia and Thailand. In more recent years, more countries in Asia and Latin America have gained from rapid trade expansion.

Entrenched forms of protectionism are now receding. Much more than before, there are opportunities for developing countries to reap the gains from growing trade. There is also a growing number of country experiences teaching the rationale, and displaying the benefits, of more open and more liberal economic approaches, as a basis for responding to the growing trade opportunities.

In this context, the role of aid must change. Now that the new rules of a more equitable world trading environment have been laid, and the route established to further liberalisation, aid must not hinder or distort them as, in some of its guises, it has in the past. Aid must not, in other words, work in opposition to freer trade but in favour of it, if donors are not to be perceived as giving with one hand and taking with the other. As was discussed in Chapter 4, there are two guises of aid which are costly and distortionary.

Food and commodity aid have been of critical importance in times of emergency. But the long-term provision of such assistance as a development resource makes it a substitute for trade and depresses domestic prices and production. Tied aid is a form of export support scheme extended by donors, motivated by export competition among them. It can be applied as a more general support mechanism, or as a specific subsidy, when it can take the form of a 'mixed credit' (in which aid is associated with a trade loan). In whichever form, aid tying is protectionism by rich countries which abrogates the efficiency criteria of freer trade.

Trade stabilisation schemes such as STABEX and the IMF's compensatory facilities, as well as preferential market access agreements, should also be phased out. As discussed above, financing facilities may provide some temporary respite from a fall in export prices but, even if they could be sustained in terms of cost and act as an income guarantee, they would continue to discourage export diversification. Preferential market access schemes have proved to be a lifeline for some small one-commodity exporters, and the rapid elimination of such schemes would have serious repercussions on the livelihoods of exporters. Some means need to be found, therefore, to ease the transition until more economically viable means of economic sustainability are developed.

If there is still a 'right' aid, then it should rather be directed at the efforts of developing countries to reform their own economies in ways that were described in the preceding section. But the 'aid' should be on the basis of trade partnership, rather than traditional donor-recipient relations. Most of the required policy decisions are domestic concerns and they need neither the patronage nor the coercion of richer countries. Much of the capital requirements - for infrastructure, trade finance, and so on - can come from domestic or foreign sources, again with encouragement from a stable and transparent policy environment. Richer trading partners, however, might assist in hosting trade fairs and in providing information on their markets. Multilateral partners, including WTO, should support the wider and more intensive participation of developing countries in the continuing process of trade negotiations.

There are also other trade-related partnership options through which countries can expand their markets, exploit complementarities, while still easing the transition from protected domestic markets to fully open ones. These are some of the opportunities of regionalism, which is discussed in detail in the next chapter.

7 Regionalism: expanding lateral partnership

During their annual summit meeting in 1996 in Lyon, the Group of Seven industrial countries (G-7) devoted a lot of attention to the international development agenda, at the instigation of the host country. Alongside the more familiar reaffirmations of commitment to aid, however, there was a reference in the final communique to the "fundamental responsibility" of the developing countries for promoting their own development, and the statement that "it is in their interest to commit themselves actively to the multilateral system and to promote regional cooperation".

Regionalism is not new to the global agenda, and it is more and more frequently bracketed with globalisation,[1] in recognition of the fact that all forms of political and economic cooperation are receiving a higher priority among countries in all regions and at all levels of development. It is also significant, however, that the G-7 should have chosen to highlight regional cooperation in the context of a statement on the future of aid, acknowledging the growing importance of inter-country partnerships in parallel with more dependent relationships.

Regionalism[2] is in vogue. Although there are a few examples of long-established regional groupings that have become stronger over time - notably the 15-member European Union and the 9-member Association of South-East Asian Nations (Box 8) - many of those established over the last three decades have been short-lived or have retained mainly symbolic political significance. From the late 1980s, however, there has been a growing commitment to regionalism, for a number of reasons.[3]

First, regionalism reflects an increased understanding of the importance of trade and economic openness. Inward-oriented development and self-sufficiency - a concept traditionally espoused by state-controlled economies - are terms disappearing from the development lexicon. Even the five largest continental developing countries - Brazil, China, India, Indonesia and Russia - have recognised the need to widen their markets,[4] and all have

---

1 Already a decade ago, the Japanese economist Saburo Okita declared that 'globalism and regionalism are the two main currents in the world today' Okita (1989).
2 Regionalism (or regionalisation) can be defined as increased cooperation across national borders within a geographically defined area.
3 Bhagwati (1993) refers to the new commitment as the 'second regionalism', a sequel to what he perceived as the 'first regionalism' movement of the 1960s.
4 These 'big five' countries account for half the world's labour force of 3.5 billion, but only 8 percent of world exports.

shown interest in regional cooperation in recent years. At the other end of the scale are the small states - 87 independent countries out of a total of 193 have fewer than 5 million people - for which membership of regional blocs can provide economic openness without exposure to the full blast of global competition.

A second allied reason for regionalism is globalisation. The real world is perceived as increasingly borderless and competitive boundaries between transnational corporations count less than national boundaries. Thus while regionalism receives official recognition in formal inter-governmental agreements, it is also manifested in the rapid expansion of privately-sponsored cross-border economic activity.

Third, in many parts of the world, there is a more conciliatory political climate. As we saw in an earlier chapter, the Cold War kept many neighbours at political odds. In its aftermath, old ideological enemies and political rivals are more willing than before to collaborate. Countries of the Warsaw Pact are now joining the North Atlantic Treaty Organisation (NATO) and seeking membership of the European Union. In West and Central Asia, there is a new Black Sea Economic Cooperation forum, and the Economic Cooperation Organisation expanded its membership in 1992 to include all the newly-independent countries of central Asia. The arrival of full democracy in South Africa also gave a new lease of life to the Southern Africa Development Coordination Conference, renamed a Development Community (SADC) in 1992. There have also been examples of stronger regionalism in East and South Asia.

Fourth, regionalism reflects collective solidarity in trade. When the latest global trade negotiations - the Uruguay Round - began in the 1980s, there were widespread hopes that they would be completed within a few years. In the event, although the Round went further than had originally been anticipated, there was much frustration at its slow pace, prompting many countries to take a 'sub-globalist' route. The creation of MERCOSUR in 1991 by Argentina, Brazil, Paraguay and Uruguay (see Box 9), and the expansion of the US-Canada free trade area to include Mexico in 1993 and form the North American Free-Trade Agreement (NAFTA) were both examples of regionalism as a sub-set of global tariff-cutting. In global negotiations, moreover, regionalism also encourages the formation of collective negotiating positions, likely to have more weight in the overall balance.

This chapter examines regionalism, and the different types of partnership inherent in regional cooperation arrangements, more closely. The purpose is to review the growing importance of such partnerships as frameworks for expanding lateral - as opposed to vertical - forms of development cooperation.

Three types of regionalism

Regional cooperation takes various forms which do not lend themselves easily to categorisation. This section describes three different forms of economic cooperation which cover the most important manifestations of economic cooperation at the regional level. All forms of regionalism assume that some measure of cross-border cooperation is a superior alternative to purely country-based economic systems. The forms differ is several important ways, however, including the extent to which regional arrangements are dependent on government initiative.

Protected regionalism: the preferential trading arrangement. Most regional cooperation arrangements (RCA) focus on trade and they are very numerous. By 1997, the World Trade Organisation (WTO) and its predecessor the General Agreement on Tariffs and Trade (GATT), had been notified over the years of no fewer than 144 regional trade agreements, of which some 80 were still in force (26 are listed in Table 4).

The majority of these agreements fall into the category of preferential trading arrangements, which we have chosen to describe as 'protected' regionalism, for reasons which will become more evident below. PTAs are usually formed among limited numbers of countries with the specific purpose of fostering more trade within the grouping by lowering tariff and other trade barriers, and implementing facilitation measures (streamlining of border administrations, common recording systems and nomenclatures for traded goods, and so on). In a customs union, common external tariffs are raised against goods imported from non-members.

The potential advantages and disadvantages of PTAs for the participating countries can be described in both 'static' and 'dynamic' terms.[5] Static factors are those resulting from once-for-all resource reallocations, while dynamic factors are the continuing and longer-term changes that can be ascribed to regional cooperation. In PTAs, static gains and losses can be determined by the extent to which trade has been 'created', rather than 'diverted' or suppressed, these terms owing their origin to the work of Jacob Viner[6] and other economists writing in the 1950s. The net economic advantages of PTAs can be determined by the extent to which trade creation exceeds trade diversion or suppression.

When a PTA is established, the members agree to lower the tariffs on certain items traded among them, thus reducing their costs. In a customs

---

5 See for example, de la Torre and Kelly (1992).
6 Viner (1950).

union, the members establish common external tariffs on some items traded with non-members; these tariff levels are usually higher than those prevailing before and result in higher costs of those items in the markets of the members. Trade is created when a partner replaces goods produced at a higher cost domestically with goods produced at a lower cost by a partner. Trade is diverted or suppressed, however, when a partner replaces goods produced at a lower cost outside the union with goods produced at a higher cost domestically or by a member country.

Box 8: ASEAN - an enduring Asian partnership

The Association of South-East Asian Nations commemorated its thirtieth anniversary in 1997. Although the celebration was muted by the economic difficulties facing several of its members, the anniversary was a significant one because ASEAN has demonstrated continuity and has grown, albeit unsteadily, in depth and breadth since its inception.

Politics and security considerations first brought the five founding members of ASEAN together - Indonesia, Malaysia, Philippines, Singapore and Thailand - with the signing of the Bangkok Agreement in 1967, during the war in Indochina. It was initially an anti-communist alliance and there is much significance in the fact that, following the adherence of Brunei in 1984, the seventh member of ASEAN was Vietnam in 1995. Laos and Myanmar joined in 1997 and Cambodia in 1999. Economically as well as politically the expansion of the membership has greatly altered the complexion of the grouping. It now comprises at least three income tiers (with Brunei and Singapore at the high end, Cambodia, Laos, Myanmar and Vietnam at the low end and the others in the middle) and different economic systems, mixing very open economies with enclosed transitional ones.

Because of the complex politics of the region, ASEAN has evolved cautiously for most of its history. The first and second summits of heads of government did not take place until 1976 and 1977, the latter as a commemoration of the first 10 years. Since 1995, there have been formal or informal summits every year. There is also an elaborate administrative and committee structure which ensures frequent contacts among ASEAN representatives, through more than 300 meetings per year. The ASEAN Ministerial Meeting (AMM), comprising the Foreign Ministers, is responsible for strategic policy and coordination and meets annually. Economic cooperation is the responsibility of the ASEAN Economic Ministers, also meeting annually. Both these committees report to the ASEAN Summits. The most active policy body is the ASEAN Standing Committee which meets more frequently and reports to the AMM. There are also many committees and forums in sectoral, technical and cultural areas coordinated in each member country by national secretariats in Foreign

Ministries. For the cohesion of the grouping, however, one of the most important developments in recent years has been the upgrading of the status of the ASEAN secretariat in Jakarta. In 1992, the position of Secretary General was elevated to ministerial status and the secretariat restructured and expanded.

Underlying the elaborate political and administrative structure of ASEAN, however, is a dynamic process of economic interchange, which predated the formation of the grouping. The people of the original ASEAN countries have been collaborating actively in economic terms for many years, the main common element being the entrepreneurial Chinese diaspora, who are prominent in the private manufacturing and service sectors. ASEAN's first objective - "to accelerate the economic growth" of the region - is largely being accomplished outside the official purview of the grouping. However, the process of economic integration is being assisted by the lowering of trade barriers. This was a very gradual and hesitant process during the first two decades of ASEAN's existence and had little impact on trade patterns in the region (ASEAN accounts for only 22 per cent of trade among the members). But in 1993, the members agreed to establish an ASEAN Free Trade Area, phasing out tariff and non-tariff barriers by the year 2003 (for the new members, it will be 2008). For a market of 470 million people - substantially larger than either the European Union or the US - this facilitation process will be an important stimulus for both trade and investment within and into the region.

In terms of customs union theory, the benefits of ASEAN are clearly more dynamic than static. Some of these benefits were not anticipated, but they serve to underline the importance of regional partnership. Expansion of the membership has now brought into the grouping several members with very different economic records, but there could be important 'dynamic' benefits in terms of encouraging the new members to adopt more liberal and outward-looking economic policies in order to gain maximum benefit from their inclusion in a dynamic and progressive economic space. In this regard, ASEAN membership is likely to have an impact at least equal to the programs of development assistance being provided to the transitional countries individually. Practice is always easier to emulate from next door.

ASEAN has also begun to promote the concept of open regionalism. In 1994, the grouping established the ASEAN Regional Forum which brings together the member countries with ten dialogue partners (US, Canada, Japan, European Union, Russia, China, India, Korea, Australia and New Zealand). The Forum is designed to promote dialogue on preventive diplomacy and confidence-building in the region. The EU is ASEAN's oldest dialogue partner and there have been attempts in recent years to builder closer ties with Europe. The first formal meeting of the Asia-Europe Meeting was in early 1997.

It is rational for countries to enter into trade agreements when the lowest cost producers of traded goods are members of the grouping. In practice, this is rarely the case and adherents to PTAs are often faced with higher costs of essential items. An example is provided by Britain, when it joined the European Community in 1973. Britain had been a large importer of food from low-cost producers in Australia and New Zealand and was obliged to phase in larger tariffs on food from these sources, switching to higher cost producers in Europe. The EC led directly to a significant diversion of trade and a substantial rise in food prices in Britain.

There are other potential 'dynamic' gains from trade within PTAs, however. To the extent that trade is increased among neighbours, transport costs are lowered. And regional agreements usually go beyond tariff reduction to facilitate the freer movement of goods among members. There are also advantages in terms of rent gains for exporters who can sell their products inside the union at higher prices, equivalent to the world price plus the common external tariff. Regional trading blocs have been described as 'natural' partnerships, since neighbours could be expected to trade disproportionately with each other even in the absence of formal arrangements.[7]

The gains from operating within a larger protected market has been called the 'internationalisation of protection'. From the 1950s, the idea has been prevalent of using trade cooperation to allow infant industries in member countries to benefit from larger markets protected from competition from more efficient lower-cost producers outside. On the assumption that this protectionism is gradually diminished over time, these economy of scale arguments are among other 'dynamic' advantages attributed to PTAs. Other advantages may be derived from the joint development of infrastructure (regional transportation and communication networks) as well as pooled research efforts.

In practice, the determination of gains and losses in PTAs is highly complex. For example, there are enormous ambiguities associated with 'rules of origin'. In today's globalised economy, more and more manufactured goods are produced with raw materials and parts from several different countries. Where these parts originate outside a regional grouping, they may attract tariffs - or they may not if they benefit from foreign investment incentives. Tariff-free or otherwise, these externally-sourced materials and parts make the final traded product partially 'foreign' to the trade grouping. Should such products benefit from the lower tariff privileges of the PTA: wholly, partially or not at all? These questions have

---

[7] Paul Krugman, 'Regionalism versus multilateralism: analytical notes', in de Melo and Panagariya, op. cit.

to be answered by carefully negotiated rules of origin. Other consequences of PTAs which have to be weighed in the cost-benefit balance are losses of tariff revenues, which can be substantial for some countries. For example Mexico, which has traditionally maintained rather high tariff levels, will lose considerable income from this source through membership of NAFTA, although Mexican producers and consumers will benefit from less costly American and Canadian goods.

With the conclusion of the Uruguay Round and the replacement of the GATT with the World Trade Organisation (WTO) in 1995, more virtue has been made of multilateralism and the Viner principles. For global trade liberalisation, tariffs cut in favour of one country, must be cut for all - the Most Favoured Nation principle. PTAs, and especially customs unions, abrogate these rules. Yet when the rules of trade were written into the GATT in 1947, they included Article XXIV which permits the formation of PTAs and customs unions as long as they eventually lead to the complete elimination of discriminatory tariffs.

For the free-traders, Article XXIV is seen as an aberration. In practice, PTAs have been quick to raise trade barriers to countries outside a grouping, and slow to phase in trade liberalisation. There is a lively debate among economists about whether regionalism should be considered as an alternative to, or as a precursor of, multilaterism: a stumbling block or a building block.

The verdict is bound to be ambiguous. In some cases of protected regionalism, such as the European Union, the path of economic and political integration has clearly taken precedence over multilateralism, and the two processes are increasingly in conflict. The EU's elaborate system of agricultural protectionism, designed to support the incomes of Europe's high-cost farmers, proved to be a major stumbling block in the finalisation of the Uruguay Round of global trade negotiations. But the existence of the WTO, its much larger membership (than the GATT) and its rules of procedure and dispute mechanisms is putting considerable pressure on Europe to unravel its Common Agricultural Policy. The Caribbean Community (CARICOM) and the Central American Common Market (CACM), among other groupings, have also made significant progress in recent years towards lower common external tariffs.

Within regional blocs, this trend towards internal trade liberalisation first and gradual external liberalisation later, and the building of closer links between different trading arrangements, particularly within the same continents, suggest that the fashionable process of protected regionalism through PTAs can contribute to, rather than detract from, a gradual global liberalisation. There are beneficial dynamic processes of lateral cooperation, in other words, that reach beyond the boundaries of the existing groupings.

But protected regionalism is nonetheless discriminatory. While the formation and consolidation of PTAs are an embodiment of the partnership principle in development, there are two other kinds of 'open' cooperation - one sponsored by governments and the other not - which deserve increasing attention, and which have important implications for the future of development assistance.

> **Box 9: MERCOSUR - the fastest emerging regional cooperation arrangement**
>
> The Common Market of the South (MERCOSUR) brings together Argentina, Brazil, Paraguay and Uruguay and was created by the Asuncion Treaty of March 1991. It was formed at a time when the Latin American countries were frustrated at the slow pace of multilateral trade negotiations, yet saw regional integration as an important step towards economic openness and trade promotion.
>
> The pace of progress has been impressive. The first three years were a period of transition but by the end of 1994, the member countries had eliminated tariffs on 90% of regional trade. During that period, the value of trade among the four countries was estimated to have grown from less than $3 billion to $12 billion per year. Intra-MERCOSUR trade in 1996 accounted for 22% of total exports, compared with less than 10% in 1990. The grouping is also the only major customs union outside Europe. It has established a common external tariff, covering all about 85% of imports from outside the region, which came into force at the beginning of 1995. The tariff schedule will be fully harmonised over the next ten years. The MERCOSUR countries have a combined population of over 200 million, a total GDP of over $800 billion and trade (in either direction) of over $70 billion per year. The grouping is thus an economic force of some consequence. In addition to creating a substantial amount of additional intra-regional trade, the grouping has also been a spur to incoming foreign investment, as companies have sought to benefit from a large and dynamic market.
>
> The highest authority of MERCOSUR is the Common Market Council, comprising the Ministers of Foreign Affairs and Ministers of Finance. In 1996, the grouping took the important step of establishing a secretariat in Montevideo, and a development bank to finance integration-related investment projects. Also in 1996, MERCOSUR signed free trade agreements with its two associate members, Chile and Bolivia, and is negotiating with Latin America's other important trade association, the Andean Group, about further expansion. An eventual merger of the two blocs could lead towards an FTA in the whole sub-continent. There is also a plan for a Free Trade Area of the Americas which would link all 34 countries of the continent. Bilateral trade liberation deals are being negotiated between Canada and Chile, and between Mexico and several Latin and Central American countries. A continuing impediment to further trade liberalisation is the denial of 'fast-track' negotiating authority to the US Government. However, there is no doubt that in the Americas, regional trade agreements are proving in the 1990s to be stepping stones towards continent-wide liberalisation.

Open regionalism: the APEC example. Regional cooperation which promotes the benefits of closer regional ties, but without selective or discriminatory trade measures, is a broad definition of open regionalism. But open regionalism - as well as many examples of the protected variety - also goes beyond trade to embrace other forms of cooperation. The Asia Pacific Economic Cooperation (APEC) forum is the best current example, which could prove to be a model for regionalism elsewhere.

APEC was an initiative promoted by Australia in 1989, partly inspired by the experience of the quasi-governmental Pacific Economic Cooperation Council (PECC). APEC embodies the vision of a dynamic 'Pacific rim' emerging in the next century and constituting the major global economic dynamo. With a membership of 21 countries[8] - spanning rich and poor and including the three largest economies - APEC accounts for 55% of total world output and almost half of world trade. It is not so much a region as a hemisphere. At its inception, the grouping was considered rather large and amorphous and its impact was uncertain. However, just as the US conversion to regionalism gave impetus to NAFTA, its interest in hosting the first informal summit (of 'economic leaders') in Seattle, Washington in 1993, vested APEC with increasing importance. At subsequent annual summits, significant progress has been made in forging the basic principles of open regionalism.

Seattle laid down some principles of partnership, which were to be based in large part on harnessing private enterprise in order to raise the general level of prosperity throughout the region. Exhortation led to a 'declaration of common resolve' the following year in Bogor, Indonesia in which the leaders made a commitment to achieve 'free and open trade and investment' in the region by the industrialised members by the year 2010, and by 2020 for the rest. The important feature of APEC trade liberalisation, however, is that it aims specifically to reduce protectionism in the region and between the region and other countries and groupings. It is thus a large interest group of one-way liberalisers, contributing directly to freer trade and investment flows globally.

The Osaka Action Agenda, agreed in 1995, was a blueprint for the process of trade and investment liberalisation, and began to develop the principles of broader 'economic and technical cooperation'. The summit in Manila in 1996 determined further that cooperation was to be concentrated on six themes: developing human capital, fostering efficient capital

---

8 Australia, Brunei, Canada, Chile, China, Hong Kong (sic), Indonesia, Japan, South Korea, Malaysia, Mexico, New Zealand, Papua New Guinea, Philippines, Singapore, Chinese Taipei, Thailand, USA and, since the Vancouver summit in 1997, Peru, Russia and Vietnam. APEC has now placed a 10-year moratorium on new members.

markets, strengthening economic infrastructure, harnessing technologies, promoting environmentally sustainable growth and encouraging small and medium enterprises.

The added dimension of economic and technical cooperation is significant for a number of reasons. First it is set in the context of a substantial and globally representative grouping of countries comprising a range of development levels and resource endowments. Second, development cooperation is seen as an adjunct to a process of market and trade liberalisation, which is recognised as the appropriate context for promoting regional prosperity. Third, it adheres to the principle that countries should contribute human, technical and financial resources voluntarily to cooperative ventures, from which all partners would derive mutual benefits.

APEC development cooperation requires further definition and refinement. However, it has been the subject of growing interest and study,[9] and it is of interest to observe that these studies have generally not construed APEC development cooperation as a North-South transfer of incomes - which would be in keeping with traditional aid concepts - but focus more on trade, investment and other facilitation issues based on partnerships.

Micro-regionalism. A third form of regionalism is gaining increasing prominence. It involves activities within contiguous economic and environmental spaces encompassing parts of national territories: hence the term 'micro-regionalism'. In the case of so-called 'growth triangles', these initiatives are largely market driven. Where there are complex political dimensions, official sponsorship helps to encourage an enabling climate for private interests. And where there are issues of joint resource management, official mechanisms can help to assure that costs and benefits are more equitably shared.

A growing number of examples of these transboundary activities are driven by private market interests, in the absence of formal inter-governmental mechanisms, and often with limited official support. Again, some of the more vibrant examples of growth triangles are to be found in East and Southeast Asia. One example is the zone comprising Singapore, the Malaysian state of Johore and Indonesia's Riau province and island of Batam. Singapore and Malaysian investors responded to the invitation to set up labour-intensive industrial activities on the island of Batam in the late 1980s. There are also privately-financed activities in the triangle to develop infrastructure and tourism. Governments have acted as faciliators of these

---

9   An important example is Andrew Elek (1997).

developments, but for the most part the resulting investments have been market-driven. Other examples in the region are provided by the Special Economic Zones of Guangdong and Fujian provinces of southern China, designed to attract private capital from Hong Kong. China's relations - or lack of them - with Taiwan have also acted as a spur to triangular informal regionalism. Hong Kong has played the role of entrepôt for Taiwanese trade and investment flows to the mainland.

There are also important instances in which market regionalism can be fostered under government auspices, sometimes with the assistance of external sponsorship. In East Asia, where politics has long proved an impediment to closer cooperation, a potentially important growth triangle is being encouraged around the Tumen river, which provides a natural border between China, Russia and North Korea. The Tumen River Area Development Programme also comprises South Korea and Mongolia and - with UN assistance - seeks to create an economic space in a relatively backward area with potentially important strategic significance. The programme has encouraged the establishment of a governing council of the five participating countries - the only such development body in which North and South Korea regularly sit down together - which identifies collaborative initiatives to facilitate cross-border movements of people and resources and to lay the ground for infrastructure development. Under the auspices of the programme, for example, North Korea is creating its first free export zone. By encouraging cooperation and building confidence in the zone, the programme aims to create the foundations on which private capital will subsequently build.

A different rationale for official sponsorship of micro-regionalism is in the joint management of natural resources. When several countries share the resources of an eco-system, it is in their interests to collaborate, so as to derive maximum mutual benefit. Major river basins provide some of the best examples, in which the riverine countries have successfully sought to establish cooperative arrangements: the Danube in Europe, the Nile in Africa and the Mekong in Asia. There are also new regional agreements around inland seas such as the Caspian and the Black Sea, in both of which water-borne pollution emanating from sources in different countries threatens to wipe out the remaining marine life.

These three examples of micro-regionalism are distinguishable by the degree to which governments - meaning national or sub-national administrations - are involved. In market driven growth triangles, governments usually play a minor role, while maintaining a regulatory presence (unless the activity is smuggling). In more complex political contexts, some inter-governmental mechanisms may be required to create a more favourable climate for market regionalism. In the case of joint resource management, the public presence is required on a more permanent basis to provide mechanisms that arbitrate among the respective interests of consumers and producers in individual countries.

Regionalism as development cooperation

This brief review of regionalism can help to demonstrate that the new wave of cooperation among clusters of countries and parts of countries could replace, not just the interest in, but also the need for, traditional forms of development cooperation.

Regionalism is an important manifestation of greater economic openness being witnessed on a global scale. Through regionalism, markets are broadened, albeit sometimes within protected boundaries. However, regionalism in the context of a WTO-led process of global trade liberalisation is ultimately contributory rather than inimical to freer trade. By bringing more countries into the fold of liberal and outward-looking economics, moreover, regionalism also contributes to continuing reform, especially in countries in a transitional phase away from central planning and management. (Policy-makers are just as likely to heed the example of their neighbours as take advice from experts based in Washington.) Hence the process is helping to change the axes of development from North-and-South to South-and-South. In the case of APEC, NAFTA and other groupings, there are no such axes at all, but emerging webs of equitable partnership.

This chapter has dwelt a lot on trade, which provides the driving force for most regional initiatives. Many, however, incorporate other dimensions of cooperation. In ASEAN, for example, there are more than twelve different sets of regular ministerial meetings on different themes and sectors, and a total of 300 meetings each year. Regional bodies also undertake important security and peace-keeping initiatives. A good example is provided by the Economic Community of West African States (ECOWAS), which has helped to broker peace agreements in both Liberia and Sierra Leone.

Regionalism in all its manifestations can give voice and respect to individual countries, expand trade, promote openness and reform, and encourage exchange of technical experience. All of these goals have been shown by experience to be consistent with development progress. The Declaration of Santiago signed by 34 heads of state at the conclusion of the Summit of the Americas in April 1998 stated: "We believe that economic integration, investment and free trade are key factors for raising standards of living, improving working conditions and better protecting the environment....we are confident that the Free Trade Area of the Americas will enhance the well-being of our peoples." Traditional North-to-South development assistance has similar objectives, but regional development cooperation is based on more equitable partnerships, without conditionality and dependence.

Table 4: Active regional groupings

Organisation	Member States	Focus Area	Population (1995 mn)	GDP (1995, $ bn)
AFRICA				
CEAO	*Communauté Economique de l'Afrique de l'Ouest*	Economic Cooperation	50.5	22.2
	Benin, Burkina Faso, Cote d'Ivoire, Mali, Mauritania, Senegal			
COMESA	*Common Market of Eastern and Southern Africa*	Common Market	253.9	57.7
	Angola, Burundi, Comoros, Congo, Eritrea, Ethiopia, Kenya, Lesotho, Madagascar, Malawi, Mauritius, Mozambique, Namibia, Rwanda, Sudan, Swaziland, Tanzania, Uganda, Zambia, Zimbabwe.			
ECOWAS	*Economic Community of West African States*	Economic Cooperation	82.9	29.4
	Benin, Burkina Faso, Côte d'Ivoire, Gambia, Ghana, Guinea, Liberia, Mali, Mauritania, Niger, Togo			
IOC	*Indian Ocean Commission*	Regional Integration	73.4	1,543.4
	Comoros, France, Madagascar, Mauritius, Seychelles			
MRU	*Mano River Union*	Customs Union	13.5	4.5
	Guinea, Liberia, Sierra Leone			
PTA	*Preferential Trade Area for Eastern and Southern Africa*	Preferential Trade Agreement (PTA)	242.6	49.8
	Angola, Burundi, Comoros, Djibouti, Ethiopia, Kenya, Lesotho, Malawi, Mauritius, Mozambique, Rwanda, Somalia, Sudan, Swaziland, Tanzania, Uganda, Zambia, Zimbabwe			
SACU	*Southern African Custom Union*	Customs Union	45.8	142.4
	Botswana, Lesotho, South Africa, Swaziland			
SADC	*Southern African Development Community*	Common Market	134.8	170.3
	Angola, Botswana, Lesotho, Malawi, Mauritius, Mozambique, Namibia, South Africa, Swaziland, Tanzania, Zambia, Zimbabwe.			

108 *Beyond Aid: From Patronage to Partnership*

Organisation	Member States	Focus Area	Population (1995 mn)	GDP (1995, $ bn)
UDEAC	*Union Douanière et Economique de l'Afrique Centrale* Cameroon, Central African Republic, Chad, Congo, Equatorial Guinea, Gabon	Customs Union	27.1	17.2

ARAB STATES

Organisation	Member States	Focus Area	Population (1995 mn)	GDP (1995, $ bn)
GCC	*Gulf Cooperation Council* Bahrain, Kuwait, Oman, Qatar, Saudi Arabia, United Arab Emirates	Economic Cooperation	26.5	216.0
OAPEC	*Organisation of Arab Petroleum Exporting Countries* Algeria, Bahrain, Egypt, Iraq, Kuwait, Libya, Qatar, Saudi Arabia, Syrian Arab Republic, Tunisia, United Arab Emirates	Economic Cooperation	158.7	327.5
OPEC	*The Organisation of the Petroleum Exporting Countries* Algeria, Indonesia, Iran, Iraq, Kuwait, Libya, Nigeria, Qatar, Saudi Arabia, United Arab Emirates, Venezuela. (Seat of Secretariat is in Austria)	Economic Cooperation	467.5	553.9

ASIA

Organisation	Member States	Focus Area	Population (1995 mn)	GDP (1995, $ bn)
ANZCERTA	*Australia-New Zealand Closer Economic Relations* Australia, New Zealand	PTA	21.7	405.9
APEC	*Asia-Pacific Economic Cooperation* Australia, Brunei, Canada, China, Hong Kong, Indonesia, Japan, Korea, Malaysia, Mexico, New Zealand, Papua New Guinea, Philippines, Singapore, Thailand, United States	Economic Cooperation	2,130.5	15,200.4
ASEAN	*The Association of Southeast Asian Nations* Brunei, Indonesia, Lao PDR, Malaysia, Myanmar, Philippines, Singapore, Thailand, Vietnam	Economic Cooperation	467.0	635.4
ECO	*Economic Cooperation Organisation* Afghanistan, Azerbaijan, Iran, Kazakstan, Kyrgyzstan, Pakistan, Tajikistan, Turkey, Turkmenistan, Uzbekistan	Economic Cooperation	340.3	280.8
SAARC	*South Asia Association for Regional Cooperation* Bangladesh, Bhutan, India, Maldives, Nepal, Pakistan, Sri Lanka	Economic Cooperation	1,219.5	431.6

Organisation	Member States	Focus Area	Population (1995 mn)	GDP (1995, $ bn)
EUROPE				
BENELUX	*Belgium-Netherlands-Luxembourg Economic Union* Belgium, Netherlands, Luxembourg	Economic Cooperation	26.0	681.5
EFTA	*European Free Trade Association* Iceland, Liechtenstein, Norway, Switzerland	PTA	11.7	453.5
EU	*European Union* Austria, Belgium, Denmark, Finland, France, Germany, Greece, Ireland, Italy, Luxembourg, Netherlands, Portugal, Spain, Sweden, United Kingdom	Regional Integration	372.2	8,398.2
LATIN AMERICA AND CARIBBEAN				
ANDEAN Group	*ANDEAN Group (Cartagena Agreement)* Bolivia, Colombia, Ecuador, Venezuela	Regional Integration	77.4	175.2
CARICOM	*The Caribbean Community and Common Market* Antigua and Barbuda, Bahamas, Barbados, Belize, Dominica, Grenada, Guyana, Jamaica, St. Kitts, St. Lucia, St. Vincent, Suriname, Trinidad and Tobago	Common Market	6.4	18.0
LAFTA/ LAIA	*Latin American Integration Association* Argentina, Bolivia, Brazil, Chile, Colombia, Ecuador, Mexico, Paraguay, Peru, Uruguay, Venezuela	PTA	409.1	1,544.7
MERCOSUR	*The Common Market of the South* Argentina, Brazil, Paraguay, Uruguay	Common Market	201.9	994.7
SELA	*The Latin American Economic System* Argentina, Barbados, Belize, Bolivia, Brazil, Chile, Colombia, Costa Rica, Cuba, Dominican Republic, Ecuador, El Salvador, Grenada, Guatemala, Guyana, Haiti, Honduras, Jamaica, Mexico, Nicaragua, Panama, Paraguay, Peru, Suriname, Trinidad and Tobago, Uruguay, Venezuela	Economic Cooperation	473.4	1,617.7
NORTH AMERICA				
NAFTA	*North America Free Trade Agreement* Canada, Mexico, United States	PTA	384.6	7,771.0

8 The information revolution

The global economy is undergoing two fundamental transformations. The first - the subject of earlier chapters - is the liberalisation and spread of trade and investment opportunities. The second is the subject of the present chapter: the information and communications 'revolution'.

These transformations - the basis of what is popularly referred to as 'globalisation' - will have far-reaching consequences for international economic relations, as well as important ramifications within countries. Like the spread of economic openness, the consequences of the information revolution could pervade all countries and their economies, making them 'informational' and 'communicative'. Connection could help to overcome isolation, and within and between countries, people and their activities could become increasingly enmeshed through exchange.

Both processes can be advanced by the deliberate policies of governments. Trade liberalisation and economic reform require re-orientations of strategy, appropriate policies, and adjustment to the unfamiliar changes that result. Embracing the information technology revolution also demands commitments to liberalise, but in ways which go well beyond the economic. The information revolution also needs investments in infrastructure, based on assumptions of returns which are much less tangible, and ultimately threatening to existing hierarchies and cultures.

For many countries, the information revolution is not inevitable. But the potential development dividends are considerable, as this chapter attempts to demonstrate. Just as trade and investment could provide financial, capital and technological resources essential to development, the information revolution could facilitate the transfer of ideas, expertise and specialised knowledge for which aid - in the form of technical cooperation - has hitherto been a principal purveyor. The information revolution could provide an extraordinary means of empowerment and greatly enhance the opportunities for partnership at every level.

Three technological 'revolutions'

The process of material and cultural change which we have come to call development has never been a smooth upward progression. For many centuries before the western Renaissance, China was indisputably the most advanced culture, and then languished in stagnant isolation for several centuries. The Spanish Empire was a predominant world power in the 16th and 17th centuries, but then became a relative laggard as the rest of Europe advanced.

From the latter part of the eighteenth century, the first of three technological transformations began in northern Europe and it was to give an irreversible impulse to the process of change. This was the first 'industrial revolution' and it was characterised by the appearance of a cluster of unprecedented technological innovations which wrought major improvements in production and distribution processes and facilitated the rapid accumulation of wealth. The icon of this first revolution was the steam engine. Innovation centred on the harnessing of steam-power for the enhanced production of textiles, other machinery, and for transportation. In metallurgy, there were advances in smelting techniques leading to the production of wrought iron.

The second industrial revolution occurred about a century later. It was also partially energy based. Steam was much further developed for rail and maritime transport. But now oil began to be used to drive internal combustion engines, transforming the means of land transportation. A new and catalytic factor in the revolution was the invention and expanding use of electric power. There were also important innovations in the area of chemicals and steel making. In anticipation of the third revolution, the telegraph and telephone were invented.

What helped to make these two phases of innovation revolutionary was what might be termed a virtuous circularity of application. For example in the first revolution, steam power begat the iron for the machines that ran on steam. In the second, fast and efficient transportation spread through railways and the steamship, bringing raw materials closer for the cheaper production of steel for rails. The telegraph grew into communication systems when linked to electricity. Indeed, in many ways, electricity was central to the second revolution and helped to precipitate changes in a variety of other fields. One of its most important attributes was its ubiquity, helping to spread factories away from primary fuel sources.

Another common feature of these revolutionary phases of change was the fact that they were centred on protestant Europe, and latterly America. This geographical concentration was significant for two reasons. In the first place, the physical proximity of the innovators and the frequency of their contacts facilitated the process of combining different inventions for useful purposes. Secondly, although northern Europe was not a unique hotbed of inventiveness, the prevailing (Weberian) socio-economic conditions were amenable to dynamic change and they favoured opportunistic experimentation. Many of the scientific concepts on which the inventions were based, were already known. But it was entrepreneurship in an open environment which perceived the opportunities for their self-sustaining commercial application.

Of course, the diffusion of these inventions was not immediate. The early material advantages of the revolutions were arrogated to the few rather than to the many, and the industrial advances which these revolutions induced were accompanied by a parallel process of urban immiserization. But while the processes of diffusion were skewed by social hierarchies, and took time to have their effect, they were ultimately the cause of irreversible material gains, at least within the northern countries.

Beyond Europe and North America, there was also a steady process of outward diffusion, but it was allied to imperial and great power ambition. Indeed, the products of these revolutions were critical to the imperial process. Economically, the revolutions helped to build up and then enforce the competitive advantages of the originating countries. These economic advantages then underscored political domination.

Now, another hundred years along, we are experiencing the third, and current, technological revolution.[1] In some important respects it has characteristics in common with the previous two, but there are also some significant differences. Like the previous two, this third revolution was preceded by inventions which were made several decades before, and which came later to be combined productively in a concentrated period of innovation. Commercial opportunism has played an important part in the diffusion process, but the nature of the revolution and its potential openness and accessibility - and the fact that the world is fully conscious of this revolution as it unfolds - hold the promise of enabling its benefits to be spread with unprecedented speed and reach.

The third technology revolution

This third information and communications technology (ICT) revolution has seen three sets of innovatory processes coming together.

---

[1] Others, including Alvin Toffler ("The Third Wave") have given even greater significance to the third revolution, citing the first as the agricultural revolution sparked by the advent of the plough many centuries ago, and the second as an extended industrial revolution spanning the eighteenth and nineteenth centuries.

Computers. The first is the emergence of the computer, which owes its origins to significant advances in micro-electronics and miniaturisation dating from the 1940s. Computers were a product of World War II. A machine sometimes described as the first computer - the Electronic Numerical Integrator and Calculator (ENIAC) - would have been hard to recognise today. Built in Philadelphia in 1946 it weighed 30 tons and was the size of a large hall. The advent of the personal computer would not have been anticipated from these cumbersome beginnings. In an oft-quoted statement, the founder of IBM, Thomas Watson, is alleged to have predicted in 1943 that the total world market for computers would be 5. On the scale of the ENIAC, that might have seemed a reasonable assumption!

At about the same time, however, in a different part of the USA, the transistor was invented and it began to make possible the large scale processing of data in the form of electrical impulses. A few years later, silicon came to be used as a substance to embed thousands of transistors together onto a miniature platform with the power to process huge quantities of digitised (electric impulse) data. The silicon chip was born and with it, the new icon for the new age. Chip production technologies improved dramatically in the 1960s and by the early 1970s their costs were falling sharply while capacity grew rapidly. In 1971, a chip already comprised some 2,300 transistor circuits. Twenty years later, it could pack together 35 million. For about three decades, the capacity of chips in terms of numbers of circuits has doubled every 18 to 24 months - a rhythm sometimes referred to as 'Moore's Law', after one of the founders of the Intel Corporation, the world's largest manufacturer of chips.

These extraordinary advances led to the miniaturisation of computers and by the 1980s, the personal computer was becoming a household good, gaining in power and convenience, falling in price, and soon commanding a mass market. This was the first pillar of the new information revolution.

Telecommunications. The second pillar was provided by related advances in telecommunications. The inventor Alexander Graham Bell made the first working telephone in 1876 and, unlike so many earlier inventions, it was immediately commercialised. He patented the telephone on the same day and the following year the first telephone company was set up. But no one could have foreseen the extraordinary applications of telecommunications a whole century later. This part of the revolution has occurred only within the last twenty years and can be characterised by three types of development.

In the first place, there has been a huge increase in telephone 'carrying capacity'. Many new lines continue to be laid all over the world, and increasingly these lines use fibre-optic cable with much larger capacity. In addition to these lines, there have been rapid increases in transmission by satellite. Measured in 'voice paths', transatlantic capacity has increased from 100,000 in 1986 to over 2,000,000 (one third by satellite) today. Across the Pacific, the growth is from 40,000 to 1,000,000 (one quarter by satellite).[2]

Secondly, there have been technological advances in telephony itself. The two most significant developments are the advent of the mobile (wireless) telephone and the use of satellites. The mobile telephone only appeared commercially in the early 1980s and already it accounts for one in seven telephone subscribers (although most have not switched systems, only added mobile to fixed). Mobile phones already use satellites, particularly for long distance calls, but developments expected at the turn of the century will vastly contribute to an enhancement of mobile systems. Several commercial consortia are putting, or planning to put, into orbit an array of 'low earth orbit' satellites which will enable a small hand-held device to communicate from any point to any other point in the entire world.[3]

A third development is commercial competition and the fall in the costs of telecommunications, and it follows directly from the other two. The huge increase in line and satellite infrastructure world wide has grown much faster than demand and created substantial over-capacity. This factor, and the falling costs of creating additional capacity, is one reason why the prices of telecommunications have begun to fall markedly in many countries. They have fallen furthest where countries have liberalised their telecommunications markets and where suppliers of different services - using the expanded range of technological means - are in direct competition. However, prices have not fallen much, if at all, in countries which have continued to maintain state monopolies for telecommunications, which are earning artificially high rents, yet failing to satisfy substantial latent demand. A very telling set of statistics from the International Telecommunication Union gives an interesting measure of frustrated demand. Out of an estimated 1,466 million (1.5 bn.) households globally in

---

2 Cairncross (1997),Table 2-1.
3 These new systems are officially known as Global Mobile Personal Communications by Satellite (GMPCS). The first limited system, Orbcomm, is already operational and uses 28 satellites. Two more are being built by the GlobalStar (48 satellites) and Iridium (66 satellites) consortia, both of which hope to have their systems operating in 1998 or 1999. A fourth consortium, Teledesic, will be the most comprehensive, able to carry a full range of data, voice, video and other communications. It will use 840 satellites, but will not be available until 2002. There are also two other consortia, ICO and Odyssey, with 10 and 12 'medium earth orbit' satellites which will also have systems to support mobile telephony within a few years. (Sources: The International Telecommunication Union, and U.S. News and World Report).

1996, 504 million (34%) have telephone service, while 286 million (20%) do not have it but could afford it , and the remaining 676 million (46%) neither have service nor can afford it. Monopolisation is one of the policy obstacles to the faster spread of the information revolution and will be revisited below.

Television. The third pillar of the information revolution is the spread of television as a medium. TV is certainly nothing new, since it was invented well before the Second World War. But until recent years, television was a local medium, like the press. Now two developments are vesting TV with a truly global reach: one is the use of satellite broadcasting, which may be said to have begun in 1962 with the launch of the first private communications satellite (Telstar), and the other is the growing use of cable connections to TV sets. Together, these technological developments are providing television audiences in a growing number of countries with a much wider choice of programmes to view, where they are prepared to pay a higher price.

As with the earlier revolutions, this three-pronged one has sprung from groups of inventors in close physical proximity, enabling rapid interaction. Silicon valley in California and Route 128 in the Boston area were indisputably the two principal founts of creativity, particularly in the 1970s. They were each adjacent to major centres of research (Stanford-Berkeley on one hand, and the Ivy League cluster of Boston Universities on the other) and they created around themselves dynamic entrepreneurial environments.

The close connections among the three components of the revolution are also characteristic. The miniaturization of electronics which facilitated the development of the personal computer has led to important technological breakthroughs in telecommunications and television. Perhaps the most important binder of technologies, however, has been digitisation. The conversion of sound, pictures and other 'analogue' mediums into a series of discrete units which can be represented by binary digits (0 and 1) and processed and transmitted through electrical impulses has given computing, telecommunications and television a common language, thus permitting the different systems to be easily combined.

The most important of these combined applications is the Internet (see Box 10) which combines computing and telecommunications in powerful ways. The uniqueness of the Internet is that it has become the fastest means of diffusing the information revolution, while itself being part of the revolution. And this time, the revolution is not owned, and it has not been appropriated, by rich and powerful interests. The Internet is neither in the public nor the private domain; it is in both, and yet it need not be confined to either. It promises to be more accessible than any revolutionary change has ever been before. As a medium it can transmit the fruits of innovation everywhere simultaneously; and it can also encourage innovation wherever it penetrates; and all innovations are everywhere visible. The sorcerer can step back gleefully and allow the apprentice a free reign.

Box 10: Origins of the Internet

The linking of computers - the essence of networking and the Internet - may be traced back about 20 years to a defence application in the US. It emerged very slowly, in stages, assisted by a series of key innovations.

In the late 1960s, researchers at the Advanced Research Projects Agency (ARPA), which had been created by the US Department of Defense to strengthen national security through sponsorship of research, developed the prototype of a network to link computers. In 1969, the first message was sent between two US universities. The original motivation of the 'Arpanet' was to decrease the vulnerability of information concentrated in particular sites by allowing it to be shared and dispersed among several computers. The Arpanet was open to military sites as well as selected universities in the US. In 1973, the first international connections were made (to UK and Norway) but by the mid-1970s it still had a limited number of participants, mainly because of different operating standards, or 'protocols', among the linked computers. There were fewer than 100 Internet 'hosts' (connected computers) in 1975.

Then in 1983, a Transmission Control Protocol/Internet Protocol (TCP/IP) - first identified in 1974 - was introduced to permit all computers, whether portable or mainframe, and whatever their make or internal operating system, to 'speak to each other'. Also during the 1980s, the market for personal computers began to grow rapidly, and another important invention ('ethernet') allowed them to be linked together in 'local area networks' (LANs). Thus the TCP/IP provided the key to a growing network-of-networks - the Internet.

By the late 1980s, however, the Internet still lacked mass appeal since it was considered a specialist tool. Two further inventions - one scientific, one commercial - then brought the World Wide Web to popular attention. The Web was invented by a researcher at the European Laboratory for Particle Physics in Geneva in 1989 and added a huge visual dimension to the Internet. It allows an organisation or an individual to present information on a 'home page' and use 'hypertext' to jump from one to another. What gave the Web mass appeal was the invention of a software system or 'browser' called Mosaic (now commercialised as Netscape's Communicator) which allows the user to move quickly from one home page - or web site - to another through a very easy mechanism. It was not long before the Web was being embellished with sound, video and other multimedia links, further enhancing the appeal of the Internet.

In 1999, there were over 40 million Internet hosts spread around the world.

Early consequences of the revolution

The information revolution is driven by the technological advances just outlined. It has led to a proliferation of new products, with enormously enhanced capacities to collect, process and transfer information. As with the previous revolutions, however, the full economic impacts in terms of costs and productivity gains, will take time to work through. There have already been important cost reductions in information processing and communications, but increases in productivity have been less apparent. Part of the reason is that investments in information and communication technology have so far been quite limited. Within American corporations, investment in information technology in now over 40% of total capital spending, but in the US, German and Japanese economies as a whole, computer hardware and software and the activities of information management are estimated to account for only 10% of GNP,[4] with a higher percentage in services (such as retailing, health care, banking, insurance, air transport and telecommunications) and a lower figure in manufacturing.

Another explanation is that the gains are hard to recognise in tangible terms. Unquestionably, the information revolution has enhanced the quality of products and services, even if the attributable rises in quantities have been small.[5] Computer-aided design has helped to improve the range and quality of many production processes. The same number of telephone calls is easier and faster to connect. Airline bookings have become more convenient and reliable. The print and television media provide more timely news from all over the world. And so on.

The real essence of the revolution is qualitative. Although based on improved technologies, it is called an information revolution because it can vastly expand access to information, and thereby enhance knowledge. Because the information revolution has such widespread ramifications, it is impossible to predict the extent of its impact. It is akin to what Thomas Kuhn described as a crisis - but in the social sciences - leading to what he has described as a 'paradigm change'.[6] Some have foreseen the advent of a globally networked society and the emergence of a universal system called 'informational capitalism' in which the ICT revolution infuses almost every aspect of economic life within countries and creates fully globalised systems of accumulation.[7] But the revolution is not all-encompassing, not now and perhaps never. There are many countries, and many people within

---

[4] Dertouzos (1997).
[5] Cairncross, op. cit.
[6] Kuhn (1962).
[7] For example, Castells (1998).

them, who are likely to remain on the margins, as they have in previous technology-led revolutions.

To benefit from the information revolution requires 'infostructure', but most of the world is poorly served. To obtain a broad overview, the following table shows the relative levels of penetration of the principal technologies - telephone, television and personal computers - by region and income level. The contrasts are rather stark, particularly in respect of computers and Internet penetration (Table 5).

Table 5: Uneven density of information technology, 1996

	Telephone lines per 100 people	Telephone lines per 100 households	Sets per 100 people (TV)	Sets per 100 households (TV)	PCs per 100 people	Internet hosts per 10,000 people
Regions						
Americas	30.4	72.2	44.4	88.3	15.9	139.2
Europe	34.6	70.6	43.0	87.0	10.0	45.7
Asia	6.0	22.3	18.2	53.8	1.3	3.0
Africa	1.9	6.1	5.6	20.1	0.6	1.4
Income levels						
High Income	54.0	102.7	61.9	90.8	22.3	171.9
Upper Middle Income	13.4	39.7	26.3	80.2	2.9	8.4
Lower Middle Income	9.7	31.0	22.7	73.3	1.7	1.9
Low Income	2.5	8.9	13.1	47.4	0.2	0.1
World	12.9	9.9	23.8	66.0	4.7	28.1

Source: International Telecommunication Union

The figures do not deceive, and they reveal large disparities of coverage. They also conceal the great disparities within countries, particularly the poorer ones. But this static picture does not take into account the potential for those regions and countries that are currently less well-endowed to make up at least part of the huge gap within a relatively short period of time. This is especially true of telecommunications and television. Because of the technological advances already described, those countries with relatively sparse telephone networks may never have to make equivalent substantial investments in expensive land-lines to link households and companies. It will soon be technically possible to create 'wireless' national networks through the use of radio[8] and satellite links. Prices of information technology appliances are also falling and the accessibility will be enhanced with further integration. There are already mobile telephone sets on which Internet messages can be read. The television set, which can be found in two-thirds of the households world-wide - and is potentially visible to a larger majority - has been developed to receive satellite signals and could soon begin to serve the functions of a computer through which different programmes and information can be searched and retrieved.

Infrastructure status and potential are not sufficient measures of knowledge and information potential. It is also necessary to take into account factors which indicate the potential for absorption of information. Two attempts to assess this capacity, using normalised indices to facilitate comparison among countries, may be cited here. The first is the 'infrastructure, experience, skills, knowledge (INEXSK)' approach which computes index values for eight different variables.[9] In addition to those on infrastructure (telephone, TV and computers), there are indices for literacy, numbers of graduates in technical disciplines, and electronic goods production and consumption. The last two variables are included as an indication of the degree to which the economies of individual countries are orientated towards the absorption and processing of information.

A second 'information imperative' index uses no fewer than 20 different variables to compare the status of a sample of 55 countries.[10] The index includes a longer list of infrastructure indicators (for example, numbers of

---

8   One new technological solution is the 'wireless local loop' which is essentially a stripped down version of a cellular telephone system. These systems have low installation and operating costs and can quickly match unmet demand in areas not currently served with telephones. According to the International Telecommunication Union, there are some 50 systems being piloted world-wide and the number of connections is expected to increase five-fold between 1997 and 2000.
9   See Mansell and Wehn (1998).
10 The Information Imperative - subtitled 'embracing the invisible revolution reshaping our world' - was developed by World Times, an organisation based in Boston.

fax machines, educational PCs), as well as data of school enrolment, newspaper readership (in preference to literacy), as well as estimates of press freedom and civil liberties. There is thus an interesting bias in favour of openness of individual countries to the use and free circulation of information. Not surprisingly, for this index also, there is a wide range of achievement. Although the sample of countries is limited, it is notable that South Africa is the sole representative of that continent, ranking 35th out of 55 countries.

Developmental impacts

Notwithstanding the growing possibilities for countries to make up for current infrastructure deficiencies by technological leap-frogging, the yawning gaps between richer and poorer countries indicated by these data have prompted pessimists to predict that the information revolution will result in a further widening of the development gap between the richer and poorer countries and make it even harder for the latter to participate in the benefits of a global economy with an increasingly strong information orientation.

The pessimists maintain that the poorer countries lack resources to invest in infrastructure on a sufficient scale to benefit from the revolution. Moreover, many people in the developing countries lie outside the monetised economy and cannot translate their individual needs into effective demand for information services. Illiteracy also inhibits access, and even for those who are literate, a substantial proportion of textual information of potential benefit to the development process is in international languages (approximately 90% of Internet content is thought to be in English, and most of the balance in languages using Latin script). As countries become more closely enmeshed in the global economy, those enterprises and entrepreneurs that are best connected and best informed will benefit most, while the information poor will be left further behind. As Nelson Mandela stated at a telecommunications conference a few years ago: "if we cannot ensure that this global revolution creates a world-wide information society in which everyone has a stake and can play a part, then it will not have been a revolution at all."

The global revolution will not happen of itself. Yet the pessimism is not entirely well founded. While the information revolution requires infrastructure, which is spreading unevenly between and within countries according to capacity-to-pay criteria, information itself - and the benefits that flow from it - is not a purchasable market item. Unlike other factors of production - capital, land, labour and traditional technologies - information is not owned, purchased or transferred, so much as it is shared (or leaked). Yet it can be substituted for other factors. Information is also not subject to scarcities like tangible resources. On the contrary, it expands as it is used, and it is capable of becoming increasingly economical in its absorption of other resources.

Information, enhanced by technologies of management and processing, can be made more ubiquitous, and more easy to apply beneficially to more products and services, than other resources. Unlike the technologies that have emerged from previous revolutions, technology-enhanced information is potentially much more widely accessible and usable. The factors inhibiting access to information are of several kinds: economic, technological, as well as political. But in every country without exception, these factors can be mitigated so as to increase access, and the fruits of the information revolution beneficially applied to a growing number of development purposes. Thus while the gap between the information-poor and information-rich will remain wide, there are nevertheless enormous opportunities for enhancing the achievement of development goals. In this section, some of the most promising of these opportunities are briefly reviewed.

The applications of information and communications technology to development may be said to be of three kinds. The first type includes the various ways in which ICT can be used to enhance development activities across a wide spectrum. The second type involves the demonopolisation of information by governments and the application of ICT to processes of governance. The third type of benefit has to do with the ways in which information can improve the working of economic markets and help to alter economic systems. Table 6 below provides some examples of ICT-enabled development projects in various countries and regions.

ICT and development. Education is allied to the harnessing and use of information and is perhaps the most important and essential area which can benefit from ICT: important because of the range of potential applications, and essential because of the critical role played by education in advancing development and in further facilitating the conversion of information into knowledge and skills.

There are many dimensions of education which can be enhanced by the use of ICT:[11]

---

11 Mansell and Wehn, op. cit.

- Place: ICT can convey educational materials across large distances, and to many places simultaneously. Learning need not be confined to schools and classrooms, but can be brought directly into homes.

- Time: the new technologies can allow more flexibility in regard to the timing of administered learning. The recording and storage of information make it possible to give access to educational materials at times convenient to individuals and groups.

- Access: materials not ordinarily available may be retrieved from different locations and presented in formats that are friendly to users. The new technologies can also be customized to the needs and interests of different cultural, religious and ethnic groups. Dissemination in different languages is easier than in formal education systems.

- Age: ICT can deliver learning materials adapted to different age-groups and expand the scope for 'life-long learning'.

- Cost: the new technologies provide the potential for much less costly delivery of educational materials, not as a substitute, but as an important supplement to the educational infrastructure of schools and teachers.

There are further ways in which ICT can improve on learning techniques, if there are the resources and infrastructural support. The barriers of illiteracy could be breached through the use of pictorial and icon-based learning media, bringing potentially much larger numbers within the reach of the new technologies.[12] Fully interactive learning systems can also be devised and deployed to facilitate individualised tuition. Above all, the new technologies can encourage environments of learning which place a premium on individual creativity and initiative, while expanding the circulation of ideas. By these means, education can become a route to individual empowerment and liberation, rather than regimentation.

Tele-medicine - meaning simply medicine at a distance - is a second important area of ICT application. There are at least two domains in which health care can be considerably enhanced by the application of the new information technologies. The first area relates to the sharing and transfer of patient records, allowing care and diagnosis to be provided remotely and obviating the need for, and expense of, direct contact between patient and doctor. The experience has been pioneered mainly in North America

12 Hans d'Orville (1996).

beginning in the 1950s, but in the 1990s remote care and diagnosis through tele-medicine have spread to many more countries. Numerous individual examples have been cited of lives saved through tele-medicine. In addition to these successes, tele-medicine should be seen as building bridges between metropolitan and rural health care systems, and extending the reach of scarce medical facilities.

The second related domain is in the enhancement of health care through the broadcasting of health information. The need is a critical one. Medical practice throughout the world is too often obfuscated by the arcane language of curative technique when more accessible information on prevention through better hygiene is called for. The advent of primary health care and the deployment of para-medics have sought to address the critical medical needs of the poorer countries, particularly in rural areas. The application of ICT to these efforts can enormously enhance their effectiveness by linking health workers to remote information sites and by making information on healthy practices and life-styles much more widely accessible through local clinics, schools and households.

Environmental monitoring and management is another area which lends itself to the expanded use of ICT. For several decades, information technology has been put at the service of the exploration, mapping and monitoring of natural resources through the use of remotely sensed data from aerial platforms (the mainstay of Geographic Information Systems - GIS). The new technologies are helping to increase access to such data, combine it more easily with other geographic information sources, and facilitate exchange and analysis. ICT can also support the collection and dissemination of information on good environmental management practises, agricultural research and extension.

The greater capacity of GIS to incorporate more layers of information, and to monitor data changes more accurately, expands the possibilities for natural disaster tracking and prevention, both of a short-term nature (e.g. typhoons) and longer-term (e.g. deforestation, global warming).

ICT and governance. The capacity to capture and manipulate information has traditionally been a source of political power. In the most extreme manifestations of the abuse of power under totalitarian regimes, the collection and use of information was considered a monopoly of the state. Following the collapse of the Soviet empire, there are few such states in which this monopoly is still exercised. However, there are still relatively few countries in which information is permitted to flow freely.

The information revolution is aptly named insofar as the new technologies have already helped to stimulate fundamental political

Table 6: Applying ICT to development

Country/region	Project	Description	Sponsors
Education			
Costa Rica	Educational Telecommunications Network	Creates ICT-based learning environments in state schools in rural areas	Private sector and Government
Pakistan	Support Trust Education	Networking facilities (EDUNET) provide teachers and students with didactic materials via Internet and CD-ROM	Government and self-financing
Côte d'Ivoire	Télé-pour-Tous	Broadcasts via battery-powered TV sets, a wide range of practical information including advice on water and sanitation, housing, access to credit	Government
Chile	"ENLACES"	An electronic Internet-based network links up 400 educational institutions around the country allowing universities to provide advice to schools on computer applications	Government
Health			
Guyana, Philippines, Thailand	Primary Health Care	Through two-way radio network, enables rural health workers to obtain medical advice and order drug supplies	Government
Global (Africa, South Asia, Latin America)	SatelLife	Satellite-linked Internet site allows 4,000 subscribers to receive medical information from global sources and communicate with physicians everywhere	User subscription
Uganda	Multipurpose Community Telecentre	Provides members of a district community with access to telephones, facsimile machines, computers and the Internet for purposes of obtaining healthcare and other information	Government and ITU
Governance			
Mongolia	Governance and Economic Transition Programme	Improved information and communications for public entities linked via the Internet; creation of remote 'citizen information service centres' allowing widespread visibility of, and communication with, public entities	Government, UNDP, other donors

Country/region	Project	Description	Sponsors
Governance (Continued)			
Southeast Asia (ASEAN)	ASEANWEB	Uses the Internet to connect the Foreign Ministries of the member countries, enhancing communication and information exchange	Government
Morocco	Public Administration Support Project	Uses ICT in the Ministries of Finance and Planning to enhance tax administration, auditing, public investment planning and increase the efficiency in budget preparation	Government
Environment			
Global	Sustainable Development Networking Programme (SDNP)	Establishes national networking nodes to facilitate the collection and exchange of environmental information within and between countries	UNDP
Indonesia	Forest Resource Information System	Combines remotely-sensed data and ground sampling into a comprehensive computer-based forest inventory used to monitor areas and densities of forest resources	Government

Sources: UNDP, ITU

changes. It was the increasing flows of information from the democratic world into the states of the former Soviet empire which played a major part in precipitating the collapse. Chinese students inside and outside the country communicating via e-mail helped to build up the protest against the Government in China before, during and after the Tienanmen crackdown in Beijing in 1989. The information revolution has contributed to growing freedom of expression since then. Other countries in political transition - Mongolia, Vietnam among them - have been hastened on their way by more openness to information. And for the future, there is no doubt that the world's last strict authoritarian regimes in North Korea and Burma could be prised apart if more information from the outside were able to reach the population at large.

Commentaries on the democratising influence of the information revolution - and particularly the advent of the Internet - are often infused with optimistic western idealism (and dominated by English-language content). The new technologies can encourage horizontal flows of information within countries and across borders, as opposed to mainly vertical flows of information between state and populace. But many governments have perceived the undermining of traditional hierarchies and state dependence as a threat to their authority, and even existence, and some have sought to ban the use of the Internet, or control access by keeping service providers within the state domain, or subject to explicit rules and codes. It is also possible to conceive of a fully wired state using information infrastructure as a means of more rather than less control over individual freedoms. Optimists invoke the Athenian Agora as a model of a newly informed society (e.g. Al Gore), but there are those who rather see an Orwellian scenario.

There are also cultural inhibitions to the full democratisation of information. The individualistic approaches to the use of ICT, which is helping to drive the revolution forward in many western countries, has no equivalent in most of the rest of the world where the influence of extended families and communities is much greater. Furthermore, while the new technologies are likely to help diffuse information more widely, the diffusion may be uneven. The main beneficiaries will be the state and civil entities with the most resources to invest in technologies to capture and process information.

These are reasons to doubt the idealistic vision of knowledge societies in which all individuals are fully empowered. However, the dilution of the hegemony of governments over the collection and dissemination of information, and the increasing porosity of state borders, which the information revolution is guaranteed to ensure, can only be beneficial to the aims of development. An important feature of the information revolution is that its presence cannot be ignored and its impact on the erosion of barriers can only be resisted through the most draconian measures of isolation. In practice, almost no countries have been able or willing to shut it out. Countries in Asia, such as China, Laos, Iran and Bhutan, which originally chose for political reasons to ban access to the Internet, found it virtually impossible to do so and have allowed it, albeit initially under strict government supervision. (North Korea and Burma continue to maintain the ban in 1999).

In the context of governance, the harnessing of the new information technologies can have substantial development benefits in terms of encouraging governments to be more transparent and responsive. There are already many emerging examples. ICT can open doors on corridors of power and allow in more public scrutiny. One of the best examples of this new openness is to be found in Mongolia, a country in rapid transition from a centrally planned authoritarian state to a market democracy. ICT is being used to create a giant 'intranet' to link all the main organs of power and enhance information exchange and communications among them; the government is also creating a series of Citizens' Information Service Centres, eventually extending to all the remotest administrative districts, which will allow widespread access to information on, and provided by, the government. The circumstances of Mongolia are not entirely typical. The government has a strong commitment to openness and the need to improve communications over vast distances among widely dispersed communities. The population enjoys high literacy levels which encourage an interest in information (available on the Internet in Mongolian language). But Mongolia is not an exception. Many other governments are harnessing ICT in order to render their operations more transparent and improve efficiency. The increasing use of digitised information can itself contribute to greater accuracy and objectivity, while improving record-keeping and facilitating evaluation. The potential efficacy of modern information management for seeking out and preventing corruption in the public sector is obvious.

There are also important applications of ICT to democratic processes. Countries from Armenia to South Africa have used the Internet to post information on candidates seeking political office, thus enabling voters to make more informed choices. ICT can be used to elicit comments on proposed legislation and on other measures likely to affect people's lives. ICT can also enhance the role of non-governmental organisations as they come to play a growing role in articulating the views of different interest groups.

The media in almost all countries have begun to benefit from the information revolution. The globalisation of television programming has done more than anything else to impart the impression of shrinking distance and global citizenship, providing information on other societies and making many more people aware of alternative political systems. Desktop publishing software, linked to improved international communications, has also seen the emergence of vast numbers of newspapers, newsletters and bulletin boards, both paper and electronic. Informed citizens are more creative and productive members of society are more able to help themselves.

ICT and economics. The information revolution is both a product of, and a stimulant to, the global spread of the market. It is a product because, as discussed above, innovations have responded to commercial opportunities. It is a stimulant because markets require better information to work more effectively. But ICT is also helping to revolutionise the way that increasingly market-oriented economies work. This section briefly examines the consequences of the information revolution for capital, trade and labour.

A major feature of economic globalisation has been the alliance of capital markets and ICT. The information revolution has contributed to the ubiquity of capital, helping it to move quickly and in ever growing quantities towards market opportunities, oblivious to national frontiers. ICT has contributed to the efficiency of fast-moving capital, which has been an important spur to economic growth and development in more and more countries.

Of course, these benefits have been tempered by other costs. The globalisation of private capital has sparked periodic crises when markets have circumvented government controls. The free working of global capital markets brought about the demise of fixed exchange rates in the 1970s, and precipitated crises of confidence in Latin America and Asia in the 1990s. Short-term finance has also become inherently fickle, reacting to non-economic and often speculative signals. But the volatility of capital is not a reason to eschew its benefits. It highlights the need to build capacity in developing and managing regulatory mechanisms to minimise its more disruptive consequences, while retaining economic openness.

Improved information technology is also transforming international trade in goods and services. For those engaged in trade, information on the nature and size of markets, tariff regimes, documentation requirements, and so on, are now more widely and efficiently accessible by electronic means. Services such as travel and tourism have been early beneficiaries. Trade transactions themselves are going on-line (electronic commerce) and payments are increasingly being made through electronic transfer. Electronic commerce began mainly between branches of the same corporations, but it is set to grow substantially. One estimate (by Forrester Research) expects global business-to-business electronic commerce to increase from less than $3 billion in 1996, to over $320 billion by 2002. (On this scale, electronic commerce presents governments with the enormous challenge of tracing sales for taxation and recording purposes.)

ICT is also having an impact on the deployment of labour, facilitating the movement of manufacturing and service activities to workers, rather than the other way round. There are many examples to be cited of how developing countries are becoming engaged in global activities through tele-working and outsourcing. International Business Machines (IBM) has hired teams of programmers in China, India, Belarus and Latvia to develop software programs for use on the Internet. Two European airlines have relocated their revenue accounting systems to India. An American insurance company processes its claims in Barbados, where it is the island's largest employer. A Swedish firm of architects has had its drawings done in Pakistan, for a client in Saudi Arabia.

Tele-working exploits two advantages of harnessing remote labour through ICT. One is obviously the cost factor, with the same skills being employed for lower wages (the payroll costs of the Swissair operation are a quarter of what they would be in Switzerland). The other factor is time: the IBM operation has programmers working round the clock. Other US companies can outsource some of their service functions to Asia and have the work done overnight. Tele-working is not going to make more than a marginal impact on the labour markets of China and India. However, for some smaller and more remote countries, the impact of the information revolution is much more significant, and it does not depend on the availability only of skilled labour.

The same principles are also being applied within countries. Rather than grouping them physically together in factories and offices, workers in some types of enterprise can perform the same functions at home, or in tele-centres. Where the work needs to be sent, it can be done so electronically or through other designated channels. It is the beginning of the reversal of one of the most important outcomes of the earlier revolutions. Factories became the mainstay of economic progress when technology began to facilitate the transport of energy. Now the days of the factory may be numbered.

Increasing the benefits of the information revolution[13]

As discussed earlier, different interpretations are being put on the likely global impact of the information revolution. It is seen by some as an additional factor in the growing divide between rich and poor countries. In the global market-place, information and communication technologies can enhance competitiveness and help to advance the development status of those countries with the best connections. But their absence will leave the 'least informed' countries further behind.

This book, however, notwithstanding its enthusiasm for global markets, does not side with those who have reduced development progress mainly to a race for global competitiveness, which is bound to throw up winners and losers. It perceives that there need be no losers at all from the information revolution, unless they are governments - and there are still a very few - that have chosen a path of almost total isolation from the rest of the world. The information revolution has been described as a 'race in which all can have

---

13 Much of the information in this section is derived from International Telecommunication Union (1998) which provides the single most comprehensive database on telecommunications and other forms of information infrastructure.

prizes'.[14]

A message of this chapter is that there are no standards of infrastructure, and no levels of literacy and skills, that are so low as to deny countries some of the benefits of the information revolution. Any measures which help to raise the utilisation levels of information within a country, and assist it to mesh more strongly with the rest of the world, will contribute to the goals of development. A key factor in the rate of progress, however, will be the attitudes of governments and the actions they take to facilitate the process of 'informatisation'. This section is about the need for those actions.

Many governments have already passed one litmus test of the revolution. In 1993, most countries had no access to the Internet; by 1996, most countries did. By the time this book appears, there will probably be Internet service providers in virtually every country of the world except the very smallest and remotest (which will be the final target). Some governments have put up a strong initial resistance to the Internet, believing it to be an insidious channel for political dissent (Burma[15]) or moral pollution (Sudan), or unwelcome exposure (Bhutan). Many countries have resisted the Internet because of the commercial threat posed to their state telecommunication monopolies. But the Internet has mostly prevailed.

This test was not an especially hard one, however. Any country with international telephone links would find it extremely difficult to keep out the Internet except through an elaborate and expensive system of control. Many countries are still attempting to censor the content of the World Wide Web, in order to screen out unwelcome criticism, pornography, damaging (e.g. racist) propaganda, or other harmful material. That too is proving to be difficult.

The challenge now is to help create the full range of infrastructure essential to speeding up the diffusion of the Internet and the other applications of ICT. The gaps are still daunting, but there are various measures that can be taken to bring about rapid improvement, both in extending the backbone of the infrastructure (satellites, broadcasting centres, telephone lines and switching systems) and encouraging the addition of end-of-pipe items (telephone receivers, television sets, computers, modems, facsimile machines). Hitherto, the task of building the backbone has been assumed largely by governments, using public resources. Governments have also mostly controlled the distribution of telephone receivers and sometimes other end-of-pipe items. Increasingly, however, it is private investors and private consumers who are taking the

14 Mansell and Wehn, op. cit., p.9.
15 In Burma, the possession of a computer with networking capability is an offence for which the penalty is up to 15 years in prison.

initiative. The critical role of governments is broadly two fold: first, to facilitate more dynamism in the creation of infrastructure; second, to provide strategic direction to ensure that the benefits of the infrastructure can be spread as widely as possible.

Facilitation. The most important of these facilitation measures will be the introduction of competition into domestic telecommunications markets. Competition will not come easily. In many countries, the communications sector has been considered of strategic importance and central to security, and governments have created state monopolies to run their telephone systems (often combined with post and telegraphy into 'PTTs'). There are strong incentives to maintaining the status quo, apart from considerations of security. These monopolies generate significant revenues for the state, provide jobs and protect market share.

But today, state monopolies are not the best means of meeting any of these goals. State PTTs have a poor record of innovation. In many countries they have left a substantial part of domestic demand unsatisfied, perhaps amounting to fully one fifth of the entire global market, as earlier cited ITU figures suggest. The introduction of commercial return and competition into the market, on the other hand, will encourage innovation and bring about expansion of services, aided by lower prices. By contributing to growth in other areas, demonopolisation can help to increase overall tax revenues for the state, while stimulating job expansion.

Demonopolisation is already gathering pace in all parts of the world, with highly beneficial results. It can take various forms. Full or partial privatisation of state monopolies has been undertaken in more than 40 countries during the 1990s, usually accompanied by targets for service expansion. In Argentina, which privatised its monopoly (Entel) in 1990, the annual network growth target was 6% and the company achieved 14%. Mexico's Telmex, also privatised in 1990, achieved a similar expansion. In Central and Eastern Europe, the Czech Republic and Hungary privatised their monopolies in 1993 and have seen substantial growth. Ghana Telecom was partially privatised in 1996 and is expected to triple teledensity within five years.

Privatisation is not sufficient, however, if it replaces one type of monopoly with another. Transparent regulatory bodies are required to prevent abuse of market domination, and competition needs to be engendered through new entrants. The private cellular phone market is providing an important competitive stimulant. In the Asia-Pacific region as a whole, the numbers of cellular telephone subscribers have been doubling every year since the mid-1990s. In the Philippines, one of the most dynamic markets of all, the government awarded five mobile cellular licenses in 1993 and seven international gateway licenses, as part of its target to quadruple the number of subscribers by 1999. Competition galvanised the incumbent monopoly into doubling its own line installation between 1993 and 1996.

Privatisation has increasingly brought foreign capital into domestic telecommunications development. Governments can, and are, also accelerating the growth of infrastructure through foreign direct investment. In Southeast Asia particularly - Indonesia, Thailand and Vietnam - governments have contracted foreign investors to build new parts of their national telecommunications networks, including (in Indonesia) in some of the remoter areas. All these schemes are expected to achieve a significant expansion in teledensity.

More openness to foreign investment and trade is a new feature of telecommunications development. Under the auspices of the World Trade Organisation (WTO), two recent agreements are expected to speed up the process of global liberalisation, to which a growing number of developing countries are subscribing. The Basic Telecommunications Services Agreement came officially into being at the beginning of 1998 and covers foreign investment, pro-competitive regulatory principles, access to international communications services and satellite facilities. Forty out of the 69 signatories of the agreement are developing countries, although not all subscribe to each part of the agreement. The Information Technology Agreement, which emerged from the WTO ministerial conference at the end of 1996 also commits more than 20 countries (several developing), as well as the European Union, to a phasing out of all tariffs on trade in information technology products by 2000.

These two agreements provide liberalisation frameworks into which countries can opt gradually. Even if there is still a long way to travel in some countries, few would have predicted this much progress only ten years ago. The Information Technology Agreement will stimulate trade in the whole range of ICT, helping to spread the benefits of technological advance not only in telecommunications, but in television and computers. In 1996, China (35 million) and India (16 million) had almost one quarter of the world's cable TV subscribers. There are now more households in India with TV than with a telephone.

Strategic direction. The advances in 'info-structure' being witnessed in many countries are demonstrating the importance of facilitation, with private interests increasingly driving the process. However, the information revolution cannot be created solely in response to market demand, which could skew the benefits in favour of economic élites and exacerbate disparities between information haves and have-nots.

The information revolution, and the creation of knowledge societies, requires partnership between the public and private sectors (including civil society). The power of private sector organisations in shaping the information revolution is considerable and they exert enormous influence on inter-governmental organisations such as the International Telecommunication Union and the World Bank, and on the setting of international standards. Individual countries must determine how they will align themselves with these trends and seek to derive maximum benefits from them. There is also a need for mechanisms at the country level to govern the judicious allocation of resources, and to establish priorities. Notwithstanding the retreat from state planning mechanisms, there is an emerging international consensus that countries should draw up national ICT strategies in response to these needs.

Malaysia provides one of the most elaborate examples of a national strategy. Starting in the early 1990s, it established the National Information Technology Council, chaired by the prime minister, to place the information revolution firmly into the country's development agenda. According to one of the principal authors, the fundamental rationale of the strategy is to complement what is described as the 'technology push' with the 'social pull'. The technology must be planned and managed. It should enable change, enhancing "national capacity to apply information technology for the ultimate purpose of achieving more intelligent use of human intelligence."[16]

Malaysia's experience may not be typical. The country's highly successful development strategy is founded on openness, maintaining high trade levels and encouraging substantial inflows of foreign direct investment. Its economy is thus strongly influenced by global trends and the country feels strongly the need to adapt its human resources and organisational culture to ICT in order to remain competitive. Other countries, with different parameters, are adopting strategies more suited to their own development needs. But these strategies contain many of the same basic objectives. South Africa sees the need to 'link basic needs with information highways' while also helping its industry to integrate with world markets. Mexico's ongoing development plan advocates the deployment of ICT so as to benefit its economic and social sectors.

Strategies are about choices. Among the most important that each country needs to address in respect to ICT policy are those between: public

---

16 Shariffadeen (1995).

and private ownership and control; monopoly and competition; strong regulation and facilitation; domestic and foreign ownership; fostering of local ICT production capacity and importation from abroad; importation of content and advanced ICT and the promotion of indigenous culture and values; intellectual property protection and diffusion.[17]

The choices made by states will determine the nature and speed of the process of diffusion from the global information revolution to the information empowerment of the individual. As this diffusion grows, the role of the state will change from command to facilitation. One of the most difficult accommodations of all will be to the losses of information sovereignty. As it proceeds, the revolution will lead to the growing porosity and diminishing relevance of country borders in the processes of information transfer.

The role of aid

Traditionally, aid has been conceived as a supplement to capital and a source of expertise. Earlier chapters have discussed the efficacy and sustainability of aid in these roles, in the light of the changing nature of the global economy. The information revolution described in this chapter has profound implications for the future role of aid as a means of knowledge transfer, i.e. technical assistance.

This chapter has set out to demonstrate that the revolution is a source of potential 'empowerment' on a scale never before experienced because it can quickly and effectively provide the knowledge factor - arguably the most important missing component in development. As mentioned earlier, the process of acquiring knowledge, through information purveyed by the new technologies, enhances other capacities and expands as it is absorbed. But what is also unique to the process is the fact that, through these new technologies, knowledge acquisition can be self-generated and interactive. ICT enables individuals - or groups of individuals, or organisations - to exert their own control over the learning process. They can express their specific needs for information and put technology to work to satisfy them. The means of knowledge enhancement becomes more demand-driven and less supply-determined.

It does not take much foresight to recognise that the revolution will begin to have a profound impact on foreign-funded technical assistance. While even the most powerful and interactive technologies will never

---

17 Mansell and Wehn, op. cit.

completely substitute for all forms of training which technical assistance provides, ICT can enable individuals and organisations to help themselves to information sources and contribute to their understanding of their problems.

While the expatriate aid expert may gradually become extinct, the information revolution points to other roles for aid in adding to the pace of change and enhancing developmental benefits, thereby helping more countries to become active international partners. The types of aid intervention are suggested by the nature of the unfolding revolution and the bottlenecks which are constraining its wider diffusion.

Countries cannot build in isolation. At the global level, they can be assisted in identifying, and in gaining access to the most appropriate international information gateways, including satellite bandwidth, international fibre-optic channels, and other international 'public information goods'. There are also important initiatives being developed in the major regions. As a continent, Africa lags quite far behind the rest of the world in levels of information infrastructure, but several new regional non-governmental and governmental initiatives are beginning to compensate. FIDOnet, a sponsored store-and-forward network which utilises inexpensive computers linked to servers with full Internet connections, has the largest number of users in Sub-Saharan Africa. Canada's International Development Research Centre is funding the 'Acacia' initiative, which encourages the search for ICT for development applications in poor communities in Africa. United Nations bodies are supporting the Pan-African Development Information System (PADIS), the African Information Society Initiative and the Internet Initiative for Africa.

There are many examples from other regions also. In addition to helping to extend the reach of information infrastructure, ICT can have a powerful role in supporting mechanisms of regional cooperation. The Association of South-East Asian Nations has built ASEANweb, designed to link the focal points in the Foreign Ministries of all nine member countries, so as to facilitate information exchange, improve communications and streamline the cumbersome inter-governmental consultation and approval process. The Economic Cooperation Organisation - comprising 10 countries in West and Central Asia with a secretariat in Tehran - also intends to harness the benefits of ICT to support cooperation.

At the 'upstream' domestic policy level, aid can support the development of national information strategies and the building of the ICT infrastructure. They can also be assisted in determining and meeting their technical requirements for domestic information networks. Downstream, aid can supply hardware to support developmental applications of information. A very important role could be played by the adaptation of technology to remoter areas where supplies of electricity are limited or non-existent. After the wind-up radio (developed for South Africa), the more isolated parts of the rural world await the wind-up computer and TV set. Solar sources of power also need to be developed to help run end-of-pipe ICT components in remote places. Aid can be a source of technology adaptation and leap-frogging, in which the interests and resources of the public and private sectors can be productively combined.

Other valuable forms of assistance include information sources and interactive communication networks. The example of SatelLife has already been cited.[18] Other sources of information available globally are numerous, and they are growing fast. There is also more diversification into languages other than the international ones. The posting of information is not enough, however. The new technologies also offer new possibilities of interactive learning which can be widely adapted and applied. The Open University in Britain has provided a model for distance learning in several other countries. In the US, the University of the World seeks to provide a global centre for developing tele-education products.

In sum, there are innumerable opportunities for new forms of aid to contribute to the enhancement of knowledge and the empowerment of the many millions who have never enjoyed an information and learning franchise. This will not be 'aid' in the traditional sense, so much as cooperative mechanisms facilitating global access and connectivity, and contributing to a benign invasion of the more isolated and the less informed individuals and communities. In the manner of the third technological revolution, the cooperation will combine the interests and resources of the private and public sectors, not patronisingly, but in the framework of a vast new global information partnership.

---

18 "An international not-for-profit organisation employing satellite, telephone and radio networking technology to serve the health communication and information needs of countries in the developing world" is how it is described on its website: http://www.healthnet.org.

9 Strengthening global development institutions

A new 'global age'

In the last decade of the century, we are seeing the advent of what we earlier called a global age. It was anticipated by recognition of growing economic interdependence. It has been made more visible by the global scale of environmental change. It has been facilitated by the information revolution, which has further contributed to an awareness of common global interests. It has been encouraged by the 'post-wall' international political consensus, which brought into clearer relief the common problems faced by humanity, without the obfuscation of ideological frameworks.

Change in the global age has come about at an accelerating rate through the liberalisation of trade, private capital flows and investment, and through the freer flow of information. These changes are mainly private sector-led and are generally equated with what has come to be called globalisation. This book differs from some of the more pessimistic commentaries about globalisation in emphasising that individual governments can take action to increase the benefits from it and minimise the costs. But their capacity to do so also depends on the existence of effective regimes of global governance.

The Bretton Woods conference of 1944 was designed to lay the basis of global economic governance. The institutions that emerged - the International Monetary Fund and the World Bank - have not fulfilled the roles intended for them, and will need to be adapted to contemporary demands for more equitable governance. The establishment of the World Trade Organisation is an important step, but it must be encouraged to work equitably. Adequate governance mechanisms for private capital flows, investment and information have yet to be developed.

Economic governance is only one component of the 'planetary interest'[1] that characterises the global age. There are many other areas of development concern, previously addressed principally at the national level, which lend themselves to collective international action. The growing importance of cross-border initiatives has already been discussed in the chapter on regionalism. Many other concerns are of global import, assuming greater amplitude and urgency in recent years. Maintaining the physical integrity of the earth's environment and protecting it from

---

1 Graham (1995).

anthropogenic sources of degradation has prompted the hasty development of a series of new governance regimes. The growth of international public 'bads' including the spread of the HIV/AIDS virus and drug trafficking demand global initiatives to complement those undertaken by countries.

These are some of the regulatory and palliative mechanisms required of global governance, to which must be added, of course the traditional role of the United Nations in peace-keeping and the control of conflict. Other international public goods and services generated by effective governance include products and technologies of developmental significance, as well as the creation of uniform technical standards to facilitate cooperation. In its more passive voice, global governance leads to the establishment of conventions and norms to encourage universal compliance with human development standards.

There is not the scope in a book of this nature, concerned with development assistance, to review the full gamut of global governance issues in the depth which they probably deserve, nor to discuss all existing mechanisms.[2] It is certain that the number and nature of global mechanisms - particularly outside the public sector - will continue to grow. This chapter examines the functions of global governance pertaining especially to the development domain, and within it, the Bretton Woods institutions and the UN system. It outlines where these institutions are falling short and how they could be reformed if effective global governance is to deliver the international public goods and services needed to facilitate development.

The original pillars of global governance

The era of global cooperation may be said to have opened with the signing of the United Nations Charter by 51 sovereign states in 1945. It is a document infused with optimism about the determination of the peoples of the United Nations - "resolved to combine our efforts" - to accomplish the aims of peaceful development. It remains perhaps the single most significant international agreement, and individual articles have been

---

2 For the most part, this chapter will be concerned with official global - but not regional - governance mechanisms, in which the constituency is one of states. This is not because the nation-state is the only, or even the most important, element of global regimes. But the governments of states are the custodians of laws, and the interpreters and enforcers of international laws and regimes at the country level. Governments command the public resources to contribute to regimes and they have the administrative capacity to help with implementation. Also, although governments are not always representative of all interests within a state, they are the official channels through which interest groups can seek representation in global dialogues.

invoked in many efforts to resolve conflicts and set norms.[3] The most important practical purpose of the Charter was to create two key pieces of the machinery of global governance: the United Nations organisation and the International Court of Justice. By 1949, the UN had already fielded its first two peace-keeping missions - which are still continuing today.[4]

Peace was the UN's main goal at the beginning, and arguably it still is. A panoply of other organisations and agencies grew up, or were absorbed, into the 'UN system' which this book has described as one of the main pillars of the inchoate aid process of the 1940s. These were functional entities, responsible for norm setting and technical assistance of a specialised kind.

Other organisations set up to administer the global economic system resulted from the UN conference at Bretton Woods in 1944: the International Bank for Reconstruction and Development (World Bank), the International Monetary Fund and the General Agreement on Trade and Tariffs. The World Bank and IMF were functioning by 1946, and GATT in 1948. Thus, if the rest of the UN system is considered as a single entity, there were four original pillars of the global system of development governance.

The architects of these institutions had intended to build an effective system of global management and it is useful to recall the context in which these objectives were determined. In the wreckage left by world war, capital was urgently required for economic reconstruction; this was the intended role of the World Bank (or International Bank for Reconstruction and Development as it was originally called), and it was expected to perform this role by recycling market funds to the developing countries until they had sufficient credit-worthiness of their own to tap these sources directly. Following the collapse of the international monetary system, a new mechanism was required to maintain order based on stable currencies; hence the International Monetary Fund (IMF), whose major role was the maintenance of an international currency system based on fixed exchange rates. The International Trade Organisation (ITO) had been intended to stabilise international commodity prices and encourage liberal trading practices. Finally, the UN system was to be the custodian of peace and the

---

3 However, the Charter has not lived up to expectations. Its harmonious spirit was breached almost from the outset, as a result of cold war which was to last more than four decades. More than 130 new signatory states have been added since the San Francisco conference, but only four articles have ever been amended (in minor ways). The absence of amendments suggests that the Charter embodied many timeless and universal principles. But some individual articles have never been complied with, and no rigorous screening of new members has ever been applied.
4 UNTSO on the border of Israel and Syria and UNMOGIP between India and Pakistan.

promoter of social and economic progress.[5]

Matters turned out rather differently. The ITO was still-born, and in its place was the General Agreement on Tariffs and Trade (GATT). The GATT succeeded in achieving limited tariff-cutting among its developed member countries (the 'contracting parties'), but its membership remained very limited and the one area of trade liberalisation which it ignored was primary commodities.

In its peace-keeping role, the United Nations has been able to mount a series of operations but it could not prevent the outbreak of hundreds of new conflicts - international and civil. The Security Council was set up to act as a watchdog, but it was plagued by numerous vetoes by one or other of its five permanent members. Only in recent years of post-cold war consensus has the UN seen some of its cohesion restored. However, its recent record in stopping conflict and building peace has been mixed. The economic and social forums of the UN, for their part, have acted as consultative bodies for the purposes of norm-setting and technical assistance - organisations such as the Universal Postal Union (UPU), the International Telecommunication Union (ITU) and the International Labour Organisation (ILO) were performing these functions long before the UN was created and they were absorbed into the system - but have not had adequate resources to fulfil the developmental ambitions expounded by the Charter.

The IMF and World Bank

As an instrument of global governance, the IMF has had a mixed history. The blueprints of the Bretton Woods conference called for a large currency reserve facility to maintain liquidity where it was most needed, and proposals advocated between one-sixth and one half of the value of total world imports.[6] Keynes's vision was of a world central bank, issuing its own currency (the 'Bancor'). Belatedly in the 1970s, the IMF was authorised to create Special Drawing Rights (SDR), but they never fulfilled their intended role. The US ran large and persistent deficits, which it chose to finance with dollars, never submitting to the discipline of adjustment and ensuring that the US dollar became and remained as the principal reserve currency. The total value of SDRs has never exceeded 3% of global liquidity.

Nonetheless, the IMF did play an important role as intermediary up until

---
5 ul Haq (1993).
6 The lower figure was advocated by the US (led by Harry White), the higher one by the UK (Maynard Keynes).

the early 1970s, when it could still be regarded as an institution operating on a global scale. In the period 1968-72, no fewer than 11 industrialised countries - including all of today's G-7 except Japan - drew on the Fund, and held the lion's share of outstanding credits.[7] Then in 1971, the US decided to abandon the pegged-but-adjustable exchange rate system and allow the dollar to float freely against other currencies. Other countries soon followed suit. As a result, a central role of the IMF as the custodian of the exchange-rate system - on which it had to be consulted before currencies could be adjusted - had been summarily eliminated. Foreign exchange transactions - and the risks that went with them - were effectively privatised. There was no longer a global monetary system worthy of the name, and no longer a basis for policy consultation and coordination. The subsequent amendment to the IMF's articles (1976) merely required the Fund to "exercise firm surveillance" over exchange rate policies.

In the 1970s, the IMF metamorphosised into a stern banker for the poorer and more vulnerable of the developing countries. For more than two decades, there have not been any credit programmes with the industrialised countries - which can readily meet their external capital needs on private markets - and the IMF has not played any significant role, as had been intended, in helping to recycle the substantial balance of payments surpluses of countries such as Japan. In the 1990s - and with the encouragement of the US Government and the Baker and Brady Plans for debt relief (discussed in an earlier Chapter) - the IMF has increasingly assumed the role of lender of last resort for the middle-income countries which have borrowed heavily in the private markets. For these countries, the IMF is less preoccupied with the current account and more with the capital account balances. In this role, the IMF is at least as important to the international banks as it is to the countries themselves. As we shall see below, the stern banker and lender-of-last-resort roles got confused in the IMF response to the Asian financial crisis.

For many of the poorer countries, the perennial concern has been with fluctuating commodity prices. In 1963, the Fund created the Compensatory Funding Facility (CFF) designed to assuage the impact of commodity price fluctuations. The understanding at the time was that the CFF would be a substitute for global commodity agreements that would have acted directly on commodity prices through buffer stock adjustments. However, although finance through this facility was intended to provide temporary assistance to countries put in difficulty by circumstances largely beyond their control, the CFF (and later the Compensatory and Contingency Financing Facility)

---

7 Bird (1995).

became increasingly tied to policy conditionalities, particularly from the early 1980s. Conditionalities were clearly inappropriate where domestic policy inadequacies were not a cause of the problem.[8]

Many of the commodity-dependent countries have also become the most highly indebted. The recurrent debt repayment obligations of these countries compound the difficulty of complying with the harsh conditions which IMF programmes often entail, acting like a tax on reform and making policy changes even harder for borrowing governments to sell politically. As the debt crisis has mounted, more new finance from the Fund has been absorbed into keeping countries financially afloat, while not reducing the debt problem. The poorer countries embarking on Fund programmes have found it increasingly difficult to disengage themselves.

The standard measures on which the Fund bases its conditions are inspired by 'monetarist' principles, insofar as they emphasize strict domestic credit controls and currency devaluation, often to the exclusion of other priorities. The primary concern is to restore or enhance the capacity of client countries to repay short-term credits to the Fund. These contractionary policy approaches have linked IMF programmes to substantial and sustained falls in investment rates, with serious consequences for output growth. This is a far cry from the 'promotion and maintenance of high levels of employment and real income' for its member countries inscribed in the IMF's first article of agreement, particularly since it would appear that the performance of the Fund has been generally less effective in low-income countries.[9]

Other shortcomings of the IMF were also exposed in its response to the Asian financial crisis. These middle-income countries - Indonesia, Korea, Malaysia, Philippines and Thailand - had been maintaining balanced or even surplus budgets, high foreign exchange reserves and low inflation. Yet when the IMF was required to intervene to shore up liquidity and restore confidence in the aftermath of a substantial flight of capital, it immediately predicated its lending on a tightening of monetary controls, the raising of interest rates, the closure of banks and other measures, which had the predictable consequence of further destroying, rather than restoring, confidence. Perhaps not surprisingly, confidence began to be restored fastest in Malaysia, which chose not to go to the IMF for help in the early phases of the crisis.

The World Bank may also be said to have missed the vocation intended for it. Part of its role in Europe - where it started operations - was eclipsed

---
8 Griffith-Jones (1993).
9 Bird, op. cit.

in the early days by the Marshall Plan, for which it was not chosen as a conduit. Subsequently, it saw its influence increase after the approval in 1960 of the International Development Association (IDA), a concessional funding arm for the poorest countries, generously funded by the richer countries. It thus became the largest single source of development assistance, as described earlier. But it never acted as a true mechanism of global economic management in recycling substantial private resources towards development. It became predominantly a development fund and - from the 1960s - its operations were also exclusively in the developing world.

An important phase in World Bank operations occurred in 1980, when the first 'structural adjustment loan' (SAL) ushered in what this book has described as the third age of aid. Policy-based lending through the SAL was a response to different currents in the Bank's management. One was the desire to enhance the position of the Bank as a full-fledged development agency, with a concern for broader objectives such as poverty alleviation, which project finance was less effective at addressing. Another was a growing impatience with what was perceived as poor economic management.[10] The former objective would have needed longer-term programme lending, which the Bank was not ready for. In the event, therefore, SALs became rather heavy-handed instruments of policy conditionality.

By the 1980s, the Bank and Fund found themselves moving more closely together, not always harmoniously. The SAL shifted the Bank firmly into territory which the Fund had come to dominate. Even the lending instruments had become more similar. The SALs were more strictly disbursed in tranches, according to performance. In 1974, the IMF had introduced its medium-term Extended Fund Facility (EFF) and in 1986 and 1987, came the Structural Adjustment Facility (SAF) and Enhanced Structural Adjustment Facility (ESAF) respectively, the latter designed for poorer indebted countries. The SAF and ESAF were on concessional terms, much more like Bank loans.

The Bank's SALs could initially be extended only to countries already under IMF stabilisation, which necessitated close coordination, and compatibility between two sets of conditionalities. Fund conditions are more purely quantitative and macro-economic, and the Bank conditions partly qualitative, but there have been conflicts which have caused confusion for borrowers. The joint Policy Framework Paper, dating from the late 1980s, attempts to set out a common understanding of the economic

---

10 Mosley et al. (1991).

situation of the borrower and the needed policy goals.

Latterly, the World Bank's role as the principal source for concessional lending has diminished, because of the growing volume of repayments. In many recent years, the transfer of funds between the Bank and the developing countries has actually been in the Bank's favour. (Although the reverse flow is dominated by middle-income countries, they and the transition countries of Europe have also been among the largest recipients of new funds). Even for the poorest countries, the positive transfers by the Bank are in some years smaller than the resources made available on grant terms by the UN system. The Bank's concerns with the capacity of its most heavily indebted borrowers to repay its loans are growing steadily. It now leans ever more heavily on bilateral partners to stump up grant funds to meet resource gaps which are increasingly accounted for by obligations to itself and the Fund. As described in an earlier chapter, this process makes aid mobilisation increasingly ambiguous.

The Bank's growing capacity to raise grant funds from donors for technical assistance is helping to build up its role as the pre-eminent development agency, with an ever-widening mandate, putting it in direct competition with the UN development system in many fields and in many countries.

Reforming Bretton Woods

As global economic interdependence continues to expand, the institutions originally established to help govern the global economy are not playing their role. The World Trade Organisation, opening in 1995, is in some measure a re-creation of the International Trade Organisation conceived at Bretton Woods, although it has yet to meet fully the goals of trade liberalisation. For the other two institutions from that conference - the IMF and World Bank - it would be neither appropriate nor feasible to seek to restore them to their original mandates. However, reform is urgently called for if they are to respond to contemporary needs of financial governance. The growing dependence on private capital markets has advantages of flexibility, but exposes countries to considerable risks when there are crises of confidence. The experiences of Mexico in 1994-95 and Thailand and Indonesia in 1997-98 provide dramatic examples of capital volatility linked to exchange rate adjustments which the IMF was originally set up to supervise, but for which there is now no global regulatory mechanism. The intransigent debt problem afflicting many of the poorest countries is still not being adequately addressed, at a time when some countries are accumulating substantial foreign exchange surpluses.

In the absence of an adequate financial governance system, the economically powerful countries have come to dominate all processes of regulation or adjustment. They act alone, or through ad hoc improvisation at annual G-7 summit meetings, or through their dominance of the Fund and Bank. The G-7 countries have become the real 'governors' of the IMF, and also the World Bank by virtue of weighted voting, with the US playing a dominant role.[11] US foreign policy dictates to the Fund and Bank on their dealings with individual countries, inhibiting their operations in 'unfriendly' countries such as Iran, Cuba and Vietnam, while ensuring speedy action in commercially and strategically important ones like Mexico and Russia. If it can still be called a system of governance, it has become seriously lop-sided.

The International Monetary Fund. It is now time to attempt to re-create the functions of a world central bank, whose role should be to bring more discipline to bear on global economic activity, regulate banks and financial institutions, provide additional international liquidity and act as a more effective lender of last resort. Most or all of these functions could be undertaken by a reformed IMF, but to gain the necessary confidence of all constituent governments, it would have to be an IMF in which the concerns of the more vulnerable countries are clearly articulated and responded to.

The resources of the IMF need first to be urgently increased. Some 70% of resources come from members' subscriptions and the balance from borrowing from members. This heavy dependence on subscriptions based on quotas determined by economic size was appropriate when it was envisaged that the IMF would be essentially a mechanism of temporary adjustment. However, if a much larger role of strategic financing is anticipated, mainly for the benefit of countries with the smallest quotas, then additional sources of finance need to be found, and the access of countries to IMF credit should be related to criteria based more on need and less on quota size. In addition to more borrowing, there have been proposals for other innovative ways to raise development funds, which might be administered by the IMF. One of the best known of these is the foreign exchange transactions levy,[12] a small tax on all foreign exchange dealings, designed to act as a deterrent to speculation and first proposed by James

---

[11] The G-7 countries command almost half the votes in the World Bank. The donor countries as a whole hold a large majority. Since some key decisions are taken on the basis of a substantial majority of the total votes, a few of the largest members voting together can effectively exercise a veto.

[12] ul Haq et al. (1996).

Tobin in 1972. There have been recent refinements of this proposal.

There are additional sources of finance which could contribute directly to the liquidity of the highly-indebted poor countries. One - already mentioned in the earlier discussion on debt - is the sale of gold, which could make immediately available several billion dollars to cancel arrears. Another source is an increased allocation of SDRs. This general increase in liquidity would improve the overall credit-worthiness of developing countries, improve the prospects for private borrowing and also contribute to a solution of the debt crisis. As with quotas, there could be more flexibility in distribution, with some countries agreeing to lend their allocations to others.

The IMF must also climb down on the conditions of its programmes for the poorest countries. With substantially more resources at its disposal, it would be able to offer more flexibility. Instruments such as the CCFF and ESAF should be extended in term and free of quota restrictions. The CCFF should not be saddled with conditionality. In tune with the philosophy of this book - and more in tune with multilateral principles - countries coming to the Fund for assistance under the ESAF and other instruments should be provided with a choice of different borrowing options agreed to by the full membership. These choices could involve a trade-off between interest-rates and conditionality, and a mixture of funding sources.

The World Bank. For the World Bank, it is clear that it never was, and will not become, a mechanism of global governance. Over time, its role as a source of development capital has diminished. As more middle-income countries are able to move into private markets for their capital requirements, its clientele is narrowing to the poorer and more heavily indebted countries. But even to them, net capital flows are diminishing. Only the break up of the Soviet Union, and the opportunities for lending to the new countries in transition, has slowed the decline in the Bank's traditional lending functions.

In the meantime, the Bank has moved into and maintained its position as the foremost development agency and, under new leadership, is actively diversifying its role. But there are at least two key concerns which now demand its attention, and both relate to its traditional role as a source of development finance.

In the 1980s, it led the trend towards policy-oriented lending, with structural (and later sectoral) adjustment loans. The rationale was to influence macro-economic management. The results were very mixed: in many cases where policies were changed, they did not stick, often because the political consensus was lacking, but also because institutions were weak. For a reformed economy to work well, there needs to be an efficient public service, a well-run legal system and clearly defined and respected property rights. Now - in this fourth age - the Bank is following the development trend of the 1990s and emphasizing the importance of strengthening domestic institutions. This is less familiar territory for the World Bank, and not amenable to the kinds of conditionalities which it has deployed in the past (with mixed success). The Bank will need to win the confidence of its clients in this area and build alliances with other organisations with the necessary experience and expertise.

The Bank also needs to find an urgent solution to the problems of indebtedness of its most important clientele: the poorest countries with limited access to private capital markets. Increasingly, the Bank acts as advisor to other creditors, while claiming that it is constrained by its charter from rescheduling its own debts. As its ownership of the debts of the poorest countries increases, it will see net transfers to them continuing to decline. Its credibility as a primary source of development finance will diminish. A more radical approach than the Heavily Indebted Poor Country (HIPC) initiative will soon be needed.

For the Bretton Woods institutions, one outstanding task of global economic governance remains, and that is the maintenance of financial stability and the prevention of the periodic economic shocks which have assailed different middle-income developing economies in recent years. The East Asian financial crisis of 1997-98 is the latest - but surely not the last - example of capital volatility temporarily undoing the economic gains and rising living standards of past decades. Some analysts have claimed that the crisis puts into question the reality of the Asian miracle. Others have seen it as a condemnation of the whole process of globalisation. Both groups cannot be correct, and it is more likely that neither is. The strong 'fundamentals' of the miracle economies, which have gained so much from and contributed to the globalisation process, are still in place. However, there is no disputing the need for countries enjoying substantial inflows of short-term and portfolio capital to develop the capacity to absorb them: palliating inflationary and exchange-rate pressures, recognising the danger signals (e.g. excessive speculative on-lending of foreign capital), and putting in place banking standards and regulations to ensure the soundness of financial institutions.

It would be wrong to say that the IMF and World Bank wholly failed to anticipate the dangers leading up to the latest crisis. But clearly, they were unable to ensure that adequate corrective action was taken to prevent it. In a general manner, globalisation requires effective mechanisms of financial governance. While the basis of such a mechanism may already be in place, it needs strengthening. Central bankers already meet in Basle under the auspices of the Bank for International Settlements, which has helped to improve the liquidity of banks through capital adequacy ratios. Securities markets can also consult through the International Organisation of Securities Commissions.

There have been many proposals to improve global economic governance. One would bring all aspects of governance - including economic, trade, social and environment issues - within a single apex body. Another proposal, put forward by George Soros, would be to create an 'international credit insurance corporation', which would underwrite market lending to borrowers in a country up to a limit determined by an objective assessment of the country's debt-carrying capacity. Both proposals point towards a solution. It is certainly necessary to strengthen the links between different existing bodies, while clarifying their areas of responsibility. More comprehensive assessments of the financial health of individual countries are also required. They should take into account the analysis of private markets and should not be left to the overly secretive deliberations of the IMF.

The IMF and World Bank should be a central part of a strengthened system of global economic governance, but their role cannot be exclusive. Their meetings (including the annual joint meeting of both bodies) and their deliberations need to reflect more equitable representation of all countries. They must work more openly with other bodies such as the Bank for International Settlements. And they must assume more responsibility for insuring that the regulatory and safeguard mechanisms are in place in individual countries to prevent or temper external economic shocks.

The World Trade Organisation. The chapter on trade liberalisation included discussion on the formation of the World Trade Organisation (WTO). The WTO is one of the key components of the new global governance structure, and its establishment was long overdue. In some important respects, it resembles the mechanism originally envisaged in the Bretton Woods conference to encourage greater trade liberalisation.

The importance of the WTO may be determined from a comparison with the General Agreement on Tariffs and Trade, which was agreed to following the failure of the US Congress to ratify the charter of the International Trade Organisation. Like the World Bank and IMF, the GATT was dominated by its so-called 'contracting parties', of which there were only 23 at the outset, mainly developed countries. Unlike the other Bretton Woods institutions, however, it was virtually bereft of implementing machinery.[13] GATT was a

---
13 See discussion in Konrad von Moltke, 'The Structure of Regimes for Trade and the Environment', in Young (1997).

periodic tariff-cutting exercise, and its contribution to trade liberalisation was limited by the narrowness of its mandate and by the development of other trade protection measures which reduced the impact of the successive negotiating rounds.

The actual working of the WTO has already been discussed earlier. The purpose here is to judge the WTO's effectiveness as a mechanism of governance. Unlike the GATT, the WTO is on its way to universal membership, with over 130 signatories and a long waiting list. Virtually all countries have perceived the advantages of joining, and the new trade regime negotiated under the Uruguay Round is seen as containing a set of trade rules that is much fairer to all parties, and a disputes procedure to which all countries have access. Countries can negotiate the terms of their membership and adjust the timetables for adhering to the different protocols. The WTO is an essential - and inevitable - mechanism to facilitate the inexorable process of global trade liberalisation.

But it is by no means perfect, and it can be made to work better. The deliberations of the WTO are not sufficiently transparent, in consideration of the fact that the outcome of its negotiations affect large numbers of people in a direct material sense. There should also be more scope to include non-governmental interests in WTO discussions. Another problem derives from the very success of the organisation in liberalising trade: the summary removal of all protection in some sectors is adversely affecting some smaller and weaker trading countries. The WTO must be sensitive to their needs, while continuing to adhere to free trading principles.

There is also criticism that the WTO's trading rules are environmentally harmful. Unquestionably, trade expansion contributes to the exploitation of natural resources and has been linked to the rapid depletion of forests and marine life. Ultimately, decisions regarding the sustainability of the environment are the responsibility of the host country, or in the case of international waters, subject to an appropriate global regime. The WTO should not be invoked as a scapegoat for responsibility abrogated in favour of the multinational private sector. However, where the rules appear to favour commercial exploitation over environmental conservation, they must be very carefully examined and rewritten if necessary in favour of sustainability. In fact, the whole concept of protectionism is fraught with ambiguity and needs clarification. As discussed below, multinational companies are using the increased protectionism in respect of intellectual property under the WTO to patent plant species and threaten biodiversity.

The future of the United Nations development system

Although the Bretton Woods institutions strayed from their original mandates, their respective roles in the governance of the post-war economy were quite precisely laid down in the 1944 conference. By contrast, the UN organisation and its incorporated system were provided with an imprecise road-map in the development field and made a rather hesitant start. While the IMF and World Bank roles evolved in response to changing global conditions and under the firm direction of the dominant economic powers, the shape assumed by the UN development system was rather more accidental.

As a blueprint for the promotion of "economic and social progress and development", the relevant articles of the UN Charter are vague (Chapter IX and articles from Chapters IV and X). Perhaps this is scarcely surprising in a document primarily intended to establish ground rules for the maintenance of international peace and security. At San Francisco, moreover, there was no exercise undertaken for the UN, equivalent to the drafting of the articles of agreement for the Fund and Bank accomplished the previous year.

There was also a considerable problem of organisational coordination. The creation of the UN development system was a brave attempt to 'bring into relationship' with the UN organisation three long pre-existing bodies (the International Telecommunications Union, Universal Postal Union and International Labour Organisation) and the Bretton Woods institutions, while facilitating the creation of 4 more UN specialised agencies over the next 5 years (ICAO, FAO, UNESCO, WHO). The relationships with the agencies was governed by Special Agreements, but they could not prevent a considerable degree of autonomy emerging. The World Bank and IMF never took these agreements seriously, asserting their independence from any external coordination by a body which they perceived as essentially political. The World Bank was fearful that a close relationship could hurt its credit rating.[14] The other agencies also had separate constitutions and assemblies, which elected their heads independently of the Secretary-General. The comportment of member governments did not assist coordination - quite the contrary. The same governments which argued forcefully in the early sessions of the General Assembly for better UN integration also sent delegates from their sectoral ministries to the forums of the specialised agencies to support those autonomous mandates.

With inadequate integration, any grand design the founders may have

---

14 Childers and Urquhart (1994).

had for the UN to play a central role in managing global economic affairs was likely to fail. Dispersion of the constituent parts was a fundamental problem, but the UN development system has also, from its foundation, lacked a centre. The coordination role which the 54-member Economic and Social Council (ECOSOC) was intended to play has never been effective. For most of its life, ECOSOC has met only once a year to consider an overcharged agenda, consisting largely of reports submitted to it by the many different parts of the system. ECOSOC has lacked authority and would have needed a strong permanent secretariat to follow through on its decisions.

Belatedly, in 1977, the Secretary General established in New York the office of the Director General for Development and International Economic Cooperation. The incumbent was supposed to be the highest-ranking UN official after the Secretary General, act as 'primus inter pares' among the heads of agencies and - in the original proposal - chair an advisory committee of selected heads of agency, including the World Bank and IMF. The DG proposal never had the whole-hearted support of the rich countries. The committee was never established, and it is very likely that, even if it had been, the Bank and Fund heads would not have attended, given their aversion to being coordinated.

The position of Director General was finally abolished in 1992 and it is evident from hindsight that any revival of the idea for the UN to play a major coordinatory role in global economic and social development is unrealistic, because it is infeasible. That is why this book does not support the proposal of the Commission on Global Governance and others for an 'economic security council' under UN auspices. As an inter-governmental entity, such a proposal is unlikely to win the approval of the G-7 finance ministers, who are content with their long-standing association with the Bretton Woods institutions.[15] But in its secretariat functions, there are also credibility problems. With very few exceptions, the UN system has never successfully attracted the kind of intellectual talent in the development field which the Fund and Bank enjoy.[16] The reasons are not hard to come by: no strong intellectual tradition was established, there was no pro-active recruitment policy to attract development specialists, and the UN remuneration and working conditions are distinctly inferior to those of the Fund and Bank. In the senior ranks of the UN, advancement should be

---

15 With the accession of Russia, the new 'G-8' grouping comprises 4 out of 5 of the permanent members of the UN Security Council, and already begins to resemble an economic security council.

16 An early exception might be Hans Singer, who worked in the UN secretariat in the early days; a late exception is Mahbub ul Haq, who previously worked in the Bank and became senior advisor to the UN Development Programme in 1989.

based more strictly on criteria of relevant professionalism and experience.

Unquestionably, the potential effectiveness of the UN development system as a mechanism to coordinate economic governance was undermined by the factors already cited. However, the new system that emerged - in somewhat haphazard manner - in 1945 had several other purposes besides development oversight. On several other counts, the UN development system has performed rather useful functions, which have not been dependent on closer integration of the different parts of the system, and which have furnished important public goods and services for global benefit.

In the first place, individual agencies of the system have organised significant world-wide campaigns to address critical human problems. One of the best known is the World Health Organisation's successful coordination of a campaign to eradicate smallpox (and its current efforts to render polio, leprosy and other infectious diseases extinct). Another is the global programme led by the UN Children's Fund (UNICEF) and WHO to conduct mass vaccinations against 6 of the most deadly childhood diseases. These programmes have led to very tangible gains, which can be measured in numbers of lives saved; the vaccination campaign probably saves the lives of 2 million children every year. UN agencies and programmes also channel between $1 billion and $2 billion into emergency relief each year, helping to maintain the livelihoods of some 20 million refugees and delivering one third of the world's food aid.

In a potentially vast development agenda, there are other areas in which the UN system has been called on to play a coordinating role. One is in the monitoring and control of narcotic drugs, where despite - but probably also because of - the enormity of the problem, there has been little tangible progress since the passing of a major convention in 1988. Another critical development concern, with global ramifications, is the fight against HIV/AIDS, on which six different UN agencies (including the World Bank) are collaborating. A third area - the management of the global environment - is of sufficient importance to justify discussion in a separate section below. In each area of concern, such as these mentioned, one or other of the UN development system agencies have taken a leading role, while others have provided support.

Secondly, there are tasks of standardisation and harmonisation which only global regulatory bodies can draw up. In the last century, when international communications by telephone, telegraph and mail were developing, it was found necessary to create global bodies to ensure the adoption of common standards and codes, and the International Telecommunication Union (ITU) and the Universal Postal Union (UPU) were set up. As mentioned above, the ITU and UPU were brought under UN auspices in the 1940s, and several other technical UN bodies were established for regulatory purposes: the International Civil Aviation Organisation has drawn up common air safety standards, and the International Maritime Organisation has done the same for shipping. Outside the communications and transport fields, the World Meteorological Organisation has fostered cooperation in weather forecasting and disaster warning and the World Intellectual Property Organisation is the custodian of global patent and copyright agreements. In addition to developing common standards, these technical agencies were important sources of technical expertise and have helped to facilitate the transfer of expertise between countries.

Thirdly, the UN system has been instrumental in the setting of fundamental development norms. These normative functions of the UN involve the determination of universal standards of human needs and rights applicable to the whole of humankind. Only through the global forums of the UN, working by consensus, in which every country has equal representation, and in which other non-governmental voices are being encouraged, can such norms be developed. Under UN auspices a large number of conventions have been agreed to - perhaps too many for each to have a significant impact. But some are of special significance and have made an important impact.

Without doubt, the most important area of UN norm-setting is in human rights, although the work of the organisation in this area is not especially well known. Equality of status and opportunity are enshrined in the Charter and in 1948, the UN passed the Universal Declaration of Human Rights. In that year, there were still fewer than 60 UN members, but some 40 additional human rights conventions have since been agreed to, to which the large majority of countries are party. Although membership of the UN has never been conditional on the observance of human rights standards, governments are expected to comply with the spirit of UN conventions. The records of all are regularly reviewed and more than half have been held accountable for violations. While it is difficult to clearly connect the UN with improved human rights protection, its work helps to expose non-compliance. The World Conference on Human Rights in Vienna in 1993 led to the creation of the post of High Commissioner. The appointment of a growing number of Special Rapporteurs has also helped to raise the visibility of the UN's efforts.

The Vienna conference was one of the eight summits convened by the UN in the 1990s (see Table 7). The first of these was of at least equal significance in terms of the rights agenda. In drawing up the Convention on the Rights of the Child - the most widely ratified of all human rights treaties[17] - UNICEF's Children's Summit set normative standards which quickly achieved almost universal recognition. Another area in which progress can be ascribed to UN initiatives is gender equality. The 1995 summit was only one step in a protracted effort on behalf of the rights of women (and the Cairo summit on population was also significant in reaffirming women's rights in respect of family planning). There have been several UN conventions on women's rights, the most comprehensive being the Convention on the Elimination of All Forms of Discrimination against Women of 1979.

Table 7: The global UN summits of the 1990s

Year (month) and Place	Title	Main Outcome	Lead UN Agency
1990 (September) New York	World Summit for Children	Adopted Convention on the Rights of the Child	UN Children's Fund (UNICEF)
1992 (June) Rio de Janeiro	UN Conference on Environment and Development (Earth Summit)	Adopted Agenda 21, global plan for sustainable development; agreed to the Framework Convention on Climate Change; agreed to the Convention on Biological Diversity; established the Commission on Sustainable Development	UN Environment Programme (UNEP)
1993 (June) Vienna	World Conference on Human Rights	Established the High Commissioner for Human Rights	UN Secretariat
1994 (September) Cairo	International Conference on Population and Development	International recognition of the need to educate and empower women	UN Population Fund (UNFPA)
1995 (March) Copenhagen	World Summit for Social Development	Commitment to global poverty eradication	UN Secretariat and others
1995 (September) Beijing	Fourth World Conference on Women	Set targets for achievement of gender goals	UN Secretariat 1996
1996 (June) Istanbul	Second UN Conference on Human Settlements	Adopted plan of action on human settlements	UN Centre for Human Settlements (UNCHS)
1996 (November) Rome	World Food Summit	Adopted Declaration of Rome and Plan of Action	Food and Agriculture Organisation of the UN (FAO)

Sources: http://www.un.org; http://www.unicef.org

17 Only two states have not ratified the Convention: Somalia and the US.

In recent years, parts of the UN development system have refined norm-setting into specific indicators of development progress. UNICEF has established targets on the status of children and carefully monitors the progress of its vaccination campaigns. In 1990, the UN Development Programme developed its 'human development index' based on attainments in education, health and income and ranked every country in the world by this measure, implicitly judging development success. The index is remeasured and published annually. (In 1991, UNDP factored human rights into performance with a 'human freedom index', but it proved highly controversial with a few countries and was discontinued).

There is a fourth function which the UN development system has performed since its formation which, in UN parlance, is called the 'operational' one: the provision of technical assistance to individual member states by the different specialised agencies. To facilitate this role, the configuration of the UN development system at its formation more than 50 years ago was to a large extent a mirror of a typical state administration. The World Health Organisation (WHO) had its counterparts in the health ministries; the Food and Agriculture Organisation (FAO) in the agriculture ministries; the UN Industrial Development Organisation (UNIDO), the UN Educational, Scientific and Cultural Organisation (UNESCO), and so on, all had their ministerial counterparts.

Alongside these specialised technical agencies a funding facility was developed, a major purpose of which was to finance technical assistance services provided by the specialised agencies. But, for reasons discussed earlier, it was never on the scale of the World Bank. The keenly debated proposal in the 1950s to establish a Special UN Fund for Economic Development (SUNFED) was scaled down to a much more modest 'special fund' to supplement the Expanded Programme of Technical Assistance (EPTA). Instead the major donor countries gave the much larger soft-loan International Development Association to the World Bank. EPTA and the special fund were combined in 1965 to become the UN Development Programme which, despite its name, was initially mainly a funding mechanism.

It is somewhat ironic that now, the reverse flows of funds to the World Bank have made the UN system a source of concessional aid of equivalent size, in terms of net resource transfers, even without taking humanitarian resources into account. However, the utility of the currently-configured UN development system in its technical assistance functions is now steadily diminishing, for several reasons.

First, because the role of the state in fostering development is waning. UN technical assistance programmes grew up and expanded during a period when state-led development was the predominant model. Given their supporting constituencies in government ministries, the instinctive response of UN agencies to development needs has been to search for interventions from appropriate parts of the public sector. But from agriculture to industry to infrastructure, privately-organised initiative, supported by private capital, is spearheading change. The role of governments is being steadily transformed from do-ers to enablers. The macro-economic environment and the existence of basic legal and financial institutions are more critical than the technical capacities of state ministries.

Second, and to the extent that technical expertise is still required, it can be found from many other sources besides the UN agencies. While the UN system can provide valuable guidance in locating such sources, it is no longer the main repository of expertise - if it ever was. Some of the alternatives are to be found in other international public service organisations, some of them created by the UN system. For example in the early 1970s, FAO, the World Bank and UNDP formed the Consultative Group on International Agricultural Research, a consortium of specialised institutions located around the world, including those which helped to propagate the benefits of the 'green revolution' which led to a substantial improvement in the yield of food crops in developing countries. In the 1990s, WHO and UNDP have collaborated in the formation of the International Vaccine Institute in South Korea to help to develop and widen the use of vaccines in health campaigns around the world. There are numerous other examples.

Third, development progresses along thematic and cross-sectoral lines, for which the existing configuration of the UN development system is increasingly inappropriate. Among the foremost themes in technical assistance are those concerned with human development needs, improved governance and environmental management, which cross disciplinary and sectoral boundaries. If enhanced food security is an objective it cannot be left to agricultural ministries to pursue only by addressing the technical challenges of increasing agricultural production, since it involves issues of income distribution, market efficiency, status of infrastructure and so on. Growth of manufacturing capacity is not a matter solely for industry ministries, but involves concerns of investment promotion, technology transfer, skills development, market size, international trade policy, among others.

The record of the UN development system over the last half century is perhaps the best guide to its future. The system never attained the status of a global mechanism for governing the development process. It could scarcely have done so without attracting sufficient financial and human resources, which the international community - and in particular its richer members - has not been willing to permit, and without a significant enhancement in cohesion and coordination.

The technical assistance role of individual agencies has received the strong support of counterpart ministries in developing countries but, for reasons just outlined, their developmental significance is diminishing and the same governments and their ministries have alternative sources to go to for technical expertise and advice.

The most important and exclusive role of the UN development system derives from its normative functions. These reflect most faithfully the spirit of the original Charter which envisaged inter-country cooperation as the basis for social and economic progress through the UN. The UN provides a unique mechanism for addressing collectively and fairly the major development challenges which individual countries cannot adequately deal with when acting alone. Growing global interdependence can only enhance the importance of this role, but to perform it adequately, the UN system must adapt and modernise its own methods. These are secretariat responsibilities. Too many global conferences can be wasteful and - if the outcome is meager - counter-productive for the promotion of an issue. The UN system must continue to encourage alternative opinions and voices in its deliberations, particularly from non-governmental and private commercial sector interests, so as to strengthen the eventual consensus.

The system must also improve its capacity to provide information through a better management of its resources. The information revolution gives the UN system an extraordinary opportunity to gather together and facilitate the dissemination of information from many sources. The proliferation of sources will reduce the need for the system itself to generate information internally. One web-master may be a much better use of resources than a team of researchers preparing information from secondary sources. Market principles should also be applied more rigorously: what cannot be sold, should not be told. Reports should at least break even to prove their utility. To compliment its normative functions, and to assist the process of monitoring progress, some of the most precious information generated by the UN itself should be data pertaining to the setting and achievement of development standards.

Notwithstanding the continuing value of the its normative functions, the future evolution of the UN development system implied by the foregoing discussion has important ramifications for its structure. The overall size of the system, and the existing duplication of activities demand urgent scrutiny. It is questionable whether the international community is willing to continue to support a system of the present magnitude and complexity, particularly in the execution of operational functions. The Commission on Global Governance recommended consolidation, including the reduction in scope or closure of a specialised agency (UNIDO) and several secretariat entities (UNCTAD and the five regional commissions), and the combining of three New York-based departments into one.[18] The Secretary General has taken the last step as part of a two-part internal reform process. He has also clustered the different parts of the UN under his direct authority - the secretariat, the funds and the programmes, comprising approximately half of the total staff of the UN system - into 5 executive committees each lead by one of the under-secretaries general. The executive committees cover peace and security, development, economic and social affairs, humanitarian and general services. It is a first step towards a possible eventual merger of more departments. Over the past few years, there have been reductions in the total number of UN staff. A further 10% cut is expected between 1997 and 1999. However, the continuing examination of the utility of all parts of the system is still needed, before any serious statements can be supported about the UN lacking resources.

Proliferation shows even more starkly in UN field operations, where many agencies and programmes have developed their own networks of country offices. In some countries there are as many as 18 separate representations of UN entities (excluding the IMF and World Bank), each with a head of office, staff and infrastructure. In many countries, 10 or more is common. Worldwide the system maintains no fewer than 1,000, including regional offices. In most countries, the head of the UNDP office also acts as the UN resident coordinator for operations and for humanitarian interventions. The incumbent at least ensures that the heads of the offices meet, but much more could be done to achieve greater harmonisation of UN system activities, and to pool administrative resources. There have been many proposals for closer consolidation[19] and the Secretary General has proposed the formation of integrated 'UN Houses' in each country, with as many UN entities as possible within common premises.

This book strongly supports field consolidation, but goes much further in proposing structural reform. With the advantages of information and communications technology, the funds and programmes of the UN system could become almost wholly decentralised into global networks. Large headquarters would become superfluous. Each country office, or cluster of offices would be effectively owned by the host country which would fund the staff and the establishment, with the exception of the international posts.

---

18 Commission on Global Governance, op. cit.
19 The Nordic UN Reform Project (1996); Browne (1993).

This practice is already followed in a few countries, but it should be generalised. The field network would be the main entry point of each member country into the UN development system from which services could be 'purchased' by additional voluntary contributions. Middle and higher income countries, which make relatively little use of the development services could agree to pay for services provided to poorer countries.

Modified funding principles should also be applied to the 'assessed' contributions paid by member states into the UN regular budget, which supports headquarters-based activities. The current formula of assessment is based on relative capacity to pay, but takes no account of the relative benefits of membership. Thus, the world's largest country, China, which enjoys permanent membership of the Security Council, pays only 0.77% of the total budget. The United States pays 25%. Unfortunately, in the latest reappraisal of contributions in 1998, the trend was towards even greater disparities, with the smallest contributions falling from 0.01% to 0.001% of the total budget.

There is no question that the world needs a UN development system more than ever. As the process of global interaction advances, the UN meets many of the criteria through which collective governance can generate collective benefits. It offers fair and open forums of equal representation; it increasingly provides for the participation of minority interests; it develops universal standards and ideals and helps to monitor their observance. It has also provided the channels through which newly-perceived global concerns can be urgently debated and acted on through the drafting and implementation of global regimes. The whole area of environmental governance has very well demonstrated the utility of the UN in this regard, and is discussed in the following section.

But while the need is beyond question, the future shape of that system is a matter of urgent debate. The 'accidental' evolution of the UN family of agencies and programmes has led to a proliferation which the international community cannot be expected to support indefinitely. When the Charter was written in 1945, a grand design of a development system was only vaguely perceived and imperfectly configured. Since then, there has been no effective effort to develop an overall strategy to support the roles which the UN performs best and phase out those of which the continuing utility is questionable, or for which alternative means have been developed. A new blueprint is now required, the attainment of which will entail more than phased reforms.

Environmental governance

Notwithstanding the shortcomings of its current orientation and structure, the UN development system's role in global management has been critical in some areas of planetary interest. Since the late 1980s, the challenge of managing the global environment has been one of the most important - and in recent years urgent - of the UN's preoccupations.

From the 1950s, the UN has sponsored negotiations on the management of the global commons leading to several landmark conventions: the Antarctic Treaty of 1959, superseded by a Protocol in 1991; and the Treaty on the Exploration and Use of Outer Space of 1967; and the Convention on the Law of the Sea of 1982.

In recent years, spurred on by increasingly visible signs of environmental degradation, governments working through the UN have reached agreement on several significant new global environment regimes, and the establishment of implementing bodies. Growing meteorological perturbations, more prolonged floods and droughts, higher incidence of skin cancers in humans, are among the signals that have prompted these actions. Also, consciousness has been raised by events such as the second Earth Summit of 1992 - fortuitously timed - which helped to advance the global environment agenda. Three of the most important of these agreements are the Montreal Protocol, the Framework Convention on Climate Change and the Convention on Biological Diversity (see Box 11).

These three global regimes illustrate both the importance and the shortcomings of international cooperation. They illustrate the importance of universality of acceptance, which all three have almost achieved. However, if one major party is absent, the objectives may fall seriously short. The success of the Montreal Protocol was ensured by the agreement of the US to comply. But the reluctance of the US to ratify the climate change convention is a threat to its success, since the country is a major source of harmful green-house gases (GHGs), and because its non-compliance sets a poor example. Similarly, American non-participation in the biodiversity convention will limit its effectiveness. The US position is strongly influenced by commercial interests. In the case of chloro-fluorocarbon reduction, good and cost-effective substitutes were found quickly. But in the case of GHGs, US companies are confronting large costs if they have to switch fuels or technologies to reduce emissions. The biodiversity convention is also perceived as a threat by some US companies which want to be assured of uninhibited access to species in host countries.

Another important feature of the new global environmental regimes is the need to be able to accommodate countries at different levels of wealth

Box 11: Major global environment agreements of the 1990s
Vienna Convention on the Protection of the Ozone Layer and Montreal Protocol
Under the auspices of the United Nations Environment Programme (UNEP), the Vienna Convention on the Protection of the Ozone Layer was drawn up and agreed to in 1985. Through this Convention, governments committed themselves to protect the ozone layer and to co-operate with each other in scientific research to improve understanding of the atmospheric processes. In 1987, the Montreal Protocol was drawn up specifying steep chloro-fluorocarbons (CFC) reduction targets for ratifying countries; these terms have been strengthened in three subsequent amendments: London (1990), Copenhagen (1992) and Montreal (1997). Under the Montreal Protocol, the richer countries were to have phased out production of CFCs by the beginning of 1996. The developing countries were given a grace period of ten more years. The Vienna Convention has been ratified by 166 countries and the Copenhagen Amendment by 78.

Linked to the Montreal Protocol is the Multilateral Fund, a financial mechanism set up under the London Amendment, to support country studies, technical assistance, information and training in order to facilitate implementation of the agreement by developing countries. The fund receives contributions mainly from the richer countries and by 1998 had disbursed some $450 million.[20]

Framework Convention on Climate Change and Kyoto Protocol
In the late 1980s, the UN started negotiations on a Framework Convention on Climate Change (UNFCCC) and it was signed in 1992, at the Earth Summit. It entered into force in 1994 and has been signed and ratified by 174 countries. However, the UNFCCC does not specifically bind the signatories to a timetable of reduced emissions. At a conference of the parties in Berlin in 1995, it was agreed to develop a protocol for this purpose. An agreement was then reached at a further conference in Kyoto at the end of 1997, which set specific limits for 38 developed countries: between 2008 and 2012, the European Union countries should reduce their emissions of green-house gases (GHGs: carbon dioxide, methane, nitrous oxide and halocarbons) to 8% below the levels of 1990; the US by 7% and Japan by 6%. Different targets were set for the other developed countries. Actual enforcement measures are to be determined in subsequent negotiations. Developing countries are only asked to set voluntary targets. The Kyoto Protocol will take effect when ratified by at least 55 countries, representing at least 55% of 1990 carbon dioxide emissions.

The Kyoto Protocol also provides for a mechanism, to be worked out in detail, of trading emission rights. Countries that fail to meet their emission targets will be able to make a deal to purchase excess quotas from countries which have done better than required.[21]

---

20 http://www.unep.ch/ozone.
21 http://www.unfccc.de.

> **Convention on Biodiversity**
> A working group was set up under UN auspices in 1988 to explore the need for an international convention on biological diversity. The group was upgraded in 1991 to an inter-governmental negotiating committee which drafted the Convention on Biological Diversity agreed at the Earth Summit in 1992. As of March 1998, it had been ratified by 172 countries, but not yet by the US. The convention requires countries to develop and implement strategies for sustainable use and protection of biodiversity and provides a forum (through the annual conference of parties) for dialogue on biodiversity issues.
>
> The Convention entered into force in 1994 and four conferences of the parties have been convened so far to refine and elaborate on the convention: Bahamas (1994), Jakarta (1995), Buenos Aires (1996) and Bratislava (1998). These conferences have given special attention to biodiversity in forestry, agriculture, inland waters, and marine and coastal areas. The financing mechanism for the Convention is managed by the Global Environment Facility, pending the establishment of an independent system.[22]

and endowment. Not all countries can, with equal ease and at equal comparative cost, make the adjustments to national policies and practices which regimes require. There must be provision for phasing. The cost of adjustment may be relatively much higher for developing countries - for example, in limiting carbon emissions. Also, developing countries can legitimately complain that the now developed countries never had to face the same limitations when they were formerly at similar levels of development. However, the differentiated observance of regimes raises free-rider concerns. There may need, therefore, to be provision for encouraging the extension of observance over time.

Compliance with environmental regimes has to depend in large part on the responsible attitudes of the governments of participating countries, 'responsible' being synonymous with 'global-thinking'. There are net costs of thinking globally. In the first place, the benefits of curbing activities which harm the environment within an individual country may redound mainly elsewhere. An example is given by the sulphur and nitrogen oxides thrown up by the industries of some western European countries, which fall as acid rain on neighbours. In general, reduced harmful emissions by one country will make a small marginal impact on the global environment, unlikely to be perceptible by that country. Another cost is the absence of measurable benefits within a near time-frame. It is always politically more difficult to justify the need for costly environmental measures when the main dividends will be reaped by future generations.

---

22 http://www.biodiv.org.

In democratic countries, observance by governments can be encouraged by the vocal representations of the general public, through the mouthpiece of non-governmental organisations. The often spectacular demonstrations staged by organisations like Greenpeace on environmental issues have helped to turn official heads. However, where corporate lobbies are particularly strong, as in the US, parliaments are less sensitive to public opinion.

There are other means to bolster exhortation. Some regimes are supported by financing mechanisms to assist developing countries to meet the costs of observance. One is the Montreal Protocol, for which quite generous funds have been provided by donors to finance the reduction in the manufacture and use of CFCs. Many countries have benefited, including major manufacturers and users such as Mexico and China. Mexico has received some $30 million in project aid from Montreal, which has helped the country to bring forward by several years its attainment of the CFC target.

After Rio, the Global Environmental Facility (GEF) was established as a fund to be jointly managed by the World Bank, UN Development Programme and the UN Environment Programme. The purpose of the GEF is to augment development resources in order to cover the 'incremental costs' - some of which are suggested above - of globally responsible behaviour. In theory, incremental costs are the difference between the costs of projects to achieve global environmental sustainability objectives and those aimed at achieving national sustainability goals. In practice, these costs are virtually impossible to measure, and the GEF is utilised essentially as a source of incentive payments to encourage countries to undertake environmentally responsible projects in three areas: climate change, biological diversity and the management of international waters.

Under the Kyoto Protocol, there is a proposal to establish an emissions trading mechanism (see Box 11), which would allow countries that reduced emissions by more than their prescribed limits to sell their over-achievement to others. This mechanism would reward successful countries and make it more expensive to fail. The principle is a very important one, although there are many intricacies to be worked out. The plan does not yet involve developing countries, but it should be designed in such a way as to provide a financial inducement for them to participate. Another proposal is for richer countries to invest in emission-reducing projects in developing countries and sharing in the resulting credits.

These financial mechanisms, in support of global regimes, point to a very important new avenue for development assistance, and a basis for new kinds of partnership: the principle of payment by the richer countries for the creation of global public goods by the poorer. There is currently a lot of concern, for example, that the more strongly protectionist rules of the World Trade Organisation with respect to intellectual property are encouraging multinational corporations to establish patent rights over plant varieties, with no compensation to the countries of origin. Mechanisms of compensation can be envisaged which are either bilateral or collective. Extending the principle to the private corporate arena under the biodiversity convention, developing countries should seek to be compensated through 'royalty' payments for the use of rare or valuable species of plant or animal.

Global development governance and aid

It is a basic contention of this book that public goods and services for national development - education, health, housing, communications, and so on - are most effectively and sustainably generated in circumstances of good national governance; which does not mean large government, but strong institutions which facilitate the provision of goods and services by the most appropriate means. Such appears to have been the experience of the development ages: good governance is not sufficient, but it is invariably necessary.

Analagously, this book also contends that, in a world of growing interdependence, development progress must rely increasingly on good global governance, on one hand to deliver global public goods - such as market access, international capital, the fruits of medical, agricultural and other research, as well as universal norms and standards by which progress may be measured - and on the other hand, to reduce or countermand global public 'bads' - including infectious diseases and pandemics, environmental degradation, narcotic drug trafficking and the burden of international debt arrears. Development assistance resources should increasingly be utilised to help develop and improve the major mechanisms of global development governance.

The global conferences of the 1940s set out to build structures of global governance. The principles were entirely sound, but the new institutions fell short of expectations. The architecture of the UN was incomplete, but the organisation was an all-inclusive one even if the conditions for participation were arguably too lenient. The Bretton Woods institutions stayed closer to their original design, but their missions became distorted with practice. They have not been sufficiently inclusive and the conditions for participation are arguably too harsh for those member states which could gain the most. Their deliberations and their decision-making procedures are not sufficiently transparent.

In the 1990s, there are promising signs of change. The ITO which died by US Congressional veto in 1948 was resurrected in somewhat different form, but with similar objectives, in 1995. Under UN auspices, several significant new regimes of global environmental management have been agreed to. Serious reforms are under way in the UN development system and in the World Bank. They are being mooted in the IMF.

Guiding this process of change is a set of criteria which, as experience has shown, help to define good global governance.[23] Some of the principles of international cooperation are those which inspired the UN's founders. Global governance has to achieve a satisfactory balance between national concerns and the global or planetary interest. The principle of subsidiarity must be respected; to be effective, different actions often need to be taken at appropriate levels: sub-national, national, regional, global. Governance at any level is an interactive process which should encourage dialogue. It should encompass the different interests of the participating parties - including the disadvantaged and marginalised interests - while remaining true to a set of central ideals. It must also be a transparent process: the rules of participation must be clear and fair, and the deliberations should be open. Above all, the merits of participating in global regimes must be self-evident to all parties, the perceived benefits outweighing the costs.

But while these principles define the objectives, the real prospects for a strengthening of global governance lie with the efforts of individual governments. At one end of the scale, the world's most powerful country can continue to exert a critical influence, for good or ill. On the positive side, where the USA's national interests fully coincide with the global, results can quickly follow. In the development sphere, there are some important examples. America's fulsome backing for the Montreal Protocol was critical to its success. American endorsement of the WTO was critical to the establishment of the new trade body. However, where there is not the same coincidence of interest, the USA sometimes tries to make the global institutions bend to its individual will (e.g. the IMF and World Bank in their dealings with individual countries, or the UN in its reform programme), and exerts financial pressure by threatening to withhold financial support.

Historically, the US has done more than any other country to create the current mechanisms of global governance. But it can do also do more harm than any other country to render them ineffective, or undermine their credibility through bad example. It is a sobering fact that the future of the global governance institutions rests in part with the outcome of successive

---

23 Commission on Global Governance (1995).

US parliamentary elections, and the will of the administration to resist the pressures of small but highly influential domestic and international lobby groups.

At the other end of the scale are the many other, smaller countries already gaining immensely from the benefits of global governance. For these countries, participation in global organisations will facilitate their sharing in collective benefits unattainable through their individual efforts. By bringing its own concerns to the conference table, each country can exert its own small influence over the agenda and expect a more relevant outcome. These international public goods and services are important inputs to the development process.

More importantly, each country can make its own particular contribution to the collective effort and expand the totality of that effort more than commensurately. In environmental management, reduction of narcotic drug production and consumption, control of cross-border crime, removal of land-mines, among many other areas, the efforts of each country can pay larger dividends when administered through a collective mechanism.

These important benefits of partnership point down one of the paths leading beyond aid. Global governance can help to change traditional donor-recipient relationships in which aid is principally motivated by the interests of the source. From charity and dependency, global mechanisms can enhance interdependence and foster the sense of what the Commission on Global Governance has termed 'shared contractual obligation'. While every participating country is expected to pay membership dues in global organisations, these organisations can help develop mechanisms to calculate the global value of benefits generated by members and encourage richer countries to compensate poorer countries for development products and services rendered. In the world beyond aid, partnership of this kind holds more promise than patronage.

10 Beyond aid

This concluding chapter is not an attempt at a full summary. However, it draws together the major themes of the book into a statement on the future of aid.

The mixed performance of aid

The first part of the book reviewed the origins of aid, its rise and its fall and the reasons for these trends. It concluded with a critique of development assistance based on the record, and found at least five circumstances in which it had been revealed as less effective. First, aid has been traditionally directed at governments, often supporting inappropriate and inefficient state dirigisme. Second, much technical assistance has been directed towards the wrong, or insufficient, types of capacity building while ignoring the importance of institutions. Third, in an inappropriate policy environment, capital assistance has been dissipated through unproductive use, or in displacing domestic capital; in a conducive policy environment, aid has been productive, but beyond the short-term it can be substituted by private capital. Fourth, notwithstanding the domestic policy environment, many of the poorest countries have become saddled with substantial external official debts, largely as a result of circumstances beyond the control of their present governments. Fifth, the effects of aid are countermanded by the consequences of protectionism by the richer countries.

If there is a sixth reason for unproductive aid, it is when recipient countries are in a state of serious upheaval, or open conflict. During these periods, the institutions of global (or regional) governance may be required to intervene, and relief assistance - which is not being examined in this book - will be needed. What is nevertheless disturbing for the record of development assistance is the extent to which previous aid - economic linked to military - may have been a contributory factor to the disruption.

The second part of the book looked in more depth at the two aspects of the global economy which must necessarily be linked to any discussion on the effectiveness of aid: debt and trade. The debt crisis has become the major external impediment to the development of the poorest countries and its solution must dominate any discussion on the future of aid. The new opportunities provided by more liberal trade relations enhance the preference for trade over aid, but countries will need to adjust to the new parameters.

Part II also examined three areas which offer growing opportunities for cooperation and partnership in an increasingly interdependent world: the expansion in horizontal relations among countries through regionalism; the realities of the global 'informational' economy; and the strengthening of the institutions of global development governance.

Are Governments falling out of love with aid?

Aside from its performance and prospects, it is evident that aid in its traditional forms is losing its lustre. Hitherto, aid has been governed by assumptions that both donors and recipients needed and wanted it. But these assumptions can no longer be taken for granted. The needs and wants of donors have changed, just as their motivations and perceptions have. Equally, there is serious questioning on the part of recipients about the utility of aid. The perceptions are even more varied outside the donor and recipient governments.

The donors. Through the aid ages discussed in Part I, there has been a steady convergence in the five principal motivations for aid - multilateral, altruistic, military-strategic, politico-strategic and commercial - on the part of the donors. The end of the Cold War removed the rationale for aid based on military-strategic spheres of influence (although it did not remove the rationale for military sales aid - through export credits - for which the middle-income countries of Asia and Latin America are still providing a buoyant market for western arms exporters).

The distinctions among the other motivations for development aid have also become blurred. It is true that emergency assistance from the donors - which is not a subject primarily addressed by this book - has continued to be driven by a spirit of altruism (even where the causes of crisis were the direct result of man's inhumanity). But development aid has become increasingly allied with other, more self-interested considerations. Multilateral development aid, which in its purest expression had subsumed national interest into wider developmental objectives, has been diluted by the rising influence of individual donors within the different UN agencies and the development banks. The 'like-minded' bilateral donors have also been adding stronger political criteria to their aid choices, exemplified by the fact that all Nordic countries have in recent years more closely integrated their aid agencies with their foreign ministries. Most bilateral donors, beginning in the 1980s, have also aligned their aid with commercial concerns.

This general convergence has been prompted by two main donor perceptions. In the first place, there is the sense that much aid often does not of itself make a critical difference to development performance, for the reasons cited in the foregoing discussion. It does not play an effective gap-filling role. It may help to catalyse processes, but only in environments which are 'friendly' and sustainable.

Secondly, donors - from their own experience as well as from their perceptions of the developing world - have determined that markets are the major sources of dynamism in development, as demonstrated by the wave of liberalisation that has overtaken many developed and developing countries in the present decade. Publicly-administered resources have a diminishing role. Increasingly the state is called upon to facilitate the freer working of markets rather than trying to substitute for them. Aid could therefore be seen as an adjunct to this facilitation process.

The recipients. The perceptions of recipients are also changing. While at global conferences there is a continuing sense of solidarity among the so-called G-77 countries-plus-China, taken individually, the traditional recipients have a changing, and increasingly differentiated perception of the utility of aid. The reasons have been suggested by earlier discussions.

First, there is the perception among developing countries that aid is tied to a development agenda dominated by the donor countries. Traditionally, population control and environmental management have been stressed by the major donors, and backed by generous assistance. In the 1990s, poverty alleviation, good governance and human rights are the additional aid-winners. Objectively, there can be little dispute about the importance of these development aims. But by adopting them as their foremost preoccupations, conceiving their own - often politically infeasible - solutions, and supporting them with aid funds, donors and aid organisations are underlining aid patronage.

Second, recipients also perceive aid as primarily serving the interests of the donors. The widespread practice of tying aid to trade distorts markets and reduces the value of aid for recipients. Irrespective of aid tying, however, some three-quarters of the financial value of bilateral technical assistance funds are retained by donors, their companies and their experts, according to the author's own research.[1]

---
1 Browne (1990).

This leads to a third concern: that donors know best. Bilateral technical assistance - and multilateral aid to a high degree also - uses predominantly donor country-based expertise. The northern provenance of most technical advice conveys the impression that those most directly involved in the development process know least. Highly specialised external expertise from anywhere can be valuable in technical areas. However, in fields of institution-building and policy development, towards which technical assistance should be increasingly orientated, the best advice may come from those with the most germane experience.

Fourth, there is also the perception that the aid machine has simply grown too large, leading to a surfeit of assistance, which is neither consistent nor coordinated. There is no development problem on which the developing countries - collectively or individually - are not advised, whether the advice is solicited or not. Usually the assistance vaunts the comparative advantage of the source, but rarely are all sources in agreement, leading to multiplicity and inconsistency in the aid effort. In the 1980s, Kenya received 18 different types of pump for its domestic water programme. In a single year, Tanzania has been host to 10,000 separate aid missions from donors. On its own, one donor sends more than 80 missions a year to Bangladesh. Recently, many aid agencies have been active in brokering advice on the 1997-98 financial crisis in East Asia. Only a fraction of this advice could have been heeded, even if it was all heard. Those who have often witnessed aid salesmanship at the receiving end know the meaning of 'less is more'.

Fifth, developing countries are becoming more resistant to aid because of the conditionalities that accompany it. There are alternatives for some countries. There is a still limited, but growing number able to raise capital on commercial markets with fewer conditions and on equivalent terms to borrowing from the multilateral finance institutions. Some reforming countries have also seen the merits of foreign direct investment. After China - by far the largest recipient among developing countries - other low-income countries in Asia and Africa have successfully attracted new investors. In India, there has been a sharp increase in foreign investment inflows on the heels of their reform programme. These alternatives have made some leaders increasingly vocal in their opposition to aid in its traditional forms, even while they continue to receive it. Ugandan President Yoweri Museveni has compared aid to an ineffectual life-support system and calls investment "the shortest route to development".

Sixth, some developing countries are 'graduating'. Those that have developed successfully and whose economies have grown at a rapid pace, such as Singapore, can now boast income per capita levels, and human and environmental conditions, on a par with, or higher than, some of the OECD DAC countries - the traditional donors. The former 'developing countries' Mexico and South Korea are now members of the rich club, OECD. Several other countries still retain membership in the G-77, but are themselves donors, with aid budgets funded from public resources. India and China are prominent examples.

Finally, and perhaps most importantly, there is scepticism among the intended beneficiaries of aid. The view of practitioners in the field is that top-down approaches to aid provision have often exacerbated social inequalities more than they have reduced them; that in some countries aid has become a considerable prize, for which undemocratic forces have fought each other to gain control. Aid has been generally heedless of considerations of human rights, ethnic balance, political legitimacy and other institutional factors, which are fundamental to sustainability.

There are millions of victims of mal-development in countries entering or returning from a state of collapse. These have traditionally been some of the most generously assisted: Haiti, Somalia, Liberia, Democratic Republic of Congo, and others. Rwanda, considered in the 1980s as a generously aided development success story, was the site of one of the century's major human cataclysms barely five years ago. The role of aid in abetting this disastrous societal breakdown - and the failure of the same donor and multilateral community to prevent the genocide - have been documented. In Rwanda, "the process of development and the international aid given to promote it interacted with the forces of exclusion, inequality, pauoerization, racism amd oppression that laid the groundwork for the 1994 genocide".[2]

Rwanda is now in a full phase of post-conflict reconstruction, for which short-term assistance can be essential. But aided rehabilitation must lead to an early restoration of normal development processes and encourage a mentality of self-sufficiency rather than dependence, which aid agencies are often disinclined to do. It is the Government which has recently stated its intention to reduce its dependence on aid in the future.

The democratization of aid

Such are some of the perceptions of governments. But aid has evolved far beyond the stage of being a government-to-government affair.

---

2 Peter Uvin (1998); also Peter Uvin (1996), 'Aid and Conflict: Reflections from the Case of Rwanda', Research for Action 24, United Nations University/World Institute for Development Economics Research, Helsinki.

Unfortunately, the voices of the real aid donors - mostly the tax-payers of the richer countries - and the real aid recipients - the poorest and the neediest in the developing world - are insufficiently represented in aid transactions. If they were, aid might already be very different.

On the donor side, the growing involvement of northern NGOs as conduits for aid funds has brought them more squarely into the aid debate. They are of course strongly pro-aid, being influenced by the need to continue to attract funds. But some NGOs have made an important contribution to the direction of aid, especially as it impacts on the disadvantaged. They can be vocal lobbyists for development causes with national governments and multilateral organisations (for example OXFAM UK on the persistent debt crisis). At global conferences, there are usually parallel NGO forums holding alternative debates; some country delegations include representatives from non-governmental interests. There is also more public discussion about aid budgets, although politicians in some rich countries still reflect opinions on aid that are out of line with public opinion (the attitudes of the US Congress towards the United Nations is just one glaring example). There is room for much greater transparency in the allocation and disbursement of public funds, even allowing for the necessary discretion that must accompany the budgetary process. In parallel, however, there are more and more private-to-private aid transactions occurring, independent of official aid channels. The magnanimous gift of $1 billion to the United Nations by Ted Turner in 1997 is a further new variant: private funds through official multilateral channels.

On the recipient side, the democratisation of aid - which must also follow the progress of democracy in individual countries - has far to go. The question 'who speaks for the poor?' has never been more important, and never more ambiguous than it is today. The intended beneficiaries of aid scarcely have a voice and considerable mistrust still prevails between them and their 'spokesmen'.

There are of course many reasons why much official aid will continue to be channelled through official bodies. Wherever aid is provided in the form of concessional loans, governments are required to act as guarantors. Some aid is destined to assist governmental machinery directly, and is entrusted to governments because they have the most comprehensively developed delivery mechanisms (food aid for targeted beneficiaries, aid for education and health). However, governments are not always either sensitive or knowledgeable about the needs which such assistance is intended to address, and the means by which these needs might be more clearly articulated scarcely exist. Communications are passed up and down through administrative hierarchies which are dominated by social elites, on which the poor and marginalised are ill represented.

If the intended beneficiaries of aid could speak, perceptions of aid needs might be very different. We might hear how aid, when it is given, has often bypassed the truly needy. The poorer landless families might tell how farmers with land have benefited at their expense in rural development projects. How in some countries the linking of bilateral and military assistance by friendly donors has put armaments into the hands of regimes which, bent on self-preservation more than development progress, have used them against compatriots.[3] We would hear why, among many millions of the intended beneficiaries, 'aid' and 'development' have become words to be feared and despised. We might hear people questioning whether there were alternatives to patronage.

The aid hierarchy

For aid is hierarchical. Just as, within countries, it reinforces systems of patronage and is as likely to widen income gaps as it is to narrow them, to disempower as much as to empower the needy, it also divides the world into two ambiguously defined parts.

Over more than half a century, an aid culture has helped to foster a notion of two 'worlds' distinguished only by whether they were givers or receivers of aid. The distinction has been perpetuated by the existence of clubs. On one side, the original recipients of Marshall Aid re-formed themselves into the Organisation of Economic Cooperation for Development (OECD) and invited Japan, Australia, New Zealand and others to join the rich club, within which most of the membership (21 countries) belongs to the Development Assistance Committee of donors. On the other side, there has been the 'Group of 77' and the Non-Aligned Movement. There has been very little crossing of the divide, although Mexico (1995) and South Korea (1996) have recently become members of OECD (but not yet the DAC).

Even in terms of income per head, the distinction is artificial, since there are many members of the 'recipient' club (Singapore, Kuwait, Israel, Brunei among others) which are 'richer' in these terms than members of the 'donor' club. As just noted, countries are graduating: some 'recipients' are becoming 'donors'. South Korea, Singapore, Malaysia and Chile are among the 'developing' countries with new and expanding aid programmes of their

---

3 Data released by the Pentagon in early 1997 reveal that four of the world's poorest countries - Liberia, Somalia, Sudan and Zaire - all of them torn apart by civil wars, together owe the USA $430 million in arms sales loans.

own. China, India and Israel (recently the largest recipient of US aid) have been both donors and recipients, having maintained active aid programmes for several decades. Moreover, on both sides of this artificial divide, there are vast economic differences in terms of size, resource endowment, openness and market orientation, to say nothing of the demographic, cultural, societal and political contrasts which make each country a special case.

It is doubtful whether - even at the beginning of the aid story - it was realistic to define the world dichotomously, in terms of resource transfers. In economic analysis, there were fashionable schools of dependency theorists, and centre-periphery relationships. But long after doubts have been cast on these bifurcated interpretations of world development, aid has tended to perpetuate them, building into an artificial two-tier gobal edifice an unfortunate culture of patronage. Today, given the comprehensive nature of the economic, social, environmental, political and other forms of interaction across borders - state-to-state, as well as between private corporations and ethnic groups - the upper-lower patronage culture is revealed as defunct.

This book has made no apologies for observing the same dichotomous distinction in its labelling of countries as donors and recipients, and developed and developing, because it is the language which has helped to define international relations hitherto. But the book seeks to demonstrate that this traditional distinction has become increasingly anachronistic. Apart from the unfortunate assumptions of stereotypical behaviour attached to the simplistic donor and recipient categories, these affiliations tend to instil into international relations *a priori* notions of superior/inferior, stronger/weaker, dominant/subordinate, independent/dependent which are increasingly meaningless in a world in which official resource flows are being supplemented and supplanted by other, more equitable, bases of cooperation, of which examples have been provided in the preceding chapters.

From patronage to partnership

Much development aid has been an unsatisfactory bargain, both for recipients and donors. Whatever the motivation for aid, and wherever the destination, the dividends have been disappointing. There is a wealth of literature on this subject, to some parts of which this book has referred. Nearly all these works conclude with proposals for improving aid, both quantitatively and qualitatively. This book also has some proposals to offer,

Beyond aid 177

but it does not see them as a sufficient solution to the shortcomings of aid. Aid must be newly construed in the light of rapid and radical changes in international relations, because:

- Aid grew up in a world dominated by systems of patronage fashioned by post-colonial relationships, and by strategic spheres of influence. These patterns are disappearing.

- It is a world no longer simplistically divided into North and South, 'first' and 'third', developed and developing. Today, there are important new geographical configurations by region and sub-region - APEC, Mercosur, NAFTA - which are helping to change the traditional development axes.

- Countries have common interests independent of geography and development level (however defined): major agricultural producers from Australia to Thailand; industrial giants from India to Russia; service economies from Singapore to Surinam; major foreign investment destinations from Britain to China, and major technology sources from Taiwan to the US. There are heavy marine and air polluters, drug producers, labour exporters, and so on, all with common interests in particular issues.

- It is a world in which states have diminishing significance in domestic governance, but growing responsibilities as global governors of universal institutions and values.

In a world of states and peoples that are both more interdependent and more individualistic, it is principles of partnership that should prevail, not those of the patronising and the patronised.

A new international economic order - so long and so unproductively debated in UN forums in the 1970s as part of a 'North-South dialogue' - is actually closer than it has ever been. The rules of the global economic game are not yet fair, but they are distinctly fairer, with one outstanding exception. That exception is the debt crisis which must urgently be resolved, not perpetually and indefinitely postponed, if the most iniquitous aspects of financial patronage are not to continue.

In many other important respects, all countries are becoming full players in the global economy. Flows of goods, services, private finance and information are freer than before. The opportunities to benefit from globalisation are biased by many factors, but foremost among the impediments are those which it is within the power of individual governments to overcome most easily. The chapters on trade and information contain numerous examples of the ways in which governments can facilitate more openness by lifting the hand of bureaucracy; clarifying and simplifying regulatory procedures; decentralising administration; establishing safeguards to promote social and environmental responsibility; encouraging private enterprise, technologies and capital; promoting competition and restricting monopolies.

Whether privatisation of state assets in western Europe, deregulation of former centrally-planned economies in eastern Europe and Asia, or the shrinking of the state in Africa, most countries in the world are in a state of transition towards more liberal, market-oriented economics. Experience demonstrates that the policy changes required sometimes incur substantial social and political costs. Over several years, the author witnessed at first hand the painful passage of a large European country through a triple transformation to statehood, democracy and market economics, during which the human costs were much higher than those of the great depression of the 1930s.[4] But, however great the difficulty, the direction of change was never in doubt. The record of successful transitions elsewhere, and the assurance they provide for sustained human development, attest to the wisdom of change.

Development agencies have tried to make aid dependent on policy change through policy-based lending and the use of devices such as the 'programme approach' in technical assistance. But experience has shown that fundamental policy change is usually not dependent on aid. The structural adjustment programmes of the Bretton Woods institutions in Africa are often cited as examples of externally-induced and funded policy transition. But the record of success is very mixed. While the IMF can be a convenient scapegoat for undertaking unpopular economic measures, the desire to avoid such programmes and their heavy-handed conditionalities has also been an incentive for change. The argument being made by this book is that the spread of the global economy and the increasingly visible consequences of globalisation themselves provide a growing motivation for desirable domestic policy changes. There is a consequently a diminishing need for leveraging through aid.

While it extols the merits of open, reformist domestic policies to facilitate liberal economic systems, however, this book takes a qualified view of the free workings of global markets. The features of globalisation described in earlier chapters - freer trade, investment, capital flows and information - are bound to become more pronounced. But freedom does not guarantee fairness, and effective global rule-making and enforcement are

---

4 Some of the these findings are in Browne (1995).

critical complements to the globalisation process. Freer trade need not hasten environmental deterioration, nor exacerbate labour conditions. There are forums and regimes established to develop safeguards, but they must be utilised. Facilitating foreign direct investment also needs clearer groundrules. The present attempt to develop them outside the machinery of global governance - through the OECD - is likely to fail. But the process is important and should be pursued multilaterally. Other aspects of governance in trade, intellectual property, environmental management and information need continuing refinement.

Participation in collective governance is the other major area of development responsibility of individual states. The book devoted a chapter to regionalism, underlining the growing importance which countries attach to harmonising their development efforts with their neighbours. Regionalism in its different forms, and as a manifestation of the internationalisation of development priorities, may be seen as a stage towards collective global action. In some circumstances it may be a superior alternative.

All states must be participants in organisations and regimes of global governance. And while states remain the principal actors, global governance should increasingly encompass non-governmental organisations and the private sector. This book holds to the basic tenet that people must increasingly take control of their own lives, and states of their own destinies. The responsibility to seek benefits from processes of globalisation, while palliating any ill effects, lies mainly with each country.

What next for aid?

Aid is in decline, but not dying. In itself, this trend is not a cause for alarm. The verdict of this book on the quantity of aid is that - developmentally speaking - much more can be done with much less. The qualitative verdict is equally strident: the priority is not on the improvement of aid, but on its nature. It is no longer a choice of 'how', but of 'what'.

This book has attempted to describe some of the major features of the world of the fourth age, and their implications for aid. This final section sets out the general principles on which aid might be based, and then summarises the main implications.

Aid should not be synonymous with development efforts. It should be a means of facilitating and accelerating beneficial change already initiated, and for which the will and commitments of Governments and other interested parties has been clearly manifested. Aid can make a permanent difference where ongoing processes of change can be catalysed through outside intervention.

The general orientation of aid should be towards:

- removing the major debt and trade impediments to the fuller participation of all countries in the global economy;
- eliminating aid which hinders and countermands the workings of markets, and perpetuates bureaucratic dirigisme, but
- assisting in the development of capacity, at national and international level, to monitor and regulate private sector activities in order to temper social, environmental and other harmful distortions;
- eliminating the functions of international and national public sector technical agencies which are duplicative, and for which there are superior sources of expertise;
- assisting countries to participate more fully and equitably in regimes and organisations of global governance;
- developing global public goods and services through cooperative means which would not otherwise result from private sector initiative;
- sponsoring closer cooperation among countries to further their collective interests;
- requiring countries to pay for public services received, from other countries or from multilateral bodies, assessed according to the value of those services rather than ability to pay.

Some of the more specific and immediate measures required are described below.

Debt. The persistence of the debt crisis renders much of the aid effort futile. Whether it is classified as aid or not, the resources must urgently be found to deliver a solution to this crisis, through the application of more generous terms of eligibility for the HIPC initiative for some countries, and through total debt cancellation for others.

Trade and investment. The principal 'aid' effort should be concentrated on eliminating the protectionism of the richest countries - particularly in agriculture and textiles - and undoing other trade distortions such as the tying of existing aid.

Aid should ensure that countries receive the best objective advice in negotiating the terms of their participation in the World Trade Organisation, including the provision of temporary transitional shelters for their own producers of good and services. Under UN or other genuine multilateral auspices, attempts should be renewed to draw up codes of conduct for direct foreign investment.

Regional cooperation. Third party aid mechanisms can help to strengthen cooperative arrangements among countries - either within contiguous sub-regions or inter-regionally - for their mutual benefit. The rationale of using aid for this purpose is to encourage individual countries to 'think cooperatively' and explore - where they might not otherwise be inclined to, for political or other reasons - collective approaches to common development problems.

Information. The progress of the information revolution is an example of the extraordinary power and effectiveness of public-private partnerships, both at national and international levels. Information has become the most catalytic of all development factors and aid can complement efforts at national level to harness the benefits of this partnership, ensure that as much information and data of developmental importance are available through accessible public domains, and assist processes of dissemination.

The phenomena of the Internet and the World Wide Web are typical of the beyond-aid era because the extraordinary growth in their use has been a reflection of individual empowerment, with the public sector playing a largely facilitatory role. The Internet and its contents cannot remain entirely ungoverned, however. Diffusion will be facilitated by international coordinating mechanisms to improve standardisation of domain names and addressing systems. An effective governance system would also ensure that the needs of all countries are more clearly articulated.

Global governance. This is the primary and privileged aid arena, where public resources should be concentrated.

The debt problem of the poorest countries has been repeatedly mentioned as a dominant priority. Its resolution should be a major preoccupation for the IMF and World Bank, if those organisations are not to be accused of using the crisis as a means of leveraging their own jurisdiction over the management of the affected economies. Relocating national economic sovereignty to Washington runs directly counter to the principles of individualism and interdependence of international economic relations supported by this book.

There is an urgent need to bring more discipline to global economic activity, regulate banks and financial institutions, provide additional international liquidity and more effective lender of last resort facilities. These functions could be assumed by a world central bank, or wholly or partially by the IMF. But if the latter, it would have to find additional sources of finance and transform itself into a more facilitatory and less disciplinary instrument of governance.

The World Bank is not, and will not become, an effective instrument of global governance. However, it is the foremost development agency and it must accommodate its operations with other organisations in order to fulfil more adequately its roles of strengthening the financial management capacities of individual countries, and facilitating access to private capital sources. Bilateral aid could also be used to an increasing degree, not to substitute for private capital, but to establish investment guarantee funds.

Innovative financial support arrangements should be applied to some of the smallest and most vulnerable economies, including in particular the small island states, which have never significantly reduced their dependence on aid. It is in their interest, and that of their benefactors, to establish self-managed trust funds into which appropriate multilateral and bilateral sources should contribute grants on a once-for-all basis. Once established, each trust fund would be managed by the country, and guaranteed by one or more of the original benefactors. The country would benefit from interest and capital appreciation, yielding flows of resources at least equal to current aid levels.

The World Trade Organisation should pursue its unfinished agenda, leading to further liberalisation in agriculture, maritime transport, other services and investment.

With the diminishing utility and relevance of its technical assistance role, the UN development system must increasingly concentrate on its more unique functions of a normative nature, including the negotiation and enforcement of universal regimes. These functions are more important than ever in the context of growing global interaction. Particularly critical is the development and enforcement of environmental regimes. Global regimes must encourage fullest participation and provide for countries to pay in full for the benefits they receive.

The international public sector responsible for multilateral aid is insupportably large. It is overdue for strategic reappraisal, which should result in a significant consolidation around those functions which are central to effective global governance. This consolidation should affect headquarters and field operations, but should also take full advantage of administrative dispersion and decentralisation made possible by modern information and communication technologies.

Bibliography
(excluding sources available on the World Wide Web)

Amin, Samir. (1970), L'Accumulation à l'Echelle Mondiale, Paris.
Andrew Elek ed. (1997), Building an Asia-Pacific Community: Development Cooperation within APEC, The Foundation for Development Cooperation, Adelaide.
Asian Development Bank, Emerging Asia: Changes and Challenges (1997), Manila.
Bhagwati, Jagdish. (1993) 'Regionalism and multilateralism: an overview' in Jaime de Melo and Arvind Panagariya eds. New Dimensions in Regional Integration, Cambridge University Press, Cambridge.
Bird, Graham (1995), IMF Lending to Developing Countries, Routledge, London.
Boone, Peter (1996), 'Politics and the Effectiveness of Foreign Aid', European Economic Review, Vol.40, North Holland.
Browne, Stephen (1990), Foreign Aid in Practice, Pinter Publishers, London.
Browne, Stephen (1993), 'United Nations country operations: the next reform priority', Mimeo, UN, New York.
Browne, Stephen (1995), 'Sustaining human development through the transition: the experience of Ukraine', Paper prepared for the Summit on Social Development, UNDP, New York.
Browne, Stephen (1997), 'The rise and fall of development aid', WIDER Working Paper No. 143, UN University World Institute for Development Economics Research, Helsinki.
Buendia, Hernando Gomez (1995), 'The Limits of the Global Village: Globalisation, Nations and the State', WIDER World Development Studies 5, UNU, World Institute for Development Economics Research, Helsinki.
Burnside, Craig and David Dollar (1997), 'Aid, Policies and Growth', mimeo, World Bank, Washington DC.
Cairncross, Frances (1997), The Death of Distance, Orion Publishers, London.
Cassen, Robert et al. (1986), Does Aid Work? Oxford University Press, Oxford.
Castells, M. (1998), The Information Age: Economy, Society and Culture; Volume III: End of Millenium, Blackwell Publishers, Oxford.
Chenery, Hollis and A. Strout (1966), 'Foreign assistance and economic development', American Economic Review, Vol. 56.
Chenery, Hollis et al. (1974), Redistribution with Growth, Oxford University Press, Oxford.
Childers, Erskine and Brian Urquhart (1994), Renewing the United Nations System, Dag Hammarskjold Foundation, Uppsala.
Childers, Erskine (1995), Challenges to the United Nations: Building a Safer World, St. Martin's Press, New York.
Clark, John (1991), Democratizing Development: The Role of Voluntary Organisations, Kumarian Press, Hartford.

Cleveland, Harlan (1997), 'The information imperative embraces liberté, egalité and access', World Paper White Paper, Summer 1997, World Times, Boston.

Colas, Bernard (1994), Global Economic Cooperation: a Guide to Agreements and Organisations, United Nations University Press, Tokyo.

Commission on Global Governance (1995), Our Global Neighbourhood, Oxford University Press, New York.

Cooper, Richard N. (1998), 'Toward a real global warming treaty', Foreign Affairs, March/April 1998, Council on Foreign Relations, New York.

Cornea, Giovanni Andrea, Richard Jolly, Frances Stewart, eds.(1987), Adjustment with a Human Face: Protecting the Vulnerable and Promoting Growth, Clarendon Press, Oxford.

d'Orville, Hans (1996), 'Technology revolution study: communications and knowledge-based technologies for sustainable human development', mimeo, United Nations Development Programme, New York.

de la Torre, Augusto and Margaret R. Kelly (1992), 'Regional Trade Arrangements', IMF Occasional Paper, Number 93, Washington DC.

de Melo, Jaime and Arvind Panagariya, eds. (1993), New Dimensions in Regional Integration, Cambridge University Press, Cambridge.

de Silva, Leelananda (1984), Development Aid: A Guide to Facts and Issues, UN-NGLS and Third World Forum, Geneva.

Dertouzos, Michael (1997), What Will Be: How the New World of Information Will Change Our Lives, Harper Collins, New York.

Drucker, Peter F. (1997), 'The Global Economy and the Nation-state', Foreign Affairs, September/October 1997, Council on Foreign Relations, New York.

Dunning, John and Khalil Hamdani, eds. (1997), The New Globalism and Developing Countries, United Nations University Press, Tokyo.

Elek, Andrew (1997), Building an Asia-Pacific Community: Development Cooperation within APEC, The Foundation for Development Cooperation, Adelaide.

Edwards, Sebastian (1998), 'Openness, Productivity and Growth: what do we really know?' Economic Journal, March 1998, , Cambridge.

Finger, J. Michael (1994), 'The high costs of trade protectionism in the Third World', in Perpetuating Poverty, Cato Institute, Washington DC.

Ganesan, A.V. (1998), 'Strategic options available to developing countries with regard to a multilateral agreement on investment', UNCTAD Discussion Paper 134, United Nations, Geneva.

Graham, Carol and Michael O'Hanlon (1997), 'Making Foreign Aid Work', Foreign Affairs, July/August 1997, Council on Foreign Relations, New York.

Graham, Kennedy (1995), 'The Planetary Interest', Global Security Programme Occasional Paper, Global Security Programme, Cambridge University.

Griffin, Keith and J.L. Enos (1970), 'Foreign assistance: objectives and consequences', Economic Development and Cultural Change, Vol. 18, April 1970.

Griffin, Keith and Terry McKinley (1996), 'New Approaches to Development Cooperation', UNDP Office of Development Studies, Discussion Paper No. 6, New York.

Griffin, Keith (1970), 'Foreign Aid, Domestic Savings and Economic Development', Bulletin of the Oxford University Institute of Economics and Statistics, May 1970, Volume 32.

Griffith-Jones, Stephany (1993), 'Towards Global Financial and Macro-economic Governance', mimeo, UNDP, New York.

Harrod, R.F. (1939), 'An Essay in Dynamic Theory', Economic Journal, Vol. XLIX, London.

Heinz Arndt (1994), 'Anatomy of regionalism', in Ross Garnault and Peter Drysdale, Asia Pacific Regionalism, Harpers, Pymble, Australia.

Hyden, Goran (1994), 'Shifting perspectives on development: implications for research' in Mette Mast et al., State and Locality, Norwegian Association for Development Research, Oslo.

International Labour Office (1997), Employment Growth and Basic Needs: a One World Problem, Praeger, New York.

International Monetary Fund (1998), Official Financing for Developing Countries, IMF, Washington DC.

International Telecommunication Union (1998), World Telecommunication Development Report 1998, ITU, Geneva..

Korten, David R. (1990), Getting to the 21st Century: Voluntary Action and the Global Agenda, Kumarian Press, Hartford.

Krauss, Melvyn (1997), How Nations Grow Rich: The Case for Free Trade, Oxford University Press, Oxford.

Krueger, Anne O. (1995), Trade Policies and Developing Nations, Brookings Institution, Washington.

Krugman, Paul (1993), 'Regionalism versus Multilateralism: analytical notes', in Jaime de Melo and Arvind Panagariya, eds., New Dimensions in Regional Integration, Cambridge University Press, Cambridge.

Krugman, Paul (1996), Pop Internationalism, MIT Press, Cambridge Mass.

Kuhn, Thomas (1962), The Structure of Scientific Revolutions, University of Chicago Press, Chicago.

Kuznets, Simon (1954), 'Underdeveloped countries and the pre-industrial phase in the advanced countries' in Proceedings of the World Population Conference, United Nations, New York.

Loxley, John (1986), Debt and Disorder: External Financing for Development, Westview Press, Boulder.

Maddison, A. (1995), Monitoring the World Economy, 1820-1992, OECD, Paris.

Mansell, Robin and Uta Wehn (1998), Knowledge Societies: Information Technology for Sustainable Development, Report for the UN Commission on Science and technology for Development, Oxford University Press, Oxford.

Miller, Morris (1986), Coping is not Enough: the International Debt Crisis and the Roles of the World Bank and the International Monetary Fund, Dow Jones-Irwin, Homewood Illinois.

Montes, Manuel et al. (1997), Growing Pains: ASEAN's Economic and Political Challenges, Asia Society, New York).

Morrisey, Oliver (1993), 'The Mixing of Aid and Trade Policies', The World Economy, Vol.16, No.1.

Mosely, Paul (1987), Overseas Aid: Its Defence and Reform, Wheatsheaf Books, London.
Mosley, Paul, Jane Harrigan and John Toye (1991), Aid and Power: the World Bank and Policy-based Lending, Routledge, London.
Nordic UN Reform Project (1996), The United Nations in Development, Government of Norway, Oslo.
Ohmae, Kenichi (1995), The End of the Nation State: the Rise of Regional Economies, The Free Press, New York.
Okita, S.(1989), Emerging forms of global markets and the nature of interdependence in an increasingly multipolar world, OECD Development Centre, Paris.
Organisation for Economic Cooperation for Development (1995, 1996, 1997) Development Cooperation Report, OECD, Paris.
Organisation for Economic Cooperation for Development (1996), Shaping the 21st Century: the Contribution of Development Cooperation, OECD, Paris.
Overseas Development Institute (1995), 'Developing Countries in the WTO', ODI Briefing Paper, London.
Overseas Development Institute (1996), 'New Sources of Finance for Development', ODI Briefing Paper, London.
Overseas Development Institute (1997), 'The UN's Role in Grant-Financed Development', ODI Briefing Paper, London.
Oxfam International (1997), 'Poor Country Debt Relief', Position Paper, Washington DC.
Pearson, Lester et al.(1969), Partners in Development: Report of the Commission on International Development, Pall Mall, London.
Please, Stanley (1984), 'The World Bank: lending for structural adjustment', in R. Feinberg and V. Kalab, Adjustment Crisis in the Third World, Overseas Development Council, Washington.
Raffer Kunibert and Hans Singer (1996), The Foreign Aid Business: Economic Assistance and Development Cooperation, Edward Elgar, Cheltenham, UK.
Riddell, Roger (1996), 'Aid in the 21st Century', UNDP Office of Development Studies, Discussion Paper No. 6, UNDP, New York.
Riddell, Roger (1987), Foreign Aid Reconsidered, The Johns Hopkins University Press, Baltimore.
Rostow, Walter W. (1960), The Stages of Economic Growth, Cambridge University Press, Cambridge.
Rostow, Walter W. (1956), 'The take-off into self-sustained growth', London, Economic Journal, London.
Ryrie, William (1995), First World, Third World, St. Martin's Press, New York.
Sachs Jeffrey D. and Andrew Warner (1995), Economic Reform and the Process of Global Integration, Brookings Institution, Washington.
Safadi, Raed and Sam Laird (1996), 'The Uruguay Round Agreements: Impact on Developing Countries', World Development, Vol. 24, No. 7, Pergamon Press, Oxford.
Sandler, Todd (1997), Global Challenges: an Approach to Environmental, Political and Economic Problems, Cambridge University Press, Cambridge.

Schumacher, E. (1974), Small is Beautiful: a Study of Economics as if People Mattered,Sphere Books, London.
Shariffadeen, Mohd. Azzman (1995), 'Information Technology Planning and Its Implications', mimeo, Malaysian Institute of Micro-electronic Systems.
Stiglitz, Joseph (1998), 'How can aid best facilitate development?' Presentation to the Second Committee of the UN General Assembly, World Bank, Washington DC.
Stiglitz, Joseph (1998), 'More instruments and broader goals: moving towards the post-Washington consensus', UNU/WIDER Annual Lecture, UNU World Institute for Development Economics Research, Helsinki.
Stokke, Olav, ed.(1996), Foreign Aid Towards the Year 2000: Experiences and Challenges, Frank Cass, London.
ul Haq, Mahbub (1993), 'The Bretton Woods Institutions: the Vision and the Reality', paper presented at the Bretton Woods Conference, September, Washington DC.
ul Haq, Mahbub (1995), Reflections on Human Development, Oxford University Press, New York.
ul Haq, Mahbub, Inge Kaul and Isabelle Grundberg (1996), The Tobin Tax: Coping with Financial Volatility, Oxford University Press, Oxford.
United Nations Development Programme (1990-1997), Human Development Report, Oxford University Press, New York.
United Nations Development Programme (1993), Rethinking Technical Cooperation: Reforms for Capacity Building in Africa, UNDP, New York.
United Nations Conference on Trade and Development (1996), Strengthening the participation of developing countries in world trade and the multilateral trading system, United Nations, Geneva.
United Nations Conference on Trade and Development (1997), Trade and Development Report, UN Publications, Geneva.
United Nations Conference on Trade and Development (1998), World Investment Report, United Nations, Geneva.
US Congressional Budget Office (1997), The Role of Foreign Aid in Development, CBO, Washington DC.
Uvin, Peter (1998), Aiding Violence: the Development Enterprise in Rwanda, Kumarian Press, West Hartford, Cn.
Viner, Jacob (1950), The Customs Union Issue, Carnegie Endowment for International Peace, New York.
von Moltke, Konrad (1996), 'The Structure of Regimes for Trade and the Environment', in Weiss, Thomas G. and Leon Gordenker, eds., NGOs, the UN and Global Governance, Lynne Rienner Publishers, Boulder.
Weisskopf, Thomas E. (1972), 'The Impact of Foreign Capital Inflow on Domestic Savings in Less Developed Countries', Journal of International Economics, Vol. 2, February 1972.
Winters, L. Alan (1996), 'Regionalism versus Multilateralism', Policy Research Working Paper 1687, World Bank, Washington DC.
World Bank (1997), Global Economic Prospects and the Developing Countries, Washington DC.

World Bank (various years): 'Annual reviews of project performance audit results', Operations Evaluation Department.
World Bank (various years), World Debt Tables: External Finance for Developing Countries, Washington DC.
World Bank (1998a), World Development Report, Oxford University Press, New York.
World Bank (1998b), Assessing Aid, Oxford University Press, New York.
Young, Oran R. (1997), Global Governance, MIT Press, Cambridge, Mass.

Index

Act for International Development (US) 11
Advanced Research Project Agency (ARPA) 117
African-Caribbean-Pacific (ACP) grouping 88
African famine 26-7
African Information Society Initiative 136
Afro-Asian Conference, Bandung 12
Aid (see Official development assistance)
Aid ages 1, 19, 29
 First age 19
 Fourth age 29
 Second age 21
 Third age 25
Aid and debt 68
Aid and global development governance 166
Aid and ICT 135
Aid and regionalism 106
Aid and trade 92-4
Aid coordination 172
Aid democratisation 173
Aid distorting trade 48, 73
Aid targets 23
Aid types 14-5
Andean Group 102, 109
Angola 35
Argentina 102-3
ASEANWEB 126, 136
Asia-Pacific Economic Cooperation (APEC) 103-4, 106, 108, 177
 Osaka Action Agenda 103
Association of Southeast Asian Nations (ASEAN) 95, 98-9, 106, 108
 Free Trade Area 99
Australia-New Zealand Closer Economic Relations 108

Baker Plan 58, 143
Balance of payments problems 43, 56-7, 89-90
Bancor 142
Bangkok Agreement 98

Batam 104
Bell, Alexander Graham 114
Berlin Wall 29
Bhutan 127, 131
Black Sea Economic Cooperation forum 96
Brady Plan 58-9, 143
Brandt Commission 26
Brazil 57, 82-3, 95, 102
Bretton Woods conference, New Hampshire 10, 141
Bretton Woods institutions, reform 146-150
Britain 14, 74, 75, 100, 137
Brunei 98, 175
Buffer stocks 89, 143
Burma 98, 126-7, 131
Burundi 32

Cairns Group 78
Cambodia 98
Canada 14
Cancun Summit, Mexico 26
Caribbean Community and Common Market (CARICOM) 101, 109
Central American Common Market (CACM) 101
Chenery and Strout 20, 25
Child labour 85
Chile 102, 125, 175
China 29, 95, 112, 127, 172, 176
Churchill, Winston 11
Cold War 12, 35, 96
Commission on Global Governance 160, 168
Common Agricultural policy (CAP) 88, 101
Common Market of Eastern and Southern Africa (COMESA) 107
Commonwealth 71-2
Communauté Economique de l'Afrique de l'Ouest (CEAO) 107
Comoros 32
Comparative advantage 47, 73, 75, 84, 91
Congo (Brazzaville) 32, 63

Congo (Kinshasa) 32, 35, 173
Convention on Biological Diversity 162, 164
Convention on the Rights of the Child 156
Convergence 89
Convergence of aid motivations 170
Costa Rica 125
Côte d'Ivoire 125
Cuba 29, 35
Czech Republic 132

Debt arrears 55
Debt cancellation 71-2
  Canada 71
  Jubilee 2000 coalition 71-2
Debt crisis, origins 55
Debt forgiveness 53
  Baker Plan 58, 143
  Bolivia 66
  Brady bonds 58
  Brady Plan 58, 143
  Ethiopia 66
  HIPC initiative 66, 71
  HIPC terms 66
  London Club 61, 64
  Mozambique 66
  Naples Terms 62, 66
  Paris Club 61-2, 64
  Tanzania 66
  Toronto Terms 61
  Uganda 66
Debt problems 25, 53, 180
  Brazil 57
  Congo (Brazzaville) 63
  Effects on social spending 65
  Ethiopia 65
  Guinea-Bissau 63
  Guyana 62-3
  Heavily Indebted Poor Countries (HIPC) 63
  Mexico 25, 57
  Mozambique 63, 65
  Nicaragua 63
  Sao Tome 63
  Severely indebted low income countries 54, 61
  Tanzania 65
  Total outstanding debt, developing countries 54
Debt sustainability 67
Declaration of Santiago 106

Decolonisation 40
Digitisation 116

East Asia 21, 30-1
East Asia crisis 32, 59-61, 144, 149, 172
  G-7 countries 147
  IMF response 144
  Indonesia 59-60, 144, 146
  Malaysia 59, 144
  South Korea 59
  Thailand 59, 144, 146
  World central bank 147
Economic Community of West African States (ECOWAS) 106, 107
Economic Cooperation Organisation (ECO) 96, 108, 136
Economic liberalisation 91
Egypt 14, 35
Electronic Numerical Integrator and Calculator (ENIAC) 114
Emergency aid 35
Emissions trading mechanism 165
Environmental governance 162-166
Euromarket 56
European Free Trade Association (EFTA) 109
European Union (EU) 36, 46, 77, 81, 88, 95-6, 99, 101, 109, 133, 163
Export diversification 92
External economies 75

FIDOnet 136
First industrial revolution 112
'First', 'second', 'third' worlds 40
Food aid 46, 93, 154
Foreign direct investment 43-45, 59, 68, 83, 91, 134, 172, 179, 181
Framework Convention on Climate Change 162-3
France 14, 32
  DOM/TOM 16
Free Trade Area of the Americas 102

G-7 countries 32, 61, 72, 95, 147, 153
G-77 countries 171, 173, 175
General Agreement on Trade and Tariffs (GATT) 10, 76, 81, 97, 141
  Article XXIV 101
Generalized System of Preferences (GSP) 80, 88
Geographic Information Systems (GIS) 124

Germany 29
Ghana 132
Global age 139
Global Environmental Facility (GEF) 165
Global public goods 166
Globalisation 21, 30, 57, 60, 68, 73-4, 92, 95-6, 111, 128, 129, 139, 149, 178-9
Gold standard 76
Good governance 31
Graduating countries 172
Great Depression 40, 76
Growth theory 19-21
  Harrod-Domar model 19
  Incremental capital-output ratio(ICOR) 19
Growth triangles 104-5
Gulf Cooperation Council (GCC) 108

Haiti 173
Havana Conference 76
Heavily Indebted Poor Countries (HIPC) 63-4, 66, 68, 71, 149
Hong Kong 88, 93
Hungary 132

ICT and economics 128
ICT and education 123
ICT and environmental management 124
ICT and governance 124, 126-7
Import substitution 90
India 14, 82, 95, 176
Indian Ocean Commission (IOC) 107
Indonesia 30, 95, 98, 126
INEXSK 120
Information revolution 181
Intermediate technology 24
International Court of Justice 141
International Development Research Centre, Canada 136
International Monetary Fund (IMF) 9-10, 22, 25, 30, 58, 62, 88, 93, 139, 141, 147, 181
  Compensatory and contingency financing facility 22, 143, 148
  Compensatory financing facility (CFF) 22, 88, 143
  Enhanced Structural Adjustment Facility (ESAF) 145, 148
  Extended Funding Facility (EFF) 145
  Gold sales 71-2, 148

Special Drawing Rights (SDR) 142
Structural Adjustment facility (SAF) 145
International Trade Organisation (ITO) 10, 141, 167
International Vaccine Institute 158
Internet Initiative for Africa 136
Internet, origins 117
Iran 127
Israel 32, 35, 176
Italy 32

Japan 32, 62
  EximBank 62

Keynes, John Maynard 19, 142
Khruschev, Soviet Premier 14
Khun, Thomas 1, 118
Korean War 12

Laos 98, 127
Latin American Economic System (SELA) 109
Latin American Integration Association (LAIA/LAFTA) 109
Liberia 32, 173
Local content 83
Lomé Convention 88
London Club 61, 64
London Inter-Bank Offered Rate (LIBOR) 57

Maastricht treaty 36
Malaysia 42, 59, 83, 93, 98, 134, 144
Manchester creed 74
Mandela, Nelson 121
Mano River Union 107
Market access 79-81
Marshall Plan 11-2, 14, 19, 46, 145, 175
MERCOSUR 96, 102, 109
Mexico 25, 132, 146, 173, 175
Military aid 7
Mixed credits 47, 93
Mobile telephony 115
Mongolia 125, 126, 127
Montreal Protocol 162-3
Moore's law 114
Morocco 126
Most Favoured Nation (MFN) principle 80-1, 84, 101

Multi-Fibre Arrangement (MFA) 77, 81
Multilateral Agreement on Investment (MAI) 83
Mutual Security Act (US) 11

National treatment 80, 84
Netherlands 14
Net transfers of resources 55-6, 64
Non-aligned Movement 12, 175
Non-governmental organisations (NGOs) 26-7, 41, 174
Non-tariff barriers 79-81
Norway 41
North America Free-Trade Agreement (NAFTA) 96, 109
North Atlantic Treaty Organisations (NATO) 96
North Korea 29, 35, 126-7

Official development assistance (ODA) 11, 15, 21, 32, 41
  Capital aid 41-5
  Decline 29, 32-6
  Grant equivalent value 16
  Relationship to growth 21, 42
  Reverse aid 32
Open and closed economies 89-92
Organisation of Arab Petroleum Exporting Countries (OAPEC) 108
Organisation of Economic Cooperation for Development (OECD) 15, 32, 83, 173, 175
  Development Assistance Committee (DAC) 32, 175
Organisation of Petroleum Exporting Countries (OPEC) 23, 108
OXFAM 65-6, 174

Pacific Economic Cooperation Council (PECC) 103
Pakistan 125
Pan-African Development Information System (PADIS) 136
Paraguay 102
Paris Club 61-2, 64, 72
Peace dividend 35
Pearson Report 21, 26
Petrodollars 56
Philippines 12, 98, 132, 144
Planetary interest 139
Plaza meeting, New York 58

Policy Framework Paper 145
Preferential Trade Area for Eastern and Southern Africa 107
Preferential trading arrangements 97, 100
Privatisation 49, 132-3
Protected regionalism 97
Protectionism 22, 47, 73, 77, 79, 82, 86, 93, 97-102, 151, 180
PTTs 132

Regional cooperation 95-109, 181
Regional development banks 58
  African Development Bank (AfDB) 11, 66
  Asian Development Bank (AsDB) 11
  Inter-American Development Bank (IADB) 11, 58, 66
Regionalism 97
  Defined 97
  Micro-regionalism 104-105
  Open regionalism 103
Regionalism and globalisation 95
Ricardo, David 75
Role of the state 31-2, 39-40
Rostow 20
Rules of origin 100
Russia 32, 35, 40, 95
Rwanda 32, 173

Safeguards 82
SatelLife 125, 137
Second industrial revolution 112
Seriously Indebted Low Income Countries (SILIC) 55-6, 64
Sierra Leone 32
Silicon chip 114
Singapore 83, 93, 98
Smith, Adam 75
Somalia 14, 32, 173
Soros, George 150
South Africa 35
South Asia Association for Regional Cooperation (SAARC) 108
South Korea 30, 42, 88, 93, 144, 173, 175
Southern African Development Community (SADC) 96, 107
Southern African Custom Union (SACU) 107
Soviet Union 11, 12, 20, 29, 40
  Bilateral aid 20
Special Economic Zones (China) 105

Index 193

Sri Lanka 12
STABEX system 88-9, 93
Static and dynamic trade effects 97, 100
Stockholm environment conference 24
Sub-Saharan Africa 34, 36, 44, 63, 87, 136
Sudan 32, 35, 131
Sweden 41
Switzerland 41

Taiwan 93
Tariffs 79-81
Tariff binding 79-80
Tariff escalation 80
 Tariff peaks 80
 Tariffication 80
Telecommunications, birth of 114
Tele-medicine 123
Television 116
Tele-working 129-130
Terms of trade 22, 45, 67, 87, 90
Thailand 30, 59, 93, 98, 144, 146
Third technological revolution 113
Three technological revolutions 111
Tied aid 47-8, 180
Tobin, James 148
Trade and domestic economic reform 90-2
Trade and labour standards 85
Trade and the environment 86
Trade balancing 83
Trade liberalisation 74, 89
Trade policy reform 90
Trade Rounds 77-8
Trade rules 81
Trade theory 73-5
Trade-related aspects of investment measures (TRIMs) 82, 86
Trade-related intellectual property rights(TRIPs) 82
Transmission Control Protocol/Internet Protocol (TCP/IP) 117
Truman, US President 11
Tumen River Area Development Programme 105
Turner, Ted 174

Uganda 125
Union Douanière et Economique de l'Afrique Centrale 108
United Nations 7, 140
 Charter 140
 Director General 153
 Economic and Social Council (ECOSOC) 8, 153
 Human rights 155
 Peace-keeping 140, 142
 Secretary General 8
 Security Council 11
United Nations system 3, 7, 20, 24, 63, 72, 82, 115, 140, 152, 182
 Department of Economic and Social Affairs (DESA) 9
 Economic Commission for Africa (ECA) 9
 Economic Commission for Europe (ECE) 9
 Economic Commission for Latin America and the Caribbean (ECLAC) 9
 Economic and Social Commission for Asia and the Pacific (ESCAP) 9
 Economic and Social Commission for West Asia (ESCWA) 9
 Expanded Programme of Technical Assistance (EPTA) 10, 157
 Food and Agriculture Organisation (FAO) 8-9, 152, 156, 158
 International Atomic Energy Agency (IAEA) 9
 International Civil Aviation Organisation (ICAO) 8-9, 152, 155
 International Fund for Agricultural Development (IFAD) 9
 International Labour Organisation (ILO) 8-9, 85, 142, 152
 International Maritime Organisation (ILO) 155
 International Research and Training Institute for the Advancement of Women (INSTRAW) 8
 International Telecommunication Union (ITU) 8-9, 115, 134, 142, 152, 154
 International Trade Centre (ITC) 9
 Special Fund 10
 Special UN Fund for Economic Development (SUNFED) 157
 UN Centre for Human Settlements (UNCHS) 9, 156
 UN Centre for Social Development and Humanitarian Affairs (UNCSDHA) 9

UN Children's Fund (UNICEF) 7-8, 154, 157
UN Conference on Trade and Development (UNCTAD) 9, 89
UN Development Programme (UNDP) 8, 10, 47, 49, 63, 157-8, 160, 165
UN Educational Scientific and Cultural Organisation (UNESCO) 8-9, 152
UN Population Fund 8, 156
UN Environment Programme (UNEP) 9, 24, 156, 163, 165
UN High Commission for Refugees (UNHCR) 7-8
UN Industrial Development Organisation (UNIDO) 9
UN Institute for Disarmament Research (UNIDIR) 8
UN Institute for training and Research (UNITAR) 8
UN Population Fund (UNFPA) 8
UN Relief and Rehabilitation Administration (UNRRA) 7
Universal Postal Union (UPU) 8-9, 142, 152, 154
UN University 3, 8
World Food Programme (WFP) 8, 46
World Health Organisation (WHO) 8, 9, 152, 154
World Intellectual Property Organisation (WIPO) 82, 155
World Meteorological Organisation (WMO) 9, 155
UN reform 159-161
Uruguay 102
Uruguay Round 22, 73-4, 78-9, 82-4, 92, 96, 101
  Disputes procedure 86
  Environmental standards 86
  General Agreement on Trade in Services (GATS) 84, 86
  Ministerial Conference in Singapore 85
  Problems for Africa and the Caribbean 87-8
  TRIMs 82, 86
  TRIPs 82
  Voluntary Export Restraints (VERs) 80-1
US aid 11-2, 32-5
  To Egypt 35
  To Israel 35

Vietnam 35, 98, 126
Viner, Jacob 97

Wireless local loop 120
World Bank 9, 19, 25, 41, 58, 61-2, 66, 134, 139, 181-2
  Consultative Group meetings 19
  Debt Reduction Facility 61
  Fifth Dimension programme 63
  International Bank for Reconstruction and Development (IBRD) 9-10, 63, 141
  International Development Association (IDA) 9-10, 17, 63, 145
  International Finance Corporation (IFC) 9
  Rates of return 41
  Structural adjustment lending 26, 145, 148, 178
  Trust Fund 71
World central bank 181
World Trade Organisation (WTO) 30, 78, 84, 86, 90, 92, 97, 101, 133, 139, 146, 150-1, 180, 182
  Basic Telecommunications Services Agreement 84, 133
  Biodiversity 151
  Information Technology Agreement 133
  WTO Council 86
World Wide Web 117, 131